PHL

54060000155399

KT-584-533

WITHDRAWN

The Dream of Flight

THE
**PAUL HAMLYN
LIBRARY**

DONATED BY
THE PAUL HAMLYN
FOUNDATION
TO THE
BRITISH MUSEUM

opened December 2000

WITHDRAWN

ALSO BY CLIVE HART

★

KITES: AN HISTORICAL SURVEY
YOUR BOOK OF KITES
STRUCTURE AND MOTIF IN FINNEGANS WAKE
JAMES JOYCE'S DUBLINERS: CRITICAL ESSAYS
(Edited by)

The Dream of Flight

Aeronautics from Classical Times
to the Renaissance

CLIVE HART

FABER AND FABER LIMITED
3 Queen Square, London

First published in 1972
by Faber and Faber Limited
3 Queen Square, London WC1
Printed in Great Britain by
Ebenezer Baylis & Son Ltd
The Trinity Press, Worcester, and London

All rights reserved

ISBN 0 571 09886 X

THE
BRITISH
MUSEUM
THE PAUL HAMLYN LIBRARY

WITHDRAWN

623.13109
HAR

© 1972, Clive Hart

For MICHAEL and ROBIN
two high-fliers

Contents

Illustrations

Preface

My purpose is to give some account of the nature, use, and conceptual bases of aerodynamic devices in Europe from the earliest times to about 1600. As no artifacts have survived, one has to rely entirely on written and pictorial evidence, in which reality and imagination are almost always indissolubly mixed. While it is impossible to discuss the subject without referring to much that is legendary or grossly exaggerated, the emphasis in this book is on the historical rather than on the fantastic. In early days many men attempted to fly, others tried to simulate the flight of birds and winged dragons by building kites and models, and still more theorised about the matter. I am principally concerned with practical attempts or with theory which had a practical end in view. Some of the most remarkable Renaissance writings on aeronautical subjects were produced by men who did not seriously believe that their fancies could have any physical reality: Cyrano and his flasks of sun-drawn dew, Godwin and his moon-based gansas, are classics of aeronautical literature. Few such works fall, however, within my period which, generally speaking, is characterised by ingenious technical speculation. While the thinking of such writers is in a sense more mundane, it is also, in another sense, more genuinely aerial.

The literature on the subject is rather scattered. With some important exceptions, the aeronautical writings of the seventeenth and eighteenth centuries have been fairly well served by the commentators and bibliographers, but, apart from the work of one man, the achievements of the earlier period have usually been passed over in a page or two of hurried comment. Rather than repeat what has so often been said about the later and in some ways richer material, I have set my terminal date very roughly at 1600, making occasional excursions beyond it as seemed useful.

Leonardo, the greatest of all the early workers in the field, is of course the one exception mentioned above. As his aeronautical ideas form such a complex unity, it is inappropriate to discuss the various aspects of his work in piecemeal fashion in the six main sections into which the rest of the material naturally falls. I have accordingly provided a survey of his achievements in my concluding chapter, seeing in him the high point of Renaissance aeronautics, and the one mind capable of exploring in detail the possibilities of most of the main aeronautical ideas of the time. Since virtually all of his aeronautical work remained unknown until the manuscripts became available in comparatively recent years, Leonardo can be relegated to the last chapter without otherwise distorting the account. Alone among the experimenters with whom I deal, he has been the subject of extensive commentary. As a fresh detailed examination of every aspect of his designs and ideas would in itself fill a volume, I have attempted no more than a general description of the character, range, and quality of his work. In his *Leonardo da Vinci's Aeronautics* Mr Gibbs-Smith considers all of Leonardo's principal designs for flying machines, of which he provides a valuable *catalogue raisonné*. In a few places I have extended that survey by examining the machines in the light of Leonardo's ideas about bird flight, and by summarising those passages in the notebooks which hint at plans for making practical attempts. Apart from the facsimiles and transcriptions of the notebooks, the works which I have found most valuable for this purpose are Giacomelli's *Gli Scritti di Leonardo da Vinci sul Volo*, and Uccelli's *I Libri del Volo di Leonardo da Vinci*.

Among the previous books on other aspects of the subject, the following have been especially useful to me, and my indebtedness to them is great: G. Boffito, *Il Volo in Italia*; J. Duhem, *Les idées aéronautiques avant Montgolfier*; J. E. Hodgson, *The History of Aeronautics in Great Britain*; Bertholt Laufer, *The Prehistory of Aviation*; Marjorie Hope Nicolson, *Voyages to the Moon*; G. Venturini, *Da Icaro a Montgolfier*. Although the last of these is virtually unknown in Britain it is by far the most important, containing a wealth of information presented with unusually copious documentation.

In Appendix C I have reproduced, in the original languages, the most important primary sources, together with a few of the more interesting commentaries. Unless there is a note to the contrary, the translations given in the main body of the text are my own. Even at the cost of occasional clumsiness of style, I have tried to stay as close as possible to the text of the originals.

In quoting from classical sources I have used the Loeb texts, where these are available; in quoting from Patristic literature I have used Migne. For both I have given only brief references in the footnotes. Fuller information will be found in the bibliography. For most of the remaining material I have used either the manuscripts or the earliest printed texts.

Specific dates for events in mediaeval Europe prior the Gregorian calendar reforms (carried out in 1582–84 in most Catholic countries, and in 1752 in England) should be understood to be given in the Old Style. Since, before the reforms, the year was usually calculated as beginning on 25 March, dates between 1 January and 24 March, Old Style, can lead to ambiguity. To avoid misunderstanding I have, where appropriate, used the dual form 1474/5, etc.

For help, advice, and the granting of copyright permission I wish to thank the following: Miss Joyce D. Bell; the Bodleian Library; the British Museum; Cambridge University Press, for a passage from Needham's *Science and Civilisation in China*; Jonathan Cape, Ltd, for permission to quote from MacCurdy's translations of Leonardo's notebooks; Mr Charles H. Gibbs-Smith; Professor David Hayman; Dr A. G. Keller; Mr Patrick Murray, Curator of the Museum of Childhood, Edinburgh; Mr A. W. L. Nayler, Librarian of the Royal Aeronautical Society, and his staff; Dr Joseph Needham; Dr Götz Quarg; Professor Ladislao Reti; Dr Bruno Thomas; Mr Colin Townsend; Mr Rex Wailes; the Trustees of the Wellcome Institute of the History of Medicine; Dr Lynn White, Jr.

Versions of parts of Chapters Two and Five have been published in *The Aeronautical Journal* and *Air BP*. I am grateful to the editors for permission to re-use the material here.

I must offer special thanks to Mrs Moira Anthony, who typed my drafts with great skill and patience, and to my wife, for enthusiastic assistance of many kinds.

CLIVE HART

Dundee
April, 1971

1

HOPES AND EXPECTATIONS

─────

When Alexander wished to preside over the air, he had the rather good idea of seating himself, so as to be carried up, on strong, flying griffons, holding roasted meats aloft on his sword. The griffons, smelling the food above their heads, pressed upwards in order to eat. When Alexander had risen very high and wished to descend, he turned the meat down below the griffons' mouths. These, still wanting the food, flew down to try to seize it and bore Alexander, unharmed and without danger, back to earth. This, certainly, whether true or fabulous, is based on the ideas of someone of genius; it indicates, however, an excess of daring in the man.[1]

So runs Giovanni da Fontana's fifteenth-century version of one of the most popular and repeatedly told stories of the Middle Ages. Alexander, either mounted on his griffons or, more often, seated with a greater degree of imperial decorum in a wicker basket, is seen at the controls of his live flying machine in innumerable drawings and paintings, in icons, in stone carvings, and under misericords.[2] The story of Alexander was one of the later forms taken by an enduring legend. Bellerophon and Pegasus, Etana the flying shepherd of Babylon, Kai Kawus the Persian King who harnessed eagles, are all manifestations of the same theme.[3] It is the theme not only of human flight in general, but of flight achieved by an extension of man's organic relationship with the natural world. Such legends greatly outnumber stories

[1] Giovanni da Fontana, *Metrologum de pisce cane et volucre*, Bologna, Biblioteca Universitaria, MS 2705, f. 77^r.

[2] R. S. Loomis, 'Alexander the Great's Celestial Journey', *The Burlington Magazine*, vol. 32, April, 1918, pp. 136–40; May, 1918, pp. 177–85.

[3] Sensitive treatment of the imaginative use of aeronautics in myth and literature may be found in M. H. Nicolson, *Voyages to the Moon*, New York, 1948.

recounting the use of mechanical contrivances. Even Daedalus, artificer of genius and constructor of many intricate devices, found a direct imitation of birds the most satisfactory aeronautical procedure.

Fortunately for the history of flying, though sometimes with unfortunate effects on individuals, Fontana's cautious hint about excess of daring was not always heeded by those who tried to find means of emulating Alexander and his legendary fore-runners. For the primitive aeronauts a great deal of daring was essential: not only physical daring, to risk one's neck with flimsy and untried machinery, but also psychological daring, to step out of one's normal element and act in apparent defiance of all the dictates of nature. For even flight conceived as an organic relationship with the natural world was a hazardous departure from the established order. The old adage 'if God had meant man to fly, He'd have given him wings' was often taken very seriously indeed, and many conventional moralists drew comfort from the repeated stories of failure. Man's physical tendency to fall to the ground was seen by some as an observable correspondence with his fallen moral nature, so that attempts to fly might be said, in a sense, to be almost blasphemous. It is understandable, therefore, that the earliest myths and legends about bird-men usually concern either magicians and men of exceptional gifts, like Daedalus, men of suspect morality, possibly devil-inspired, like Simon Magus,[1] or kings and rulers, like Alexander, whose exalted earthly position gave them at least half an excuse to defy the God-ordained nature of things. In Britain, the story of the legendary king Bladud,[2] which competed in popularity with that of Alexander, was frequently cited as the classical example from which all modern attempts derived:

> This Bladud . . . taught this lore of Negromancy thorough his Realme. And fynally toke in it suche pryde & presumpcion, that he toke vpon hym to fle into the ayer, but he fyll vpon the temple of his god Appolyn and theron was all to torne, whan he had ruled Brytayne by the space of .xx. yeres leuynge after hym a sone named Leyr.[3]

As speculations about flight descended from legend to reality, so the practice of the

---

[1] For a convenient summary of the accounts of this apocryphal story see L. Thorndike, *A History of Magic and Experimental Science*, 8 vols., London, 1923, etc., vol. 1, pp. 422–7.

[2] H. C. Levis, *The British King Who Tried to Fly*, London, 1919.

[3] Fabyan, [*The Chronicle*,] 1516, f. viii[r]. The earliest extant account of the flight is in Geoffrey of Monmouth, *Britannie utruisque regum et principum origo et gesta insignia*, [Paris,] 1508, f. xiii[r]: *paratis sibi alis ire per summitatem aeris tentauit: ceciditque super templum Apollinis intra vrbem ternouatum & in multa frusta contritus est.*

half-formed art descended from kings to commoners. But if even a king could fall on to the Temple of Apollo, it is not surprising that the Italian gentlemen Danti and Guidotti should crash through the roofs of Christian churches, which silently reproved them for their folly.

Most of my material falls into the period 1250–1600. While one cannot, of course, make many valid generalisations about a period of three and a half centuries, a number of persistent physical and mechanical ideas continued to influence the practical approach to flying throughout that time. Most of these ideas were versions of the Aristotelian tenets about the elements, the atmosphere, and motion. Although Aristotle's views were by no means universally accepted, causing, indeed, a great deal of controversy among the more progressive thinkers, the central position which they had long held in philosophy had left them as thoroughly entrenched in the day-to-day thinking of most ordinary educated people as Newtonian concepts have been since the seventeenth century. While many of those who experimented with practical aerodynamic devices were of course unlettered men, touched by such ideas only indirectly and in so far as they formed part of the conceptual climate of the time, Leonardo, though certainly the greatest, was by no means the only aspiring aeronaut with a highly trained, alert mind. Danti was a mathematician, Guidotti aspired to be an all-round intellectual, Fontana was a physician and a very competent theoretical technician. Some brief comments on general intellectual assumptions of the time may be relevant to our understanding of the work of such experimenters.

Where would mediaeval aviators have imagined themselves to be going when they succeeded in getting off the ground? In the first place, they would have expected to pass through three distinct regions of air, of markedly different characteristics, from the warmth of the lower regions, via the colder middle parts, to the supposedly hot upper atmosphere. The first region was warmed by the reflection of the sun's beams; the second was a cold layer, reaching to the top of the highest mountains and containing watery vapours held in a congealed state prior to precipitation; the third, beyond the mountains, was heated by proximity to the region of 'fire'. While the cold middle region of the atmosphere was obviously uninviting, the uppermost was generally thought to be of great serenity, sharing, indeed, some of the characteristics of the celestial spheres. While it was therefore to some degree attractive, it was also dangerous, both because of the tenuousness and dryness of the air, and because of its great heat. On the whole man had better be content with the unpredictable conditions of his natural station and fly, if at all, near to the earth.

The three regions of air, having opposed characteristics, existed in a state of strife and were separated by turbulent boundary layers which were responsible for the formation of 'meteors' (*i.e.*, any weather phenomena).[1] The lower strata of the atmosphere contained sub-regions in which the different types of meteor were formed, the special characteristics of these sub-regions being defined by the commentators in a variety of ways. In the first book of his *Meteorologica* Aristotle analysed the formation of shooting stars, aurorae, comets, rain, clouds, mists, dew, hoar-frost, snow, hail, and various kinds of wind, all of which he attributed to differing conditions at differing heights in the atmosphere.[2] In a discussion of seven such regions of the air, Michael Scot (*d.* 1235) spoke of dew, snow, hail, rain, honey, laudanum, and manna.[3] It was believed that, as a consequence of the distinct characteristics of the regions and of the turbulences where they met, the density and viscosity of the atmosphere varied greatly from place to place, the variations creating a potential hazard for anyone who contemplated passing through them.

Air, or gaseous matter in general, was of course one of the four basic elements from which, according to Aristotelian physics, all things beneath the sphere of the moon were constituted. The elements were not to be identified in all respects with earth, water, air, and fire in the everyday sense, but were the pure principles of which those were more or less crude manifestations. In its unmixed form each element had a natural place in one of the four main, roughly concentric regions which comprised the sublunary world. Below the air were the readily observable regions of water and earth, while above it was the region of elemental fire.[4]

The nature of any physical substance was primarily determined by the proportions of the elements from which it was constituted, and since the elements in their pure state moved towards their proper places in the world, unless forcibly prevented from doing so, any object in which one of the elements was markedly predominant was also thought to have a strong tendency to move to the region appropriate to it. These ideas formed the basis of most mediaeval interpretations of the phenomena of

[1] S. K. Heninger, Jr., *A Handbook of Renaissance Meteorology*, Durham, N.C., 1960, pp. 40–2, 44–6, etc.

[2] Aristotle, *Meteorologica*, I. (Loeb, pp. 1–121.)

[3] *Liber introductorius*, Oxford, Bodley MS 266, ff. 32ᵛ–35ʳ. See Thorndike, *A History of Magic and Experimental Science*, vol. 2, p. 324.

[4] Aristotle, *On the Heavens*, II. iv. (Loeb, pp. 152–63.)

'lightness' and 'heaviness' (*levitas* and *gravitas*) which greatly exercised those who attempted to explain them.[1] Following Aristotle, and in radical distinction to our post-Newtonian ideas about gravity, both heaviness and lightness were thought of as positive qualities. Lightness was not merely the absence of weight, but was an inbuilt tendency of some things to move up towards the outer regions of air and fire, while heaviness was a tendency to move down to the centre of the universe. Aristotle had suggested that earth was characterised by pure heaviness, and fire by pure lightness, while water and air showed both heaviness and lightness in differing proportions, air being, of course, predominantly light. Mediaeval commentators subjected Aristotle's formulation of these ideas to a great deal of careful scrutiny, giving special attention to the question of absolute and relative heaviness, in order to explain, for example, such observations as that wood is heavy in air but light in water. Despite variations in detail, Aristotelian ideas continued to dominate.

In discussions of the potentiality for flight of various physical objects and creatures, careful consideration was given to the proportions of the elements from which they were constituted. Birds were thought to contain a high proportion of elemental air, together with a comparatively large amount of water. In his discussion of the general nature of birds, Bartholomaeus Anglicus (*fl.* 1250) says that as they are formed from the two elements intermediate in density between the heaviest and the lightest, this gives them their two most fundamental capacities: first, to rise, and then to 'swim' in the air.[2] Largely because of Genesis 1:20, which, in the early Latin versions, states that God caused the birds to be created from the water, stress was sometimes laid on the watery parts of birds as well as on their airy constituents. The passage as given by Saint Ambrose (*ca.* 340–397) reads: *producant aquæ reptilia animarum viventium secundum genus: et volatilia super terram secus firmamentum cœli secundum genus.*[3] In attempting to account for this scriptural oddity, St Augustine (354–430) had drawn a distinction between the upper and lower atmospheres:

> Clouds are formed from water, as anyone will feel who has occasion to walk in the
> hills among the mists or on the plains through fog. And it is in air of this kind that

[1] Aristotle, *On the Heavens*, IV. (Loeb, pp. 326–69.)

[2] Bartholomaeus Anglicus, *De proprietatibus rerum*, [Cologne, 1472?] f. c^v: *Nam ex duobus elementis inter summe graue & summe leue intermedijs auium substancia est creata.*

[3] *Hexaemeron*, V. xiv. 45 (Migne, Series Lat., vol. 14, col. 226). *Cf.* the Vulgate: *producant aquae reptile animae viventis et volatile super terram sub firmamento caeli.* These readings are in fact inaccurate. *The New English Bible* reads 'Let the waters teem with countless living creatures, and let birds fly above the earth across the vault of heaven'.

birds are said to fly. But in the rarer and purer form, which is properly called air by everybody, they are not to be found, since owing to its tenuousness it will not support their weight. In this, moreover, it is said that no clouds are formed, and that no turbulences exist. There, indeed, no wind blows, as is the case on the top of Mount Olympus, which is said to rise beyond the humid air . . .[1]

Augustine goes on to say that the thicker, humid regions of the lower atmosphere might as well be called tenuous water as dense air.

In addition to the lightness produced by the elemental air contained in its basic substance, a bird was helped to rise by the quantities of common air which it could capture within the small interstices between the constituent parts of the feathers. Bartholomaeus Anglicus is explicit: 'the air contained within the concavity of the feathers lightens the bird and helps to make it rise more easily.'[2] Capturing the air was equivalent to capturing 'lightness', and as the air had a natural tendency to stay in its proper region, above the earth, the bird would be drawn up with it. It was largely this 'air-holding' capacity of feathers, which to us now seem flimsy and out of proportion to the needs of human flight, which led to their being so commonly adopted by the makers of artificial wings. Although not all wings were built of feathers, other substances such as woven cloth might also be made to capture quantities of air. Two of the winged men whose stories I give in Chapter Six,[3] Eilmer of Malmesbury, who used feathers, and the Turk of Constantinople, who wore 'a long and large white garment, gathered into many plites and foldings', were said to have stood on a height holding out their wings to 'gather the wind' before launching themselves into space. Even with the help of such equipment, man, being predominantly earthy and therefore heavy, was nevertheless struggling against the natural tendencies of his physical substance when attempting to fly.

Not all birds are, of course, equally endowed with the capacity for flight, and there was little point in trying to emulate the structure and movement of, for example, the predominantly earth-bound domestic hen. While kites and eagles were most commonly quoted as the examples which should be followed, there was a tradition that another and smaller bird, the *apis indica*, was still more naturally suited

---

[1] Saint Augustine, *De Genesi, liber imperfectus*, XIV. 44. (Migne, Series Lat., vol. 34, cols. 237–8. See also his *De Genesi contra Manichæos*, I. 15. Migne, Series Lat., vol. 34, col. 184.)

[2] *De proprietatibus rerum*, f. cᵛ: *Aer enim inclusus inter pennarum concauitatem auem leuigat & vt leuiter feratur sursum ipsam disponit & habilitat et adiuuat.*

[3] See pp. 91–4.

to the element of air. It was, indeed, thought neither to have nor to need feet, for it was said to spend its whole life in flight. Fenton, summarising the various beliefs about it, says:

> Like as this bird . . . is both monstrous & wonderful: euenso she yeldes sufficient matter to trouble al the Philosophers in the world: wherfore who so wil consider the great maruels of nature which be found in this little foule, neede not dout to confesse that the aire wherein she makes hir continual abode, norisheth nothing at all more straunge or worthy of admiration: For, for the first part, ther hath no man handled hir aliue, she liues alwais with the dew, & hath no fete, which is wholly re-pugnant against the opinion of Aristotle, who wryteth that there is no bird without feete . . .[1]

It was recognised that although feathered wings were the norm, flight could be achieved without them, as the example of the bat clearly demonstrated. That nocturnal creature, always associated with the strange and sinister, was, however, considered anomalous, a freak of nature, and perhaps even unnatural. It was some-times feared, almost universally despised, and commonly referred to by such terms as *animal ignobile* and *hoc vile animal*.[2] Aristotle had placed it midway between the birds and the quadrupeds, pointing out that it lacked some characteristics of both.[3] To imitate such a distasteful anomaly was obviously hazardous, and almost no one seems to have thought to try it.[4] Men with bat wings are occasionally seen in illuminated manuscripts (Plate 6) but it is significant that while bird wings commonly adorn angels, bat wings are usually reserved for devils.

Apart from their having inspired the probably apocryphal story of Regiomon-tanus' iron fly, winged insects exerted, as far as I am aware, no influence whatever on mediaeval and Renaissance aeronautics. Those cold-blooded creatures were felt to fall into a different category altogether. As they were 'rudderless' (that is, tailless), they could not be classed as aerial swimmers, and Albertus Magnus, or whoever wrote the *De motibus animalium* attributed to him, went so far as to deny to some of them, at least, any genuine capacity to fly. Speaking of such insects as the locusts, he suggested that their passage through the air was no more than a sustained jump,

---

[1] E. Fenton, *Certaine secrete wonders of Nature*, London, 1569, ff. 114r–116v.

[2] Saint Ambrose, *Hexaemeron*, V. xxiv. 87. (Migne, Series Lat., vol. 14, col. 240.)

[3] Aristotle, *Parts of Animals*, IV. xiii (697. b. 1ff). (Loeb, pp. 426–9.)

[4] Leonardo provides a well known exception. For an amusing passage about the possible use of bat wings, see Benvenuto Cellini's *Vita*, I. xxiii. (English trans. by R. H. H. Cust, *The Life of Benvenuto Cellini*, vol. 2, London, 1910, pp. 20–2.) Cellini lived from 1500 to 1571.

initiated by the legs and somewhat prolonged by the action of the wings.[1] Albertus
may have been thinking of a comment by Aristotle:

> The flight of flying insects is slow and weak, because the growth of their wings is
> not in proportion to the weight of their body; for their weight is considerable,
> while their wings are small and weak; so they use their power of flight like a merchant-
> ship attempting to travel by means of oars.[2]

In any case there was clearly nothing here for men to imitate.

It was one of the cardinal principles of Aristotelian physics that the elements
could be freely transmuted.[3] The easily observable tendency to rise, exhibited by
'vapours', 'exhalations', and warm air, was attributed to changes in elemental
balance brought about by the actions of heat and combustion. The products of such
changes, finding themselves out of their proper places in the scheme of things,
moved towards the regions of air or fire where they now belonged. The gentle
action of the morning sun on overnight moisture brought about one such trans-
formation which was frequently commented upon, and even in the seventeenth
century it was still entirely reasonable of Lauretus Laurus, for example, to suppose
that one might reproduce the famous artificial dove of Archytas of Tarentum by
enclosing within a light, bird-shaped framework an eggshell filled with dew which
would tend to rise if left exposed to the sun's rays.[4]

Several times during the early Middle Ages it seems that writers may be about
to hit upon the principle of the hot air balloon. In the *De celo & mundo* of Albertus
Magnus (*ca.* 1200–80), there is a passage of great interest which seems headed in this
direction. Albertus, discussing heaviness and lightness, recognises that a bladder
which one blows up with air warmed by the lungs will be measurably lighter than
when empty.[5] As he was involved in theoretical considerations, Albertus did not
attempt to follow up the practical aeronautical possibilities of this observation, but
the rising of hot air continued to intrigue commentators on Aristotle's ideas about
lightness. By the early fifteenth century the idea of applying the lifting force to
raise a man appears fully developed in Giovanni da Fontana's *Metrologum de pisce*

---

[1] Albertus Magnus [?], *De motibvs animalivm*, II. iii: 'De motu volantium & natantium'.
(*Opera*, vol. 5, Lugduni, 1651, p. 129.)

[2] Aristotle, *Progression of Animals*, X (710. a. 15). (Loeb, pp. 518, 519.)

[3] Aristotle, *On the Heavens*, III. vi–vii, etc. (Loeb, pp. 302–17.)

[4] See pp. 50–1.

[5] Albertus Magnus, *De celo & mundo*, Venetijs, 1495, f. 70ᵛ.

cane et volucre, only to be dismissed by him as impractical and dangerous.[1] As has happened so often in the history of technology, the concept remained dormant for several centuries before developments in other areas brought it back into prominence.

A further set of contemporary beliefs about the physical world, ultimately dependent once again on Aristotle, influenced attitudes to freely moving aeronautical objects. Aristotle had held that for the motion of a projectile to take place, the moving force must remain in physical contact with the object. As nothing seemed to be applying a force to a freely moving projectile, Aristotle had to resort to the notion that the initial act of propulsion imparted to the air which surrounded the projectile a moving force of its own; this was transferred to the layer of air next in front, and so on through a series of instantaneous transferences of motive power until inevitable losses caused the motion to cease.[2] This theory aroused a good deal of controversy, and was superseded in the later Middle Ages by the *impetus* theory of Jean Buridan (*fl.* 1350) which was widely accepted throughout the fourteenth, fifteenth, and sixteenth centuries. For the external moving force Buridan substituted an inner force, an *impetus* imparted to the body at the moment of projection. Buridan's *impetus* has certain analogies with Newton's concept of momentum, and the implications of the theory were far-reaching, but we are concerned here only with its application to simple projectiles.[3]

The *impetus* persisted until reduced by air resistance, by impact with an obstacle, or by gravity, but in accordance with Aristotle's tenets that a simple body can be endowed with only a single simple motion and that if two such motions are applied one will destroy the other, it was generally believed that a projectile could be given so much *impetus* that in the initial part of its movement the tendency of the object to be drawn to the earth (its *gravitas*) was altogether overcome. Although in the curving flight of a gently thrown object *gravitas* was thought to be progressively destroying *impetus* until the former alone would prevail and the object would fall vertically, in the case of a fast moving projectile like a cannon-ball the initial path was thought to be quite straight. When the *impetus* was no longer sufficient to prevail, gravity began to destroy it, thus creating a curved, middle part of the

[1] See pp. 110–11.

[2] Aristotle, *The Physics*, VIII. x. (Loeb, vol. 2, pp. 404–25.)

[3] For a convenient summary of the *impetus* theory and reactions against Aristotelianism in general, see A. C. Crombie, *Augustine to Galileo: The History of Science A.D. 400–1650*, London, 1952, pp. 212ff.

trajectory. This was followed in turn by purely vertical motion. It was on these principles that gunners calculated their aim until as late as the eighteenth century (Plate 7). The idea that the initial part of the trajectory of a projectile is a straight line was, as I discuss in Chapter Three, one of the fundamental assumptions which underlay the reasoning of Giovanni da Fontana when he explained the application of his rocket-bird to the measurement of heights.

Perhaps the most important, and potentially the most disruptive, of the mediaeval assumptions having a bearing on aeronautics were some virtually universal misconceptions about the mechanisms of a bird's flight. Although as early as the first half of the thirteenth century Frederick II (1194–1250) had set down with great meticulousness many remarkably acute observations of the physical characteristics and modes of flight of birds, he wrote from the point of view of the naturalist and keen falconer and did not attempt any detailed analysis of the aerodynamic problems.[1] The error made by everyone who did attempt such an analysis arose from the easy analogy with swimming, which encouraged the belief that birds move their wings downwards and backwards, pushing against the air. This explanation, supported of course by the contemporary readings of Genesis 1:20, was given added authority by a number of Patristic writers, including Saints Basil (*ca.* 330–379) and Ambrose (*ca.* 340–397).[2] In fact, as high-speed photography has shown, birds move their wings downwards and slightly forwards, the propulsion and lift having nothing to do with the rowing action of the arms in swimming. In normal flapping flight

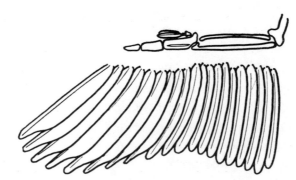

Fig. 1. Schematic representation of a bird's wing,
showing the primary and secondary feathers, and the *alula*

[1] Frederick II of Hohenstaufen, *De arte venandi cum auibus*, Augustae Vindelicorum, 1596.
[2] Saint Basil, *Homilia VIII in Hexaemeron*, 2. (Migne, Series Gr., vol. 29, col. 169.) Saint Ambrose, *Hexaemeron*, V. xiv. 45. (Migne, Series Lat., vol. 14, cols. 225–6.)

most of the bird's lift is produced by the inner third of the wing, which moves less than the rest, the flow of air over its cambered structure causing the pressure on the under side to be relatively greater than that on the upper. Most of the forward propulsion is created by the nearly vertical motion of the outer extremity of the wing. The feathers of the bird's 'hand', that is, those at the wing-tip, are known as the 'primaries'. In most land birds the outer primaries are characterised by their asymmetrical shape, the vane on the trailing edge of the quill being broad, while that on the leading edge is narrow. (The narrowing of the forward vane is known as emargination.) In flight these emarginated feathers twist, owing to their unbalanced shape, so that their motion through the air is oblique. They thus act in the same way as the blades of an aircraft propeller, pushing the bird forward. Sea birds, whose wings are long and narrow, together with bats and a few land birds, have closely integrated wing-tip assemblies which twist as a whole to perform the same function.[1] These movements were not, however, even partially understood until the seventeenth century. The writer of the *De motibus animalium* was emphatic in stating that flight and swimming are merely variants of the same action.[2] The same opinion was later held by Leonardo, and it was still among the basic assumptions of Aldrovandus, when he published his *Ornithologiae* in 1599.[3] This belief accounts in part for the innumerable designs, some of them produced as late as the nineteenth century, for flying machines propelled by oars, fins, outsize tennis racquets, and various other forms of 'swimming' or 'rowing' apparatus. It was not until 1680, when Borelli published the first part of his *De motu animalium*,[4] which corrected some (though not all) of the misconceptions about the action of a bird's wing, that the inadequacy of the human musculature to sustain flight was clearly demonstrated. Even if men had possessed the necessary strength, the incorrect movement of the arms would nevertheless have rendered all 'ornithoptering' vain. Any who managed to leave the ground in a brief glide must have completely unbalanced themselves when attempting backward swimming strokes.

While some of the bird-men may well have become airborne for long enough

[1] J. H. Storer, *The Flight of Birds*, Michigan, 1948. For Aristotle's views on the flight of birds, see *Progression of Animals*, X. (Loeb, pp. 514–19.)

[2] Albertus Magnus [?], *De motibvs animalivm*, II. iii: *Volantia autem & natantia in multis communicant: eò quod natatio quidam volatus est, sicut & volatus est quædam natatio.*

[3] U. Aldrovandus, *Ornithologiae*, vol. 1, Bononiae, 1599, p. 695: *Volatui sanè natatus ualde similis est.*

[4] G. A. Borelli, *De motu animalium*, vol. 1, Romae, 1680, pp. 322–6.

to make a brief 'hop', all the stories which speak of really successful flights are doubtless exaggerated in some respect. In many of them an archetypal pattern can be discerned, a pattern of hazardous launch, followed by a brief period in the air, followed again by a fall which more often than not is said to have broken the aeronaut's legs. This crippling result is found in the case of Eilmer, Danti, Damian, the Nürnberg cantor (who also broke his arms), and Guidotti. No doubt the legs are particularly vulnerable when one is descending from an almost uncontrolled glide, but both Danti and Guidotti, who fell through roofs, might have been expected to break some other parts of their bodies as well. Irrespective of the truth or falsehood of these accounts, I believe that there may be a more general, psychological, and archetypal reason for the frequency with which the historians seize on this matter of leg-breaking. It is, perhaps, an especially fitting punishment for Fate to mete out to those who act with 'excess of daring'. Too much movement in the air is answered by an appropriate curtailment of movement in man's proper sphere, on the ground.

One may summarise the principal ideas and beliefs determining the character of mediaeval and early Renaissance experiments with aerodynamics as follows: (a) birds are able to fly because the balance of the elements from which they are constituted gives them a natural affinity with the lower regions of the atmosphere, (b) lightness is a positive physical quality which may be artificially concentrated and manipulated, (c) wings made of feathers, which are especially 'airy' and endowed with lightness, may help a man to adjust his elemental balance to approximate to that of birds, (d) birds move forward by making swimming strokes with their wings, (e) although the nature of the free motion of a projectile is unclear and in dispute, it may perhaps be maintained by the circulating movement of the displaced air, (f) as the texture of the atmosphere is uneven, some parts of it will be better able to sustain flight than others, (g) the legitimacy of human attempts to fly is at best doubtful.

Although the beating of wings attached to the arms was the most common and most spectacular approach to experimental aeronautics, it was, as I show in the chapters which follow, by no means the only approach. There was also much unsystematic investigation of unmanned aerodynamic devices, some of which were seen as potential means of human flight. The materials and techniques used by winged men remained, as far as one can tell from the scanty reports, largely unchanged from century to century: cloth, cane, cords, leather thongs, and, of course, feathers, were always available in much the same form, and only limited variations in design procedure can have been possible. In dealing with the unmanned devices, however, technological advance and the importing of exotic ideas and materials become important considerations. Although the kite had been used from the earliest times as a man-lifter in the east, it appears to have been unknown in Europe before the fourteenth century, and only after it had been flown there for several generations was its man-carrying potential vaguely glimpsed. Rockets, the aeronautical possibilities of which were apparent to some adventurous minds from the beginning of the fifteenth century, were not seen in Europe until about 1300. Clockwork machinery grew steadily more sophisticated, but although it may have been tried in flying models from as early as the fifteenth century, one can be fairly certain that no success, however limited, was achieved with any such device before the seventeenth century at the earliest. The evolution of these and other techniques was haphazard and the results hardly encouraging. It was very rare for either a man or a model to become airborne, and the most consistent successes were achieved with a device which was soon to be relegated to the status of a toy: the kite. The tenacity and ingenuity displayed by those who attempted to master the forces of the air were nevertheless remarkable, revealing again and again the intellectual, psychological, and spiritual importance of man's desire to fly.

2

BANNERS, WINDSOCKS, AND FLYING DRAGONS

Mediaeval aeronautics may be said to begin with an unlikely object, the spectacular *draco*, or windsock banner, which was a familiar sight in Europe during the later days of the Roman empire, and which played a rather curious role in the early history of unmanned flight. It consisted of a carved open-mouthed head, of dragon-like appearance, attached to the top of a pole. Behind the head was fixed a tube of cloth which billowed out in the wind when the standard was held aloft by the *draconarius*. This standard appears to have been used in the first place to terrify the enemy and to inspire courage in the troops of the cohort, but it may also have been used for signalling, and it could have served to help archers to judge the strength of the wind. It was certainly used for ceremonial purposes.[1]

The origin of the *draco* is obscure, but it seems to have arisen somewhere in central Asia, where it continued in use at least until the Middle Ages. Whether it was ever used in China is uncertain, but what may have been a Chinese windsock standard is depicted on a beautifully decorated dish, of the K'ang-hsi period (1662–1722), in the Fitzwilliam Museum (Plate 8). The banner looks three-dimensional and seems to billow out from a ring attached to the pole,[2] but the appearance may be deceptive, and may be attributable to the modelling of the thick layers of under-glaze blue. Similar scenes are found on many Chinese plates and dishes from the period, and, in every other example that I have seen, the banner, although given something of the same billowing appearance, is unmistakably flat. While it is therefore possible that windsock standards were known,

[1] C. Renel, *Cultes militaires de Rome: les enseignes*, Paris, 1903, pp. 206–11.

[2] In a private communication, dated 1 January 1969, Dr Joseph Needham expresses his agreement with my interpretation of the standard.

1. Daedalus and Icarus, by Marie Briot. In J. Baudoin, *Recveils d'emblemes divers*, vol. 1, Paris, 1638, pp. 114, 362

2. Alexander, about to step into his griffon-drawn basket. Bodley MS 264, f. 80ᵛ, *ca.* 1340

3. Alexander in flight. Attributed to Hans Leonhard Schäufelein (1480–1539 or 1540)

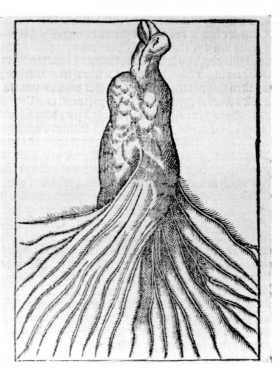

4. The three regions of the air. G. Reisch, *Margarita philosophica nova*, VII.I.41, Ex Argentoraci veteri, 1515

5. The *apis indica*, said to spend its whole life in the air. E. Fenton, *Certaine secrete wonders of Nature*, London, 1569, f. 114ʳ (after Gesner)

6a, b, c. Men and grotesques with bat wings. (a) Arras, Bibliothèque municipale, MS 657 (139), f. 89ʳ; (b) MS 1043, f. 7ʳ. Both late thirteenth century. (c) Arras, Musée Diocésain, MS 47, f. 31ʳ, early fourteenth century

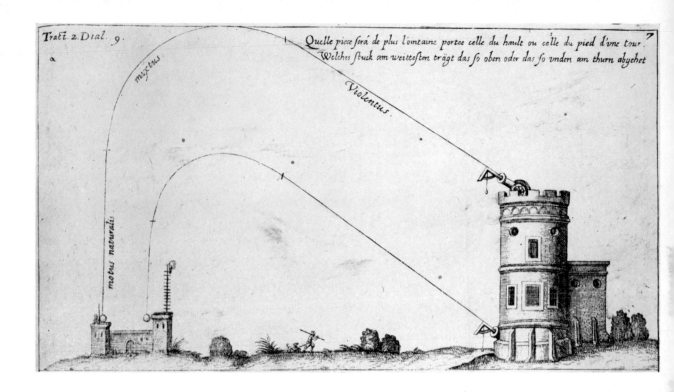

7. The old belief about the three phases of the flight of a projectile: (a) violent motion, (b) mixed motion, (c) natural motion. R. Norton, *The Gunner*, London, 1628, opposite p. 96

8. Standard, probably a windsock. Porcelain dish, Chinese, mark of Ch'eng-hua (1465–87), period of K'ang-hsi (1662–1722). Fitzwilliam Museum, C.33–1931

9. Fire-breathing windsock standard. St Gallen, Stiftsbibliothek, codex 22, *Psalterium aureum*, p. 140, ninth century A.D.

10. The *draco volans*. Conrad Kyeser, *Bellifortis*. Göttingen, Niedersächsische Staats- und Universitätsbibliothek, codex philos. 63, f. 105^r, 1405

11. *Draco*, type A. (Winged, five-parttail, free-flying.) Chantilly, Musée Condé, MS XX.C.14, f. 135^r, early fifteenth century

12, 13. *Dracones*, type B. (Wingless, three-part
tail, free-flying.) Plate 12: Karlsruhe,
Badische Landesbibliothek, codex
Durlach II, f. 119ʳ, *ca.* 1410? Plate 13:
Weimar, Thüringische Landesbibliothek,
codex fol. 328, f. 218ᵛ, *ca.* 1430

14, 15, 16. *Dracones*, type C. (Winged, four-part tail, fixed to pole, vestigial line on pole.) Plate 14: Göttingen, Niedersächsische Staats- und Universitätsbibliothek, codex philos. 64, f. 92ʳ, early fifteenth century. Plate 15: Erlangen, Universitätsbibliothek, MS 1390, f. 169ᵛ, 1500. Plate 16: Vienna, Österreichische Nationalbibliothek, codex 5278, f. 145ʳ, fifteenth century

if not common, in seventeenth- and eighteenth-century China, the date of this dish is much too late to be used as evidence of Chinese origins of the *draco*. There is, however, no doubt that more than a thousand years earlier the standard was well known to the Scythians, Persians, and Dacians, among others.[1] At some time around the third century A.D. this form of standard was adopted by the Romans. While at first it appears to have been used only by auxiliaries, it later became the regular standard of a cohort, being second in importance to the *aquila* of the legion.[2] Although it continued to be found in Europe after the fall of Rome, it was most commonly associated with the eastern 'barbarians'.

Fig. 2. Dacian windsock standard on the column, Trajan early first century A.D.

Fig. 3. The windsock standard extended by the breeze

The dragon standards were often made to look very realistic, with the result that some reports seem to attribute animal life to them. Lucian is scornful of one such gullible commentator:

> . . . he has seen everything so keenly that he said that the serpents of the Parthians (this is a banner they use to indicate number—a serpent precedes, I think, a thousand men), he said that they were alive and of enormous size; that they are born in Persia a little way beyond Iberia; that they are bound to long poles and, raised on high, create terror while the Parthians are coming on from a distance; that in the encounter itself at close quarters they are freed and sent against the enemy; that in fact they

[1] *E.g.*, Arrian, *Tactics*, 35. 2ff.; Lucian, *How to Write History*, 29. For further references see the article on the *draco* in *Paulys Realencyclopädie der Classischen Altertumswissenschaft*, ed. G. Wissowa, Stuttgart, 1893, etc.

[2] Vegetius, II. 13 (14): *primum signum totius legionis est aquila: quam Aquilifer portat. Dracones etiam per singulas cohortes a Draconariis feruntur ad proelium.*

had swallowed many of our men in this way and coiled themselves around others and suffocated and crushed them . . .[1]

The dragons on the Trajan column, which are shown as forming a part of the accoutrement of the defeated Dacians, certainly look real enough (Fig. 2), while Ammianus Marcellinus provides a vivid description of the lifelike ceremonial *dracones* which surrounded the emperor:

> And behind the manifold others that preceded him he was surrounded by dragons, woven out of purple thread and bound to the golden and jewelled tops of spears, with wide mouths open to the breeze and hence hissing as if roused by anger, and leaving their tails winding in the wind.[2]

The continuity of the *draco* can be traced through its appearance in the *Psalterium*

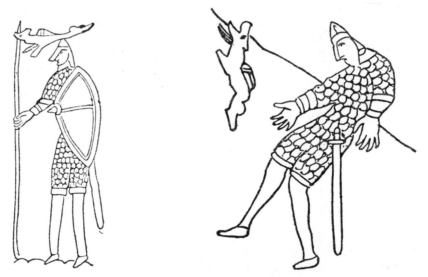

Figs. 4, 5. Windsock standards from the Bayeux Tapestry

aureum (Plate 9), in the Bayeux Tapestry (Figs. 4, 5), and in the *Chanson de Roland*, where it is attributed to the pagans, in contrast to the flat banner of the Christians.

At some time during the early Middle Ages there arose the practice of enhancing the appearance of the dragon by placing a lighted torch in its mouth, thus causing it to emit fire and smoke, as may be seen in Plate 9. It is possible that the red dragon

[1] *How to Write History*, 29. (Loeb, vol. 6, pp. 42, 43.)
[2] *Rerum gestarum libri qui supersunt*, XVI. 10. 7. (Loeb vol. 1, pp. 244, 245.)

used to such good effect by Merlin was an imaginative recreation of the fire-breathing standard:

> . . . then Merlin turned the dragon in his hand and it shot forth flames of fire from its mouth so that the air was quite reddened . . .[1]

The first definite written evidence of the use of such fire in the dragons is a well-known passage in Długosz's *Historia polonica*, describing the battle of Wahlstatt, near Lignica, in April, 1241:

> Among other standards there was, in the Tartar army, an immense banner on which a sign like an X was to be seen. And at the top of the enemy banner was the representation of a hideous, jet-black head with a bearded chin. During the pursuit on the slopes, when the Tartars had withdrawn to the distance of a *stadium*, the standard-bearer began with all his strength to shake the head which was on top of a spear, and from it there poured forth vile-smelling steam, smoke, and fumes, which engulfed the whole Polish army. Because of the horrible and intolerable fumes, the Polish warriors, nearly unconscious and half dead, were weak and unable to fight.[2]

The later development of the fire-breathing *draco*, as I shall point out, grows rather confused, the confusion arising from errors of interpretation by both mediaeval and modern writers on the subject.

In the late nineteenth century it was noticed that among the most spectacular inventions included in mediaeval technological treatises was something superficially similar to a kite, but having a body in the shape of an elongated dragon. The main part of the body was usually drawn in a manner suggesting suppleness, while instructions for building it, which sometimes accompanied the illustrations, indicated that it was made of wood, parchment, and cloth. As such kites were shown flying from the ends of cords, it was apparent that a form of sustentation was implied, at least in theory. Occasionally wings were drawn, though they were sometimes very small, and four of the creatures are shown emitting fire and smoke. Until recently it has been assumed that these were primitive hot-air balloons, the fire and smoke pointing to the use inside the dragon's mouth of a slow-burning match which warmed the air within the fabric sufficiently to produce sustentation.

When one examines the published work concerning these so-called 'semi-kites',

---

[1] *Lestoire de Merlin*, ed. H. O. Sommer, Washington, 1908, p. 225: *lors sen tourne merlins le dragon en sa main qui ietoit brandons de feu parmi la goule que li airs en deuint tous vermaus* . . .

[2] J. Długosz, *Historiae polonicae libri xii*, Lipsiae, 1711–12, col. 679.

it becomes apparent that the interpretation both of their form and of their method of flight has been supported by only two passages of contemporary text, bolstered by a substantial amount of supposition. The textual evidence is found on ff. 104^v and 105^r of Conrad Kyeser's *Bellifortis* (1405).[1] On the latter page Kyeser's miniaturist has drawn a dragon-kite which has become very familiar to aeronautical historians (Plate 10). This illustration is intended to accompany a ten-line text written, like most of *Bellifortis*, in bad Latin hexameters. The text describes the structure and mode of flight: 'This flying dragon may be made with parchment for the head, the middle of linen, but the tail of silk, the colours various. At the end of the head let a triple harness [bridle] be attached to the wood, moved by the middle of the flail [-shaped reel]. Let the head be raised into the wind, and when it has been lifted two men may hold the head while a third carries the reel. It follows him while he rides [or, 'he follows it as he rides']. The movement of the line causes the flight to vary up and down, to right and left. Let the head be coloured red and made to look real, the middle should be of moon-silver colour, the end of several colours.'

On the previous page (104^v) there occurs a passage, headed *Ignis pro Tygace uolante*, which gives details of a recipe for making fire-producing materials. It has been assumed that the fire was intended for the *draco*, and, therefore, that the *draco* and the *tygax* were identical. This explanation has gained currency largely due to the work of Feldhaus and Romocki.[2]

The supposition that the two texts were meant to accompany one another has led, in the first place, to the idea that the *draco* on f. 105^r consisted of a hollow tube into which a dish containing the fire could be introduced, and in the second place to the development of an extensive theory to account for the origin of this technologically sophisticated object.

It was not unnatural that, given the passage containing the fire-producing recipe in Kyeser, commentators should have believed that his *draco*, though flying free on a cord rather than held on a rigid pole, carried fire in the same way as did the old dragon standards. Someone had noticed that the hot air produced buoyancy in the dragon's tail, and had hit upon the idea of allowing the whole thing to rise on the end of a string. While the theory is attractive at first sight, it does not withstand

[1] Göttingen, Niedersächsische Staats- und Universitätsbibliothek, codex philos. 63.
[2] F. M. Feldhaus, *Die Technik der Vorzeit*, Leipzig und Berlin, 1914, cols. 650–9; S. J. von Romocki, *Geschichte der Explosivstoffe*, vol. 1, Berlin, 1895, pp. 160–2.

close scrutiny. In the first place, it is plainly impossible that, using the materials available at the time, dragons could have been made light enough to rise when filled with hot air. This objection loses some force, of course, if we treat the semi-kite, like many other objects drawn in manuscripts of the Kyeser type, as imaginary. As I go on to discuss below, it is nevertheless possible to interpret the *draco*, in an entirely different sense, as a reasonably accurate representation of reality.

The second and more serious objection concerns the relationship of the passages on ff. 104^v and 105^r of codex philos. 63. In a little-known article published in 1940, F. Denk questioned the relevance of the one to the other, suggesting that the word *tygax* might refer rather to a firearm illustrated on the same page.[1] The problem is the more acute in that *tygax* appears to be a *hapax legomenon* of unknown meaning. Denk seems to have failed, however, to notice that the *tygax* page is the last in an interpolated passage not written by Kyeser himself, but based on the *Liber ignium* of Marcus Graecus.[2] The consequences of this are twofold: first, the ten-line text on f. 105^r is the only evidence of Kyeser's own intention regarding the *draco*, and, second, the interpolated passage, if it does indeed refer to the *draco*, represents someone else's interpretation of its nature and function.

The rest of Kyeser's short text, taken alone, bears no implication of three-dimensionality. Furthermore, the *draco* is very similar to a kite described some twenty-five years later in Vienna codex 3064, one of many mediaeval 'fireworks-books' (Plate 32).[3] The description in this case is lengthy and detailed, and the object is undoubtedly a kite of the plane-surface type. The kite in the 'fireworks-book' was certainly built and flown, the description being written in a manner which indicates very clearly that the writer was a practised kite-flier. The Kyeser drawing could, without difficulty, be interpreted as a representation of a kite similar in all important respects to that in Vienna codex 3064. Both the scanty details of its construction and the comments on its mode of flight are consistent with the latter text. Such an interpretation would therefore retrieve the *draco* from the realm of fantasy. I think it highly likely that Kyeser meant to depict a real plane-surface

---

[1] F. Denk, 'Zwei mittelalterliche Dokumente zur Fluggeschichte und ihre Deutung,' *Sitzungsberichte der Physikalischmedizinischen Sozietät in Erlangen*, vol. 71, 1939, pp. 353–68. (Published Erlangen, 1940.)

[2] G. Quarg, 'Der BELLIFORTIS von Conrad Kyeser aus Eichstätt, 1405,' *Technikgeschichte*, vol. 32, no. 4, 1965, pp. 318–20.

[3] See below, pp. 65–7.

kite which could be built and flown, and that the *tygax* page, if it refers to the drawing, was meant to provide a fire-producing recipe for a three-dimensional kite of an imaginary kind, based on a misinterpretation of the *draco* by the writer of the interpolation.

A possible source of confusion of windsocks and plane-surface kites is to be found in the description of the kite in Vienna codex 3064 (Plate 32). In the notes for its construction the writer says that it would be best to 'cut it open down the middle of the back for two or three ells, starting from the head, and then insert and sew in a piece of silk cloth one and a half spans wide, more or less, and pointed at both ends, following the shape of the body'. He points out that the effect of this insertion is to create a sail-like fulness which, he claims, both improves the flight and makes the kite appear to have a three-dimensional body or back. It may be that the use of such wind-filled pockets led to confusion, in the minds of some early interpreters of Kyeser, about the structure of the *draco*. Alternatively the pocket may, of course, have been an attempt to produce a simple practical realisation of the probably imaginary windsock-kite.

A great deal of light is cast on the nature of Kyeser's *draco* by the many versions of the illustration which are found in later copies of the text.[1] These fall into a number of categories, many of the illustrations closely resembling one another in certain respects. The similarities are no doubt due to the genealogy of the manuscripts, but the present state of Kyeser scholarship is not sufficiently advanced to allow definite conclusions to be drawn.[2] I must nevertheless briefly refer to one important textual matter. Although the Göttingen manuscript from which Plate 10 is reproduced (codex philos. 63) represents, in general, Kyeser's final intentions with respect to his text, it is a fair copy (not always accurate) of earlier, fragmentary drafts which have not survived. While the *draco* in Plate 10 clearly suffers, as do other drawings of it, from copyists' errors, it is found in a manuscript which is probably closest, among those that are extant, to the text of the original drafts. As most of the later manuscripts appear also to derive from those sources by lines of descent which do not include codex philos. 63, their versions of the *draco* may

---

[1] Some of these are reproduced in Feldhaus, *Die Technik der Vorzeit*, and elsewhere. Others are reproduced here for the first time.

[2] The partial chronology given in the introduction to Quarg's facsimile edition (see p. 143, note 1), pp. xxv–xxxii, is certainly faulty in several respects. I have insufficient space here to enter into the palaeographical issues involved.

contain structural features which are closer to the truth than those of Plate 10, despite its being a fair copy. All versions of works such as *Bellifortis* are in any case of value in revealing what the copyists thought about the material with which they were dealing, and hence in revealing, to a certain degree, the common apprehensions of the time. This interpretative process is especially useful in the case of the *draco*, which is drawn in Plate 10 with more elegance than technological accuracy.

Not all copies of Kyeser's text contain a representation of the *draco*, and at least one manuscript (Berlin codex 117) has been lost in recent times. Other texts exist in fragments only, while there is every likelihood that some have disappeared without trace. One case where the *draco* has certainly been lost is particularly unfortunate. An interesting copy of *Bellifortis* in the *Bibliothèque de la ville de Colmar*[1] once contained a representation of the *draco* which has, however, been cut from the page and removed. This copy would have been especially valuable in view of the accompanying text, which is a paraphrase and adaptation of the hexameters, written in a late southern Middle High German dialect:

> This is a flying dragon which should be made thus. The head should be of parchment, the middle and tail, except for the head, of silk of many colours. A three-part string should be attached to the parchment by means of a connecting-link. Item, this string should be held by a reel, and it should be as long as the height to which one wishes to make the dragon fly. And when one wants it to rise, one should turn its head against the wind; when the wind blows on it, pull it up by the string, which should be held in the hand by means of a handle [*i.e.*, reel]. Thus it will rise into the air and you may let it out.

At the beginning this version remains fairly close to the Latin original, but departs from it increasingly towards the end. Even the earlier passages, however, show evidence of misunderstanding, or of corruption in the Latin text used by the translator. The redundant phrase 'except for the head' (*ussgenomen das hopt*) probably arose from misreading *fine capitis* as *sine capitis* (*sic*), while the phrase about the 'connecting link' appears to be a desperate attempt to make sense of *zona ligno coadiuncta*. After the mid-point, the translator seems to have thought it best to abandon Kyeser's text altogether and to write from his own knowledge of 'flying dragons'. Some similarities here with the description of the kite in Vienna codex 3064 suggest, once again, that the two objects are virtually identical. Given the difficulty

[1] MS 491, f. 72r.

which many of the copyists experienced in understanding the reel and the bridle, it would have been most interesting to see how these were rendered in the lost illustration.

I have reproduced all copies of the *draco* from the extant texts known to me (together with a copy of an old reproduction of Berlin codex 117). The principal distinguishing characteristics of the various types of illustration are mentioned in the main captions for each group of plates. The copyists have interpreted the *draco* in four principal ways: free-flying windsock with wings; free-flying windsock without wings; winged windsock fixed to a pole; free-flying plane-surface kite in the shape of a pennon. Other minor variations increase the total number of types to seven.

Type A. The one example of this type is alone among the copies in representing the *draco* as a winged windsock while at the same time retaining all the other principal features seen in Plate 10. Among the various possible interpretations of Plate 10, the most convincing hitherto has been that advanced by Mr Gibbs-Smith, who suggested that Kyeser intended to depict a free-flying windsock sustained by the kite-like action of a pair of large wings which have been omitted from the picture. The *draco* in Plate 11, which is realistically drawn, provides the best evidence so far discovered in favour of Mr Gibbs-Smith's theory. Its similarity in other respects to the 'non-fliers' (Plates 14–18) nevertheless leads me to believe that this copyist's interpretation of the *draco* is merely fanciful.

Type B. These examples look more like the kite in Vienna codex 3064 than does the *draco* of Plate 10. In neither case has the draftsman made any attempt to show the attachment of the bridle. The three-part tail (also seen in Plate 19) may indicate a misunderstanding of the passage about the bridle, the *tripla zona*. (Compare, however, the four-part and five-part tails in Plates 11, 14, 15, and 16.)

Types C and D. That the copyists did not fully understand the nature of the material they were copying is revealed by the presence, in Plates 14–16, of the vestigial line wound uselessly on the top of the pole, and by the cranked shape of the pole itself, which derives from its original purpose as a reel. The addition of wings in these examples may simply be an attempt to make the dragons more lifelike, but it is also possible, as I shall discuss below, that they have some genuine aerodynamic significance. Plates 14–18 bear a close relationship to the old *draco* standard. The draftsmen seem to have interpreted the Kyeser kite as a rigid standard to be borne into battle, a supposition which is supported by the vigorous use of the spurs by the armoured rider in Plate 17, and by a four-line passage of text associated with that example, the only one I have come across in these copies which differs wholly from Kyeser's original: 'Make a dragon of thin cloth, as you know how; put varnish in the head and set it alight and it will give forth great flames.'[1] Although in manuscripts such as these it is often difficult to distinguish fantasy from reality, the matter of fact tone of this brief note may perhaps indicate the continued familiarity in the fifteenth century of the fire-breathing *draco* standard. The misinterpretation of Kyeser's relatively unusual kite would thus become all the more readily understandable.

Type E. In these, the most naive of the copies, the bridle has been converted into a halter which seems to be causing the beast some distress. The copyists clearly had no idea what they were looking at. Plate 19 seems in other respects to bear a close relationship to Plates 12 and 13.

Type F. The draftsman, while allowing his imagination a great deal of scope in interpreting the dragon itself, which here looks rather like a flying pig, has made some attempt to indicate the bridle, which he only partly understands. The diagram to the right of the drawing in codex philos. 63 (Plate 10) apparently illustrates the general shape of the bridle, as seen from the top of the *draco*, looking down along the plane of the head. The copyist of Plate 21 seems to have begun by including Kyeser's supplementary diagram to the right of his illustration also. This, however, he later erased, perhaps after suddenly realising what it was meant to indicate. (Traces of the outline are still visible on the original page.) At all events, he has put a three-leg bridle, of sorts, on his dragon.

Type G. In this example we have, I believe, the true interpretation of what Kyeser had in mind. The similarity to the kite in Plate 32 almost amounts to identity. Alone among the copies, this one seems to have been drawn by someone who was familiar with plane-surface kites.

Some, but not all, of the illustrations are accompanied by a passage of text. Except in the cases of Plate 17 and of the mutilated manuscript referred to on page 39, this is always a copy of the verses which are to be found below the *draco* in Plate 10. There are a number of variant readings, none of which is significant from the present point of view.

While the fifteenth-century reality depicted in the *dracones* was probably a large, brightly coloured, and perhaps somewhat frightening plane-surface kite,

---

[1] Vienna, Österreichische Nationalbibliothek, codex 3062, f. 128ʳ.

the imaginary objects created by the copyists have their own interest. As seems suitable for such unnatural creatures, most of the wings are bat-derived, but those on the *draco* in Plate 11 are drawn, still more unnaturally, as hybrids, the bat-wing structure being covered with feathers. Although winged windsocks were probably imaginary, all the wings appear to represent artificial rather than living things, and may therefore tell us something about the structures used by aeronautical experimenters of the time. While some of the wings, such as those in Plates 18 and 21, are plainly impractical, others might be made to withstand reasonably large air pressures. The relatively straight leading edges shown in Plates 15, 16, and perhaps 11, may indicate the intention to use a rigid rod extending across the *draco* and carrying the fingers which would help to stiffen a cloth cover. Although it is found on *dracones* which are among the non-fliers, the hint of a genuine aerofoil camber in the wings of Plates 17 and 18 is interesting, and may suggest more care in the copying of nature than is indicated by any contemporary descriptions of these and other aerodynamic devices.

Fig. 6. Kite, possibly a windsock, in Walter de Milemete's *De nobilitatibus*, Oxford, Christ Church, MS 92, ff. 77ᵛ–78ʳ, 1326/7

As none of the *dracones* is bird-winged, the lack of any structure simulating a bird's tail may not be significant, but in so far as the *draco* in Plate 11 is intended to depict a model of a live flying creature, the flexible streamers at the rear emphasise how inadequate was the contemporary understanding of the tail's function.

These considerations about the Kyeser manuscripts may have some bearing on our interpretation of the dragon sketched in Walter de Milemete's *De nobilitatibus* (1326/7).[1] This is the earliest known illustration of a European kite (Fig. 6). Since, unfortunately, it occurs in that part of the manuscript which is only sketched in, ready for later completion by the illuminator, the construction of the kite is unclear. Some features of it suggest that it could have been three-dimensional (that is, that its body was a windsock). The loop in the tail, which may represent a knot, is one such feature. A knot might have been intended to close the rear orifice and so retain the wind, but this, as with so many other details from mediaeval manuscripts, may represent convention or supposition rather than fact. Dragons were commonly drawn with knotted tails (see Plate 23). A second feature of interest is the provision of wings. These, though drawn very small, may in reality have been large enough to provide the necessary sustentation for a windsock.

The Milemete kite could, on the other hand, have been of the plane-surface type, the wings being no more than a projection created by a cross-stick to which a covering was attached. There can be no certainty about the matter, and it is in any case very unlikely that such a kite ever carried a bomb in battle, but there is, I believe, some reason to think that Milemete's kite was indeed a plane-surface structure. A close examination of the original manuscript, using an ultra-violet lamp, reveals that under the drawing there is a very faint preliminary sketch of the same scene which has been inked over to produce the illustration as we now have it. The sketch differs in certain minor details, including the disposition of the line, which was evidently intended to pass directly over the winch, instead of by-passing it, as it does in the final draft. Of greater importance are three differences in the sketching of the kite itself. First, only one wing, the upper one, is drawn (though the lower one may have been lost owing to fading), and it is substantially bigger than those in the final draft; second, the outline of the front half of the kite is drawn with two parallel lines about 2 mm apart, suggesting, perhaps, a wooden frame similar to that on the well-known modern arch-top kite; third, the rear end of the

[1] Walter de Milemete, *De nobilitatibus sapientiis et prudentiis regum*, Oxford, Christ Church, MS 92, ff. 77ᵛ–78ʳ.

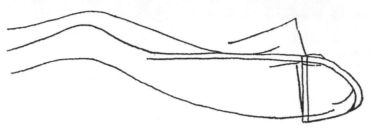

Fig. 7. Reconstruction of part of the original rough sketch of the
Milemete kite

kite is drawn with a number of fluid lines, recalling the tail of Plate 22, and suggesting that this part of the Milemete kite, at least, is simply a flat cloth pennon (Fig. 7).

As most books of military engineering contain comparatively little text (in some
cases no text at all), having been drawn up for practical rather than literary purposes,
they did not become a part of the mainstream of literary manuscripts and figure
very little in the works of commentators of a more general and non-military bent.
Thus, in trying to assess the full significance of the *dracones* one cannot appeal to
such intelligent later observers as Cardano or Scaliger. Apart from Vienna codex
3064, I know of no later written comment, outside the military tradition, which
refers unequivocally to the *dracones*. Plane-surface kites both of the dragon-shaped
type and the better-known pear and diamond shapes were becoming increasingly
common (see Chapter Four). They more frequently caught the writers' attention,
and were undoubtedly confused with the three-dimensional windsocks. Thus there
appear, in the seventeenth century, several fanciful descriptions of windsock kites
which were probably attempts to translate into reality the imaginary three-
dimensional shape which had been suggested by the dragons. A particularly interesting example of this process of translation is to be found in Daniel Schwenter's

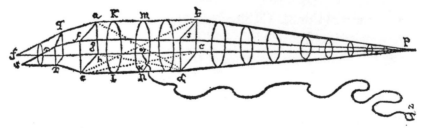

Fig. 8. Structure of a windsock kite. D. Schwenter, *Deliciæ physico-
mathematicæ*, pt. 1, Nürnberg, 1636, p. 474

Deliciae physico-mathematicae.[1] Although his ultimate source is a well-known chapter in della Porta describing what is certainly a plane-surface kite, Schwenter, in recasting the description in the vernacular, distorts the plain meaning of the original text so as to provide, instead, details of a large windsock. Although no wings are shown in the diagram (Fig. 8) they are mentioned briefly in the text. Schwenter mentions the use of windsock kites to carry lamps and musical instruments, a subject which is taken up a number of times by Athanasius Kircher, whose illustrations of windsocks look, however, still further removed from reality (Figs. 9–11).

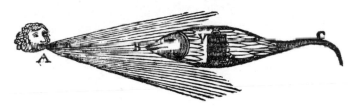

Fig. 9. Hypothetical windsock kite. Athanasius Kircher,
Musurgia universalis, Romae, 1650, vol. 2, p. 354

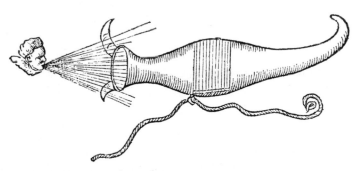

Fig. 10. A redrawing of Fig. 9. *Athanasii Kircheri e Soc. Jesu.
phonurgia nova*, Campidonae, 1673, p. 147

[1] D. Schwenter, *Deliciæ physico-mathematicæ*, pt. 1, Nürnberg, 1636, pp. 472–5.

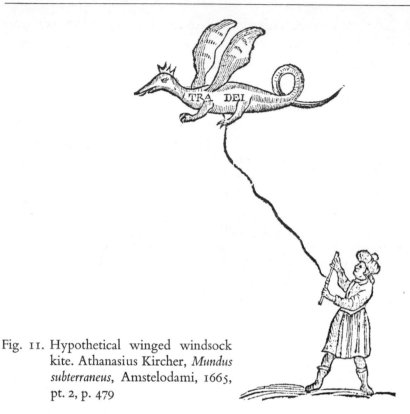

Fig. 11. Hypothetical winged windsock
　　　kite. Athanasius Kircher, *Mundus
　　　subterraneus*, Amstelodami, 1665,
　　　pt. 2, p. 479

As I have suggested, some of the copies of Kyeser's *draco*, especially Plates 17 and 18, seem to indicate that the *draco* standard, in the form of a windsock of frightening appearance and capable of carrying fire in the mouth, survived into early Renaissance times. The existence of free-flying windsocks, lifted by wings, seems much less likely, but the accounts in Schwenter and Kircher may perhaps reflect the reality of winged windsocks built and tested in the sixteenth and seventeenth centuries. As such objects would have been both difficult to construct and aerodynamically very inefficient, they were probably uncommon, to say the least, and in any case no more is heard of them after the seventeenth century.

A possible reason for the persistence of the dragon-shaped kites and standards until the years of the New Science is to be found in their physical similarity to the natural phenomenon called the *draco volans*, or 'fire drake', one of the more spectacular celestial events regularly noted by mediaeval and early Renaissance meteorologists. The 'fire drake' was believed to consist of a dragon-like conglomeration of vapours in the lower air. William Fulke describes its formation:

When a certen quantitie of *vapors* ar gathered on a heape, being very near compact, & as it wer hard tempered together this lompe of *vapors* assending to the region of cold, is forcibly beaten backe, whiche violence of mouing, is sufficient to kindle it, (although som men will haue it to be caused betwene ij. cloudes a whote & a cold) then the highest part, which was climming vpward, being by reason more subtil & thin, apeareth as the Dragons neck, smoking, for that it was lately in the repuls bowed or made crooked, to represent the dragons bely. The last part by the same repulse, turned vpward, maketh the tayle, both apearing smaller, for that it is farther of, & also, for that the cold bindeth it. This dragon thus being caused, flyeth along in the ayre, & somtime turneth to & fro, if it meat with a cold cloud to beat it back, to the great terror, of them that beholde it, of whom some called it a fyre Drake, some saye it is the Deuill hym selfe, and so make report to other. More then sixtene yeares ago, on May daye, when many younge folke went abroade early in the mornyng, I remember, by sixe of the clocke in the forenoone, there was newes come to London, that the Deuill the same mornynge, was seene flyinge ouer the Temmes: afterward came worde, that he lyghted at Stratforde, and ther was taken and sett in the stockes, and that though he would fayne haue dissembled the matter, by turning hym selfe into the likenes of a man, yet was he knowen welinough by his clouen feet. I knowe some yet alyue, that went to see hym, & returning affirmed, that he was in deed seen flying in the ayre, but was not taken prysoner. I remember also that som wyshed he had been shoot at with gons, or shaftes as he flewe ouer the Temes. Thus do ignorant men iudge of these thynges that they knowe not, as for this Deuill, I suppose it was a flyinge Dragon, wherof we speake, very fearefull to loke vpon, as though he had life, because he moueth, where as he is nothing els but cloudes & smoke . . .[1]

Although I know of no texts which make an explicit connexion between the two kinds of *draco*, illustrations of the atmospheric 'flying dragon' (Plate 23) are often very similar to the artificial simulacra in Plates 11, 21, etc., and it seems possible that the fire-breathing monster which some experimenters had hoped to make fly at the end of a cord was conceived as a crude man-made reproduction of the frightening 'meteor' with its satanic associations. Starting as a simple length of cloth on the end of a pole, the standard had, over the centuries, developed both increasingly lifelike and increasingly aerodynamic characteristics. The putative free-flying windsock with its sinuous movement and threatening mouth was potentially capable of transforming into reality the old stories of griffon-borne Alexander. The potentiality must, however, have seemed too daring an idea for the courageous

[1] W. Fulke, *A Goodly Gallery*, London, 1571, ff. 10ʳ–11ʳ.

contemporary dabblers in aeronautical science, for no one suggested that the 'flying dragons' might be used to lift a man. The *dracones* were nevertheless of importance in shaping the history of flight. For two or three centuries they gave direct practical experience of the manipulation of wind forces, and they firmly established the kite in Europe. Had there been no *dracones*, virtually the only well-known aerodynamic objects in Europe before 1600 would have been passive and active windmills, whose potential importance for aeronautics was still less appreciated than was that of the kite.

Following the establishment of the New Science, 'observations' of such things as the meteoric *draco volans* grew less frequent. With the simultaneous growth of popularity of the simpler pear and diamond kites, the old dragon shapes, both plane-surface and three-dimensional, went entirely out of fashion, so that by the eighteenth century winged windsocks ceased to be thought of as practical possibilities. The final disappearance of the *draco* may be said to date from the time of Guyot, who mentioned the spectacle of the flying dragon of realistic shape, but believed that this could be achieved only by supporting it with a pear-kite, from which the impotent and lifeless creature was to be suspended (Fig. 12).

Fig. 12. Dragon suspended from a plane-surface kite. E.-G. Guyot, *Nouvelles récréations*, Paris, 1786, vol. 2, Plate 44

3

ROCKET BIRDS

A possible source of some of the copyists' confusions and misinterpretations of the dragons of the preceding chapter is to be found in the development of an independent stream of rocket-propelled birds, some real and some imaginary. As far as most mediaeval commentators were concerned, their origin lay in the tradition that Archytas of Tarentum, the Pythagorean friend of Plato who flourished *ca.* 400–350 B.C., built and flew a wooden dove. The earliest known account of this invention is a passage in Aulus Gellius, who quotes and paraphrases Favorinus: '. . . not only many eminent Greeks, but also the philosopher Favorinus, a most diligent searcher of ancient records, have stated most positively that Archytas made a wooden model of a dove with such mechanical ingenuity and art that it flew; so nicely balanced was it, you see, with weights and moved by a current of air enclosed and hidden within it.' Favorinus' own statement, in Greek, says, further, that 'whenever it lit, it did not rise again'.[1]

It has sometimes been suggested that Archytas derived the idea for his dove from eastern sources, and it is of great interest that a strikingly similar story should be found concerning the Chinese inventor Mo Tzu, who was a contemporary of Archytas:

> Mo Tzu made a wooden kite which took three years to complete. It could indeed fly, but after one day's trial it was wrecked. His disciples said 'What skill the Master has to be able to make a wooden kite fly!' But he answered 'It is not as clever as making a wooden ox-yoke peg. They only use a short piece of wood, eight-tenths of

---

[1] Aulus Gellius, *Noctium atticarum libri xx*, X. 12. 8–10. (Loeb, vol. 2, pp. 244, 245.) The fragment by Favorinus is not elsewhere extant. See Favorino di Arelate, *Opere*, ed. A. Barigazzi, Firenze, 1966, pp. 241–2.

a foot in length, costing less than a day's labour, yet it can pull 30 *tan*, travelling far, taking great strain, and lasting many years. Yet I have worked three years to make this kite which has been ruined after one day's use.' Hui Tzu heard of it and said: 'Mo Tzu is indeed ingenious, but perhaps he knows more about making yoke-pegs than about making wooden kites.'[1]

There appears, however, to be no sound reason to suppose that this simultaneity is other than fortuitous.

The Archytas story was cited as frequently as the myths of Daedalus, Bladud, and Alexander by those considering the possibilities of artificial flight. Opinions as to the practicability of making such a model varied greatly. Some writers, like Scaliger (1484–1558), held the construction of the bird to be quite simple—*volantis . . . columbæ machinulam . . . uel facillimè profiteri audeo* ('I venture to declare the artifice of the flying dove very easy')[2]—while others, like Gaspar Schott (1608–66),[3] found it difficult to believe that such an object could be made to fly at all. There was a deal of speculation on the possible mechanisms of the dove's flight, some of the ideas being of great ingenuity. The most commonly adopted explanation was that which centred on Gellius' words *aura spiritus inclusa*, taken to refer to some form of compressed air or steam propulsion. While the practicability of such a device in classical times is doubtful, the use of steam jets was suggested at least as early as the aeolipile of Heron of Alexandria[4] (? *ca.* 60 A.D.), and it is not impossible that Archytas hit upon the principle, if not upon the means of putting it into effect. Athanasius Kircher, a man of rich imagination, took a more original line, suggesting that it could have been made to rise by means of magnetic forces (Plate 24). Some of the ideas were still more imaginative. In his *Magia universalis* Gaspar Schott quotes the Jesuit Lauretus Laurus (1610–1658), whose writings have otherwise disappeared. Among other speculations he stated that eggshells filled with dew, or leather balls filled with a mixture of nitre, sulphur, and mercury will be drawn upwards when exposed to the sun.[5] These, he suggested, might be encased in a light structure having the shape of a bird. In making such unlikely suggestions,

[1] J. Needham, *Science and Civilisation in China*, IV. 2, Cambridge, 1965, p. 573.

[2] J. C. Scaliger, *Exotericarum exercitationum liber quintus decimus, ad Hieronymum Cardanum*, Lutetiae, 1557, f. 444ᵛ.

[3] G. Schott, *Magia universalis naturae et artis*, 4 vols., Herbipoli, 1657–59, vol. 3, pp. 268–72.

[4] *Heronis Alexandrini opera qvae svpersvnt omnia*, 5 vols., ed. W. Schmidt, vol. 1, 'Pnevmatica et avtomata,' Lipsiae, 1899, pp. 228–33.

[5] Schott, *Magia universalis*, vol. 3, pp. 271–2.

Laurus was merely repeating some familiar beliefs which had been passed on from writer to writer. Thomas Lupton, for example, admitting that he is dependent on J. J. Wecker for his information, gives versions of both of Laurus' ideas:

> Put quicksyluer in a bladder, and lay the bladder in a hotte place: and it wyll skyp from place to place, without handling.

> To make an Eg ascend into the ayre. In the month of May, fyll an Eg shell cleane emptied, with dew, and stop the hoale well, wherin you dyd put the dew, then lay the Eg in the hotte Sunne about noone: and it wyll be lyft vp. But if you set a staffe by it, it wyll ascende the more easylyc.[1]

A little later Lupton returns to the idea of the flying egg, providing it this time with an animate prime mover:

> Make a hoale in the ende of a Goose egge, and put all the whyte and yolke out of it, then put into the shell, a Backe [*i.e.*, a bat] that flyes about in the euening, and then glew or close it fast on the toppe, and you shal see the Backe flye away with the same Egge shell: to the great maruayle of them that knowes it not.[2]

The fundamental misconceptions here about the nature of flight need no comment, but the idea may have been inspired by the supernatural associations of bats.

The suggestions of Laurus and Lupton, although ridiculous, have some tenuous connexion with observable physical fact. The same cannot be said, however, of some frankly magical prescriptions for producing similar effects. The writer of the *De mirabilibus mundi*, attributed to Albertus Magnus,[3] gives a recipe for making a house appear to be full of flying creatures. One should take the brain and tail feathers of a bird, wrap them in a recently used funeral cloth, and roll the whole package tightly together so that it may be used as a wick for a new, green, oil lamp. If this is then lit, using olive oil as fuel, green and black birds will be seen flying through the house. As with so many such recipes from 'books of secrets', the writer gives no hint as to why one should wish to have one's domestic peace disturbed in this way.

Some writers sought a solution to the problem of Archytas' dove in the more realistic application of fire-power which was provided by rockets. Lauretus Laurus

---

[1] T. Lupton, *A Thousand Notable things, of sundry sortes*, London, 1579, pp. 269, 281.
[2] Lupton, *A Thousand Notable things*, p. 282.
[3] *De mirabilibvs mvndi*, [Venice, 1472?] f. 26ᵛ.

again, in speculating about a possible reconstruction of the dove, hoped to avoid the difficulty of the brevity of its flight by equipping it with a series of rockets arranged to fire one after the other at carefully timed intervals. 'He thinks it would be flying,' says Schott; 'I think it would be more like a jumping lamb.'[1] Perhaps the most interesting of the speculations about the dove, that of Cardano (1501–76), which is discussed in Chapter Five, ends with a brief dismissal of the possibility that the propulsive power was provided by any form of fire: 'But it is not certain that it may be done by the power of fire or of burning torches. In this way it might rise of its own accord and move its wings, but would immediately cease, because the fire would not remain in it. Apart from the [fire producing] materials, it would also have to be very light.'[2]

While it is virtually certain that no fire power could have been used by Archytas, there is good reason to believe that when rockets became available in Europe they were applied to bird-like constructions which may have been genuinely aerodynamic devices. The first, and fullest, account of such an experiment, written more than a century before Cardano's book, is to be found in Giovanni da Fontana's treatise *Metrologum de pisce cane et volucre*.[3] Fontana was born in Venice, probably around 1395. He studied in Padua, where he took a degree in medicine, but he seems to have spent most of the rest of his life in his home town. The date of his death is unknown, but he was still alive in 1454.[4] The *explicit* of the *Metrologum* suggests that it may have been Fontana's first work:

> Here ends the treatise on measurement by means of the fish, the dog, and the bird, which the most famous doctor of arts and medicine, Johannes Fontana, of Venice, wrote in his youth.[5]

The date of the tract is uncertain, but *ca.* 1420 seems likely. It deals with a new method of measuring distances on land, in the water, and through the air. Special clocks of Fontana's own devising, and capable of measuring with accuracy very short periods of time, were to be operated in conjunction with moving models—of a fish, a bird, and a hare—which were powered by rockets. There is nothing

[1] Schott, *Magia universalis*, vol. 3, p. 272.

[2] G. Cardano, *De rerum varietate libri xvii*, Basileae, 1557, p. 440.

[3] Bologna, Biblioteca Universitaria, MS 2705, ff. 95ᵛ–104ᵛ.

[4] A. Birkenmajer, 'Zur Lebensgeschichte und wissenschaftlichen Tätigkeit von Giovanni Fontana (1395?–1455?),' *Isis*, vol. 17, 1932, pp. 34–53.

[5] Fol. 105ᵛ.

fanciful in the suggested use of rocket-power. Although not common in Europe at the time, rockets had been known since about 1300, and had been used in 1380 in a battle between the Genovese and the Venetians.[1] There is no doubt that the creation of rocket-propelled animals as described by Fontana was a practical possibility in the fifteenth century.

While Fontana seems to have read widely and to have had at least some acquaintance with the Islamic technological writers, the relevant passages of the *Metrologum* contain nothing to indicate to what extent, if at all, he was dependent on earlier inventors. The manner of his writing suggests, indeed, that the devices were his creations. He was certainly quite proud of them and, towards the end of the work, includes a charming admission of concern for technical ingenuity rather than for the practical value of his inventions:

> . . . I decided to explain what I have said about the fish, the dog, and the bird, not because I knew that it would provide, nor because I wanted it to provide, any precise certitude of measurement, but in order to give my attention to a new invention and to the more subtle establishment of principles; and so that a new form of the art of measurement might be set up, never before explained in such a way by others.[2]

Such is the spirit which keeps the intellectual imagination alive.

The following are the passages from Chapters Seven and Ten of the *Metrologum* which deal with the aerial part of the invention. (Another passage from his Chapter Seven is treated in Chapter Seven of this book.) With a certain youthful earnestness Fontana explains everything in the greatest detail, as if he were talking to a child. He is meticulous to the point of fussiness and is obviously delighted by his own ideas. The extent to which his enthusiasm is for the ideas themselves, rather than for their physical application, is indicated by his admission, in Chapter Ten, that the carefully worked out triangulation processes are unnecessary, and may be replaced by the direct measurement of a cord attached to the rocket.

> I have seen and experimented with the tube filled with gunpowder which flies through the air. When it is ignited this, indeed, is sent upwards by the force of the fire which is emitted behind, until the powder is consumed. And so I once thought of making, from paper and thin wood, models of a raven and a devil, with open wings fixed on to springy steel or bronze, and in their bellies I placed a good many tubes filled with gunpowder; and the ends which were to be ignited were terminated under

[1] J. R. Partington, *A History of Greek Fire and Gunpowder*, Cambridge, 1960, pp. 59–60, 174.
[2] Fol. 102ʳ.

the tail, so that the fire should be seen to emerge from the anus and should have the power to drive the models straight and with their heads up. When they moved the wings shook and they looked as if they were real devils, either in their own shape or changed into that of a raven, flying through the air and leaving behind them smoke and stench.

Similarly, with care you will make, from wood and cloth and paper, a great and really astonishing dragon which will fly through the air, if in the aforesaid manner you place a thick, long tube of powder in the interior of its belly, along its length, whose fire emerges through the anus. But in order that the strength of the fire should be greater, and that the same fire should be seen coming out of the mouth, you may make another similar tube running back from the neck, by which means the fire from it, coming out of the mouth, together with that which emerges from the anus, will drive the dragon more powerfully in the same direction.

But with these creatures it is necessary to attach a long tail stretched out behind, sufficient to keep the models upright; indeed, if this tail is not attached, the spurting of the fire at the upper end may turn the models over and not draw them through the air as it should. Moreover, the tail should not be made too heavy, lest it act against the power of the fire to produce upward motion. Thus in this as in other artifices a necessary proportion should be observed, for when the artificer wishes to make these or similar things, he should first consider the power of the fire, to know how much weight it can raise into the air, and he will not be able to operate a heavier moving object with that fire or one of equal power. And as I had experience of this I judged that my taper or candle, when ignited, would be sufficient to support itself in the air for some time if made from an equal proportion of fire and other materials. When I first noted that the fire was capable of lifting the candle, I then made a sensibly heavier candle with an equal strength of powder, and hence of fire, and I discovered that it stayed on the ground and was not raised, on account of its weight. Then as I straightaway thought of making a candle much heavier than the first and lighter than the second, I arrived at the point of equilibrium of the fire and the resistance of the weight of the materials. When thus made it remains stationary wherever it is placed in the air; it neither falls nor rises, since the fire works against the action both of its weight, viz. its total weight, and its lightness.

But care should be taken that the candle or taper or other such composition which is to be drawn upwards or to be suspended in the air by the fire should not be made of heavy materials or of unsatisfactory shape, for too much fire will be required and consequently a great deal of powder or combustible material, which will cause the machine to be large, or of slight staying power. Hence the fire should be of the sort which is difficult to extinguish. If the fire is easily separated from the combustible materials, the machine will fall dead to the ground by virtue of its weight. Comets, indeed, which appear in the sky are sustained because as their material is inflammable and perhaps viscous it stays with them inseparably until the material is burned up and owing to its lightness it remains in the air; thus materials with a proper balance of lightness and inflammability will stay up for a long time.

Chapter Ten, concerning the bird which can measure heights.

In order to measure heights, you may make an eagle, or peacock, or swallow, or other species of flying creature which can rise to a height. This should be of very light materials in which, nevertheless, the qualities of air and fire are dominant, so that it may be drawn up through the air, yet without excessive speed, as has previously been shown to be possible. The slower the movement, the more certain will be the measurement, and it will be adequate if, from paper or cloth or very thin and very light wood or metal, a bird is made with a hollow interior, into whose belly a tube of inflammable powder may be placed, terminating at the back, under the tail. There it should be ignited, and long tails should be attached, so that the movement may be straighter. An arrow, in truth, moves straighter through the air if it is long rather than short. Now if it is short, it keeps turning with a twisting movement and flies irregularly; therefore the short jet of flame runs at random through the air and into places which it burns and destroys. If however its shape were a great deal longer it would move like an arrow. The tail, therefore, will be as a rudder to steer its motion, just like the rudder of a ship. The fire, however, must be arranged so that the tail is not burned; alternatively the tail may be made of material which will not be ignited by the fire, such as very thin bronze or iron. When these things have been prepared, you should have one of the aforementioned clocks, or a similar one, with which to measure first the velocity of the bird in reaching any known height, after the following manner: Standing at the foot of a tower of known height, for example a hundred ells, holding the tail of the bird so that it hangs perpendicular, you should ignite the powder and allow it immediately to ascend, and at the same time the clock should be started, and when you see that the bird has reached the summit, then note the time on your clock, for the time or the elapsed period shown by this clock corresponds to the motion, at that speed, for an altitude of a hundred ells. Next, if you can retrieve the bird, if it falls to the ground and has not been burned up because made of metal, or if you take another exactly like it in shape and weight and strength of fire, you may ignite it at the base of another height and adjust your clock and note its reading when the bird has reached the summit. And, in the same way, take note of the reading of your clock, which you may compare with the reading of the same or a similar one used in the first experiment, and whatever the ratio in this case, that also will be the ratio of the unknown height to the hundred ells; therefore if the proportion of the second reading to the first is double, the second height will be two hundred ells.

But if the bird cannot ascend along a perpendicular line to the summit, which may happen either because the height is sloping, as for instance in the case of a mountain, or because it is impossible to reach the bottom on account of some obstruction, or because the measurer wants to stand at a distance from the height, then special care is needed in arranging the bird when it is to be ignited, for which reason I thought out something of a geometrical nature. Beneath the wing, close to the root, a very thin thread may be suspended, with a very small plumb-bob which should be less than a drachm in weight or just sufficient to keep the thread drawn straight; and let the thread be of such a length that it hangs a little below the bird's belly.

Thus when I wish to measure a height I hold the bird in my hand and place my eye next to the end of the tail and look along the back of the bird at the height; and if I see the summit, that is well. If not, however, I raise or lower the bird's head until along the direction of the back, that is, from the tail to the head, I can see the summit; and without allowing it to move from that position I note under the belly the place designated by the drawn-out thread and mark it with some wax, or the like. And I note the place where my feet are, calling it, say, F. Then I go to another place whose height is known to me, and holding the bird in my hand as before, with the thread falling across the mark on its belly, I walk back and forth until, by looking along its back, I see the summit of the known height, with the thread falling across the aforesaid place, and then with the clock adjusted as mentioned above, I ignite the powder and permit the bird to move up to the summit, and if it has been well made it will move straight along the line of sight. When it arrives there I note the reading on the clock, which we may call (a), and let this known height be 50 feet. Then I take the bird, after it has fallen to the ground, or another similar in all respects, and going to the first place, designated F, and standing there, I hold it in the same way, looking at the summit of the first, unknown height, and when the powder has been ignited the clock and the bird are allowed to start at the same time. And when it has reached the height I note the reading of the clock, which we may call (b).

These things having been done, I may say that as (b) is to (a), so is the proportion of the first, unknown height to the second, which is of 50 feet; whence if (b) is the triple of (a) the first height will be 150 feet.

Now if this operation is closely considered, it will be seen that equiangular triangles are created there, which consequently have sides in the same ratio, since from the line of sight drawn from the eye to the summit (that is, from the longest side) and from the intersection, near the base or bottom part of the height, whether hidden or visible, of the horizontal lines from the same eye, imagined as drawn to the height, and the line dropping perpendicularly from the summit (that is, from the other two sides of the triangle) a right-angled triangle is formed, similar on both sides [to the triangle formed in the other half of the experiment], which a geometer understands, and thus you have the height of the other[s] by a similar method of measurement.

However, just as in the case of the water it was said that [the waters measured] should be similar in all respects, so one should be careful that these movements be not made in places of which one seems to have an air heavier, mistier, or clearer than the other. Also to be avoided are winds and rain and other things which experiments may show to be unsuitable because of their always hindering the balance of the various conditions in the instrument.

. . . Now, indeed, whether or not the aforesaid creatures are able to move evenly through the water, over the ground, or through the air, with the following invention, which does not involve the use of the clock, you can, no less than with the travelling measurer, know the depth of the fish, the progress of the quadruped, and the flight of the bird.

Therefore make, on a strong axle, a reel which may easily be unwound and which can be held in the hand, and around the reel wind a long, flexible thread or thin cord of known quantity, as for example a hundred paces, and you may, if you wish, mark the paces, and you will be able to count them more easily. . . . Similarly, if you make the bird which is driven by fire or impelled in some other way from the base to the summit of a height, attach in such a way sufficient cord, strongly tied to its tail, and when the bird is driven through the air the thread or cord will be pulled out from the reel. And when the bird has reached the summit, hold the reel so that no more is pulled from it and note the mark on the cord, which then wind in and you will have the length of the bird's flight. And if the bird rises along a perpendicular line, that will be the measure of the height. If however it rises obliquely, take once again the measurement of a smaller, known height, as we have described above, since from the geometry of similar triangles you will arrive at a knowledge of the unknown height . . . But in experimenting with these it is wise not to let the reel be unwound too fast, so that no more cord is unwound than is required, which may easily happen if the force on the reel is great. The hand should therefore be held lightly on the reel, or around the thread which runs off it, and it should be allowed to revolve gently. In this way the cord is pulled out sufficiently, and it will be easier to see when the creature has reached the end of its movement. But if you do not wish, or are unable, to make the creature return to yourself when it has reached the end of the measurement (which in the air or on the ground, may be seen, and in the water may be judged when the cord is no longer pulled out because the weight has touched the bottom) note the mark on the cord near the reel and see how much cord has remained around it, and take that amount away from the total quantity of cord and what remains is the true quantity of cord which was extended between the reel and the animal, and thus, in consequence, you have the exact measure of the place, which you desired.

Although the pages of the manuscript leave space for the inclusion of a good many illustrations, these were never inserted. Fortunately, however, Fontana later included one illustration of the basic ideas of the *Metrologum* in his sketchbook of military and other engines (?*ca.* 1440), now known as the *Bellicorum instrumentorum liber*.[1] Towards the top of the picture he has written *de pissce aue et lepore habes tractatum meum sufitientem* ('concerning the fish, the bird, and the hare, you have my tract, which will suffice'), the quadruped having over the passage of years suffered a mutation from the dog of the original (Plate 25).

While some of this detailed and often over-explicit account is no doubt merely speculative, many passages read like factual reports and I see no reason to doubt that Fontana had built, and tested, his rocket-powered bird. It is, of course, an open question to what extent the bird should be thought of as in any real sense an aerodynamic device. If the wings were purely decorative, it would have been no more than a rather cumbersome and inefficient sky-rocket. If, as Fontana says, they were indeed made to flap or shake, they would probably have been more of a hindrance than an aid to flight, but, as the attachment to spring steel or bronze suggests, the flapping may have been slight, in which case well-made wings could have provided a certain amount of sustentation. Furthermore, a proper adjustment of the propulsive power and of the lift from the wings could have produced at least an approximation to the straight-line flight which Fontana describes, but which must otherwise be interpreted as an observational error conditioned by the contemporary beliefs about the straight-line path followed by projectiles in their initial moments.

As I mentioned at the beginning of this chapter, the rocket bird appears to have had some influence on the interpretations of Kyeser's *draco*. That the *Metrologum* was read by at least some of the writers of the later military treatises is clear from illustrations in two of them (Plates 27 and 28). Both these texts are of the Kyeser type, and both include reworkings of much of *Bellifortis* itself. The two related fire dragons, while clearly showing a close relationship to the Kyeser kite, appear to be illustrations of Fontana's *magnus draco*, attached to its measuring line. The bird having been scaled up to the size of an impressive winged dragon, the reel, originally to have been held in the hand, has of course had to become a proportionately large and powerful winch. In the foreground is the rocket-powered dog, but the fish is absent. The star-shaped object appears to be some sort of fire bomb. Both of these illustrations probably derive from an earlier and lost original, perhaps by Fontana himself. In both cases the fire is shown emerging from the

---

[1] Munich, Bayerische Staatsbibliothek, codex icon. 242, f. 37[r].

creatures in the wrong direction, but that is a natural error for a copyist to make. (*Cf.* the correctly shown propulsion in Fontana's own illustration, Plate 25.) If, as I have supposed, rocket propelled birds and dragons of this kind were indeed tried in the early fifteenth century, we should have an added reason for the posited misinterpretation of Kyeser's *draco* both by the later copyists and by the writer of the interpolated *tygax* passage in Göttingen codex philos. 63.

The ease with which such ideas may mutate during the process of transmission is again clearly revealed by an illustrated passage in a German fireworks book dated 1584 (Plate 26). The illumination, which appears to be a direct descendant of Fontana's original, shows not artificial animals but a real dove and a real cat carrying fire-bombs into enemy territory, a technique which had been familiar to military engineers for centuries. As so often happens, the peaceful ingenuity of the inventor has been misinterpreted and applied to destructive ends.

Fontana's dragon was not the only invention of its kind to have been used in the fifteenth century. Another description of a bird-shaped rocket, though in this case presented with much less detail and applied in no such original way, is to be found in Vienna codex 3064, which was approximately contemporary with the *Metrologum*. Of particular interest is the technique of using a removable mould on which to form a paper bird stiffened with glue.

> If you want to make a flying fire or bird, make from clay or wood a mould in the shape of a bird. Cover this with paper which should be cut and coated with joiner's glue so that it covers the mould closely and neatly. But let it remain open at one end so that the mould may be removed, and put gunpowder into it, placed up at the head, and if the bird is as big as a blackbird or of about that size, the quantity of powder should be about as much as could be contained in a beanpod. And when the powder has been placed in it, stick it together with the glue or with paste, so that it is completely closed up. And with a small pointed piece of wood bore a little hole into it behind, and right through it, and stick into it a quill which is filled with gunpowder and is one finger long and which has one end inside the model and the other end outside it. And place the bird on the ground or wherever you wish and light the powder behind at the quill and go away from it. And it is best if the powder inside the bird is up near the head, or in the head. And so light it and when you have lit it go one or two paces from it before it shoots off.[1]

Such devices continued to be used in later centuries. Athanasius Kircher[2] describes

[1] Vienna, Österreichische Nationalbibliothek, codex 3064, f. 21^{r-v}.

[2] A. Kircher, *Mundus subterraneus*, Amstelodami, 1665, pt. 2, p. 480.

and illustrates one which he says he saw in Germany (Fig. 13). After giving details of its construction he goes on to say:

> This invention is full of wonder, and such a spectacle is marvellously useful for discouraging an enemy, especially if the letters of some name are shown in the air.

Fig. 13. Kircher's rocket bird.
Mundus subterraneus, Amstelodami, 1665, pt. 2, p.480

Finally I must mention the many non-flying dragons which had been developed by the pyrotechnicians to a high degree of perfection. Rocket-propelled monsters moved either along the ground, as in the case of Fontana's dog and hare, or on wires suspended between trees, posts, or the walls of buildings. Sometimes two or more fiery effigies were allowed to meet and clash in battle, a favourite subject for such a display being the struggle between St George and the dragon. The following is taken from a contemporary description of the festivities held in 1613 for the marriage of Elizabeth, daughter of James I:

> . . . in a most curious manner, an artificiall fire-worke, with great wonder, was seene flying in the ayre, like unto a dragon, against which another fierie vision appeared, flaming like to Saint George on horsebacke, brought in by a burning in-chanter, betweene which was then fought a most strange battell, continuing a quarter of an hower or more; the dragon being vanquished, seemed to rore like thunder, and withall burst in peeces, and so vanished; but the champion, with his flaming horse, for a litle time, made a shew of a tryumphant conquest, and so ceased.[1]

[1] *The Mariage of Prince Frederick, and the Kings Daughter* . . ., London, 1613. (Somers' *Tracts*, 2nd edn., ed. Walter Scott, London, 1809, etc., vol. 3, p. 37.)

While rockets of this sort lie, strictly speaking, outside the scope of an enquiry into aeronautical concepts, they bear, because of their structure and appearance, some relationship to the flying dragons. Many of the fairly numerous Renaissance books on pyrotechnics contain illustrations of funicular monsters of the kind in question (*e.g.*, Plate 29). A comparison of the drawings of these dragons, which are known to have existed, with those of the possibly hypothetical creatures in the copies of Kyeser, reveals a similarity of treatment which may indicate that the depiction of the latter has been to some extent influenced by a disposition to think in terms of the former. Furthermore, the wings which the pyrotechnicians built for their dragons must occasionally have provided partial sustentation, and the hurtling creatures' consequent tendency to rise and lessen the tension on the rope or wire may have been noticed with interest by those who aspired to achieve free flight with rocket-powered structures.[1]

[1] Further study of manuscripts of the Kyeser type will almost certainly add to our knowledge of the *dracones* and rocket birds. One potential source of information which I have not been able to examine is the third part of MS II Varia 374, in the State Archive of Sibiu, Romania. See D. Todericiu, 'Raketentechnik im 16. Jahrhundert,' *Technikgeschichte*, vol. 34, no. 2, 1967, pp. 97–114. According to Todericiu, the manuscript contains speculations on rocket flight, an illustration of a flying cat, and a further variation on the rocket-carrying dove.

4

KITES

Although from time to time it has been suggested that some form of kite was known in the days of ancient Greece and Rome, there is no real evidence to support such an idea. If it ever really existed, the wooden dove of Archytas may possibly have been a kite, but it is more likely to have been a glider or an attempt at the rocket bird. In search of further classical evidence, aeronautical historians puzzled for about a hundred years over a scene depicted on a Greek vase in the National Museum of Naples,[1] which could have been interpreted as a girl or woman flying a kite (Plate 30). Plischke suggested that, because of the slackness of the line, this might rather depict a game still played in his day by Thessalonian children, in which a piece of paper was allowed to blow in the wind at the end of a cord, a game differing from kite-flying in that no lift is produced.[2] The correct interpretation, which now seems obvious—the object on the end of the string is a spinning-bobbin—did not find its way into print until comparatively recently.

As far as I know, the first clear record of a European kite is the drawing in Milemete's *De nobilitatibus*, discussed in Chapter Two,[3] but the origin of this and of the several other kites which are recorded in the next couple of centuries is not at present known. That kites had been flown in China for some centuries before Christ is well documented, and it may be that all European kites will ultimately be traced back to Chinese origins, but the possibility of independent invention and

[1] The suggestion that the object was a kite was first made by H. Heydemann in 'Drachenspiel,' *Archäologische Zeitung*, vol. 25, Dec., 1867, cols. 125–6. For a discussion of the vase and of other matters relevant to this chapter, see my *Kites: an Historical Survey*, London, 1967, pp. 61–80.

[2] H. Plischke, 'Alter und Herkunft des Europäischen Flächendrachens,' *Nachrichten von der Gesellschaft der Wissenschaften zu Göttingen*, Phil.-Hist. Kl., N.F., Fachgr. 2, vol 2, no. 1, 1936, p. 4.

[3] See above, pp. 42–4.

development cannot be dismissed. That so many different types of kite have been flown, for so many different purposes, by primitive peoples in widely separated parts of the world leads me to believe that the rigidly diffusionist theory which would postulate a single point of origin, although plainly able to account for the appearance of the kite in some eastern civilisations, may not be entirely satisfactory in other cases.

The various theories which have been put forward to account for the origin of the kite are applicable to many regions and cultures. Dr Joseph Needham wonders whether a Chinese hat on the end of a string might have provided the initial idea.[1] Arthur Waley thought, rather improbably perhaps, of the early Chinese fowling, carried out 'not with an ordinary bow and arrow, but with a dart, about five inches long, shot from a specially constructed bow. To the dart was attached a long string, which enabled the fowler to draw towards him the prey which he had shot, exactly as one draws in a kite'.[2] A. C. Haddon, who was concerned with the role of the kite as a religious symbol, suggested that 'the kite itself is merely the liberated sail of a canoe. Amongst a seafaring folk [such as the early Indonesians] this accident must often arise, and the excitement of hauling down a sail that had blown away might very well lead to the process being intentionally repeated on a small scale'.[3] The pennon-shaped kites of the fourteenth and fifteenth centuries have led me to wonder whether they might not have originated as liberated banners or flags. There is some evidence to support such a connexion. Kites flown in eighth- and ninth-century Islam appear to have been generally flag-like. Al-Djāḥiz (*ca.* 776–869) spoke in his *Book of Animals* of 'flags of the boys which were made of Chinese carton and paper; to these tails and wings were attached, little bells were tied to their fronts, and on breezy days they were released into the air from long and firm threads'.[4] The banner-like nature of the decorated kites flown by Thai mandarins has been remarked on,[5] and although neither the kite in Vienna codex 3064 nor any of the Kyeser *dracones* is depicted as a banner or pennon, the pictorial relationship

[1] J. Needham, *Science and Civilisation in China*, IV. 2, Cambridge, 1965, p. 577n.

[2] A. Waley, [Review article], *Folklore*, vol. 47, no. 4, Dec., 1936, pp. 402–3.

[3] A. C. Haddon, *The Study of Man*, London, 1898, pp. 251–2.

[4] B. Laufer, *The Prehistory of Aviation*, Chicago, 1928, p. 37.

[5] It appears that ancient Thai kites were also used for carrying fire bombs, suggesting a possible connexion with the Milemete drawing (Fig. 6, above). See P. Schweisguth, 'Note sur les jeux de cerf volants en Thailande,' *Journal of the Siam Society*, vol. 34, pt. 1, April, 1943, p. 3. Schweisguth gives no dates.

of the Kyeser miniatures to many representations of pennon-carrying horsemen in the manuscripts of the period is strikingly close. Again, there is great structural similarity between the European pennon kite and a type of kite still flown in Cambodia (Plate 31), suggesting the possibility that the European version bears some historical relationship to the old, banner-like Thai kites. As I have discussed in Chapter Two, the process of development from pennon to kite was repeated in reverse when the free-flying *draco* was reinterpreted as a windsock standard rigidly fixed to its pole.

At least one period of importation of eastern kites into Europe can be demonstrated beyond doubt, but the extent, if any, of far eastern influence before the sixteenth century is difficult to assess. There is rather more reason to believe that at least some European kites owe their origin to contacts with Islam, where they appear to have been flown as early as the time of Mohammed himself. It is said that at night the false prophet Musailima, a contemporary of Mohammed, flew kites equipped with 'hummers' (*i.e.*, taut strings arranged to create a musical harmony when vibrated by the wind) in order to give the impression that he was communing with the angels.[1] A search through the literature in translation, and through the relevant items in Pearson's *Index*,[2] has failed, however, to reveal any other evidence of the use of kites in Islam during the period in question, nor have I come across illustrations of anything at all kite-like in the Arabic works on technology available to me. Further study of this question is needed before the extent of near-eastern influence can be determined.

Whatever the origin of the pennon shaped kites seen in the fourteenth- and fifteenth-century manuscripts, their physical existence in mediaeval Europe is beyond question. The text which accompanies Plate 32 was undoubtedly written by someone with first-hand knowledge of such things. The description of the construction and of the mode of manipulation, though repetitive, crude in style, and occasionally obscure, is entirely factual and is an accurate reflection of physical reality. Although nothing is known of the author, the manuscript has been dated *ca.* 1430, about a generation after *Bellifortis*, and its late Middle High German dialect suggests that it was written somewhere near the Tirol. It may be remembered that Kyeser came from Eichstätt, in southern Germany. The pennon kite seems especially associated with this region of Europe.

[1] Laufer, *The Prehistory of Aviation*, p. 37.
[2] J. D. Pearson, *Index Islamicus, 1906–1955 . . .*, Cambridge, [1958].

17, 18. *Dracones*, type D. (Winged, tails indeterminate, fixed to pole, no vestigial line.) Plate 17: Vienna, Österreichische Nationalbibliothek, codex 3062, f. 127^v, fifteenth century. Plate 18: Berlin, Kriegsarchiv des Grossen Generalstabs, codex 117, 1453. (The manuscript appears to have been destroyed during World War II.)

19. *Draco*, type E. (Wingless, no reel.) Cologne, Historisches Archiv, codex W fo. 232X, f. 79^r, fifteenth century

20. *Draco*, type E. (Wingless, no reel.)
Vienna, Österreichische
Nationalbibliothek, codex 3068, f. 88ʳ,
early fifteenth century

21. *Draco*, type F. (Winged, reel, bridle, flier
on foot.) Innsbruck, Museum
Ferdinandeum, Codex 16.0.7, f. 103ʳ,
early fifteenth century

22. *Draco*, type G. (Wingless, no reel, square
head.) Strasbourg, Bibliothèque
nationale, MS 2259, f. 27ʳ, fifteenth
century

The flying Dragon, Goates of fyre leaping, the hye way to saint James in Galyce.

Ther impressions there be, as flames of fyre that mounteth . Other as flaming of fyre that goeth sydeway . Other as styll fyre that bydeth long . Other there is that maketh great flames & bydeth not long . Other also as candles sometyme great and sometyme lyttle, and this they se in the ayre and on the earth . Another

COLVMBA magnetica   ARCHITÆ ante exhibita

Cum studio ΑΡΧΥΤΣ uolat ecce Columba per orbem.
Non rota, nec uentus, Sed lapis urget opus.

23. The meteorological *draco volans. Kalender of Sheepeherds,* London, [?1560,] Mi^v

24. Kircher's magnetic explanation of Archytas' dove. *Magnes,* Romae, 1641, opposite p. 358

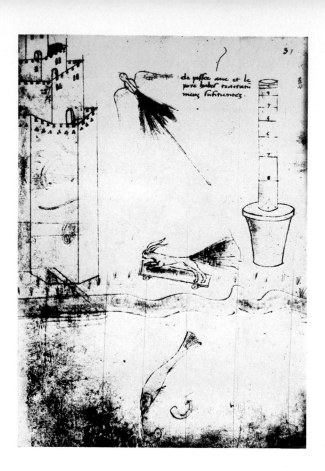

25. Fontana's rocket bird. Munich,
    Bayerische Staatsbibliothek,
    codex icon. 242, f. 37^r, *ca.*
    1440

26. Fontana's rocket bird
    transformed into a fire-
    carrying dove. London,
    Wellcome Historical Medical
    Library, MS 272, f. 123^v, 1584.
    By courtesy of the Trustees

27. Rocket dragon. Frankfurt am
Main, Stadt- und
Universitätsbibliothek, MS II,
40, f. 104ʳ, *ca.* 1490

28. Rocket dragon. Berlin,
Staatsbibliothek der Stiftung
Preussischer Kulturbesitz, Hs.
germ. fol. 94, f. 198ʳ, *ca.* 1540

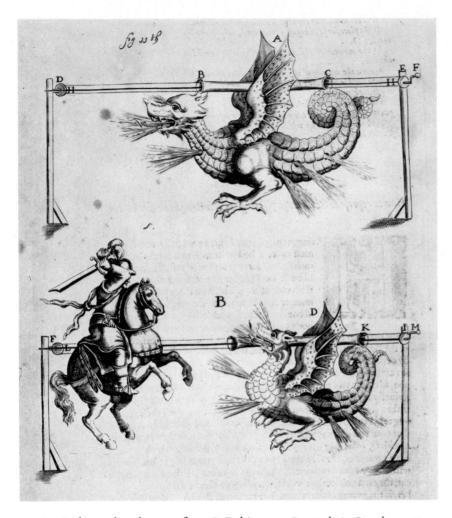

29. Funicular rocket dragons from J. Babington, *Pyrotechnia*, London, 1635,
p. 40

30. Greek vase, fourth century
B.C. Naples, Museo
Nazionale, no. 3151. The
spinning bobbin was once
taken to be a kite

31. Snake kite from Cambodia.
Its structure is very similar to
that of mediaeval European
pennon kites

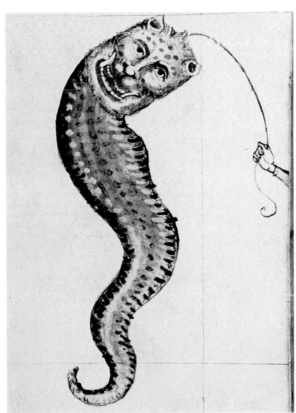

32. Pennon kite in Vienna, Österreichische
Nationalbibliothek, codex 3064, f. 6ʳ, *ca.* 1430

33. Modern reconstruction of the pennon kite

34. Landing a meteorological kite by the 'underrunning' method. Photograph by the National Oceanic and Atmospheric Administration

35. Icon, St Nicholas' Church, Nizhni-Novgorod, showing what is probably a pennon-kite, top-right

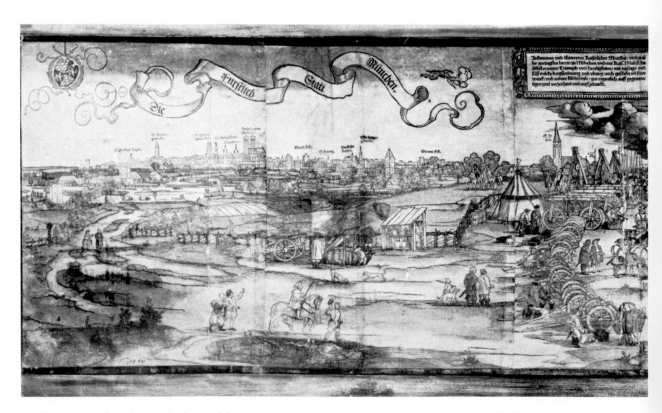

36. Large woodcut by Nicholas Meldemann, 1530, showing the ceremonial entry of Charles V into Munich. Munich, Stadtarchiv

37. First European illustration of a kite of diamond shape. J. Cats, *Silenus Alcibiades*, Middelburg, 1618, opposite p. 106

38. Artificial singing birds. A. Ramelli, *Le diverse et artificiose machine*, Parigi, 1588, f. 315ᵛ

39. Design for a devil automaton. Giovanni da Fontana, *Bellicorum instrumentorum liber*, f. 63ᵛ, *ca.* 1440

40. Tethered bird. Dutch, seventeenth century

41. Tethered insects and a tethered bird. London, British Museum, MS Royal 2.B.VII, f. 163ᵛ, first quarter of the fourteenth century

42. The flight of Kaspar Mohr, as depicted on the ceiling of the monastery library at Schussenried

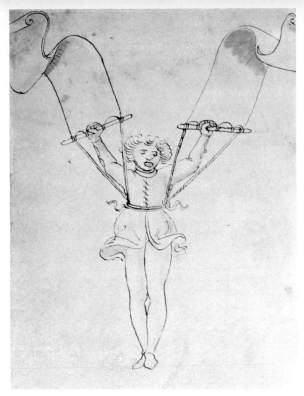

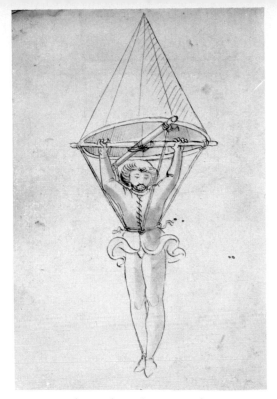

43. Proto-parachute from British Museum Add. MS 34113, f. 189ᵛ, *ca.* 1480

44. Conical parachute from British Museum Add. MS 34113, f. 200ᵛ, *ca.* 1480

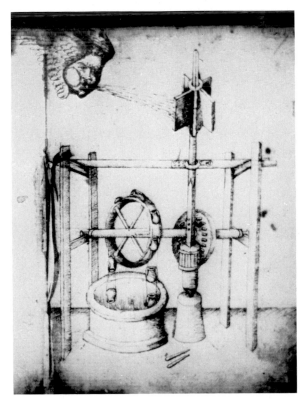

45. Veranzio's square, sail-derived parachute. *Machinae novae,* Venezia, [1615–16,] Fig. 38. (Composed *ca.* 1595.)

46. The earliest known European illustration of a vertically shafted mill. Florence, Biblioteca Nazionale Centrale, MS Palat. 766, f. 37ʳ, 1432/3. Taccola, Notebook

47. Earliest known illustration of a horizontally shafted windmill. New York, Pierpont Morgan Library, MS M. 102, f. 2ʳ, late thirteenth century

48. Horizontally shafted windmill. Valenciennes, Bibliothèque municipale, MS 838, f. 55ʳ, late thirteenth century

49. Horizontally shafted windmill. Vienna, Österreichische Nationalbibliothek, codex 5278,
f. 173ʳ, 1428

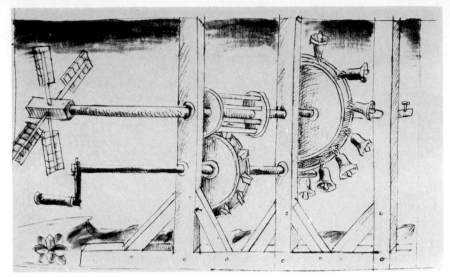

50. Windmill-operated bells. Donaueschingen, Fürstliche Fürstenbergische Hofbibliothek, codex 860, f. 117^r, mid fifteenth century

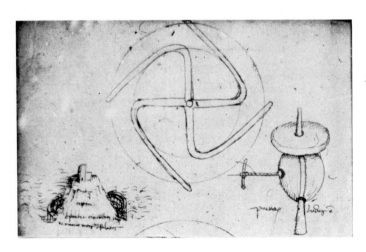

51. Child's string-pull helicopter. Munich, Bayerische Staatsbibliothek, codex lat. 197, f. 74^v, *ca.* 1438. Taccola, Notebook

52. *Moulinet*, possibly a toy helicopter. Copenhagen, Det Kongelige Bibliotek, MS 3384.8°, f. 27^r, first quarter of the fourteenth century

How you can make an artificial kite and how to handle it so that it hovers in the air and moves as if it were alive.

Take a piece of silk cloth of red, green, or other colour; alternatively the cloth may be of mixed colours, like a snake if you wish. The red colour, however, stands out much the best when it is seen in the air, and especially against the sun, as though it were something fiery. Or again you may take or prepare gilt cloth, so that it is very bright and fiery. But in any case let it be of very lightweight cloth. And have the kite cut out of the cloth and shaped according to the design of the figure drawn opposite, and so constructed that it have a head made of a sheet of parchment which is fine but nevertheless strong enough to keep the face stiff. And the head should be of the same size as a broad sheet of parchment; the total length of the body behind the head, together with the tail, should be eleven ells; and the body at the sheet which forms the head should be as wide as the head; and in the middle, at the sides, there should be placed something billowing or winglike, so that it have a dragonlike appearance. It is especially advisable, if the kite is to be exactly right, to make an incision two or three ells in length from the head down the middle of the back, and to sew into the middle of it a piece of silk cloth a span and a half wide, more or less, and pointed at both ends like the [lower end of the] kite itself. Then, if the wind strikes it, it fills out in the manner of a sail and flies up more lightly into the wind and takes on the shape of a raised body or back, which makes it much better and more lifelike, as you find in the figure given here. [These and other details are not, in fact, shown in the illustration.] Nevertheless, if you do not make this insertion it will be quite adequate. And when the body has been made in this way, have the head painted with a striking dragonlike face on the parchment sheet, which should be kept quite bright and shiny by the use of light colours. And then sew the head on to the body and at each corner of the parchment make two or three little loops formed of three or four strands of thread, and let both sides of the head-sheet, where the loops are attached, be strengthened with little patches of parchment, so that the loops will cut through it the less. And then obtain small batons which have been cut and split from good new tough fir sticks, so as to be one finger broad and half as thick as a rye-stalk [?]. Place the batons crosswise over one another on the head and fix them in the loops so that in the middle they are bowed out from the face to a distance of two fingers' breadth; and at the middle of the cross they may be bound with another loop as a protection against the wind, as you find drawn in the picture. If the wind is very strong, and you think the head may bend too much and the batons break, you may place another baton outside the kite, over the head—also [? held by] a loop—and across all this one [baton], or as many as may be needed, over the skull, from the middle of the head where it meets the back, as far up as to the forehead. If the wind is still stronger you may make this baton thicker. Or if it

5

is very strong indeed you may place a stick of a finger's breadth over the skull, from the back to the forehead, as stated before. After that you should make three loops between the eyes, from the forehead down to the nose, as is shown here. And push the string, from which you wish to fly the kite, through one or the other of them and tie it to the third, that is, the lowest, as you also find drawn. However, if the wind is too strong, put the string through the topmost and wind it around the middle one. If the wind is yet stronger, wind it on to the top one alone. If it is still too strong, however, place the thick stick over its head, as described before, and tie the string to the stick at the top of the forehead and let it fly as it will. If you now wish to make it fly, go where you have wind and hold it upright so that the wind strikes it in the face and in the body, and when the wind blows fairly strongly lift it right up and let it go with the string; thus it will rise, and you must all the while let it out carefully. If the wind is rather weak, walk against the wind so that the kite is opposed to it and in this way you will force it with the wind as high as you wish. When it has reached the height of one or two towers, and is well up in the air, you may guide it where you wish, using these methods of control, as long as the ground on which you are walking is sufficiently even: If you want to make it move into the wind, pull it gently and [then] let it have free rein, and it will go further and higher. If you want it to fly away with the wind [?], you must walk towards it and gently release it and it will move away. And it is good to ease it out very slowly, almost as if it were stationary, and then it will move in a soaring manner wherever you wish, and will not seem to be moving back. And then if it has flown over a town or a hill you can pull it back or across wherever you wish. But you should take note whether the wind is too weak. If the kite hangs its head or bends towards itself you must run quickly against the wind so that the wind blows against it and it rights itself. But when it raises its head you may direct it where you wish, using the techniques which have been described. When you want to bring it down again, walk some distance back so that when it has almost come down, in case the wind is then almost still, it will not fall to the ground before you have brought it right in or it may be caught in a tree or bush. If people threaten to approach and pester you to see it when it is being brought down, get your assistant to hold the string as if it were he who were bringing it down and take the string under your elbow and hold it in the other hand so that in case it breaks under your elbow you still have it in your hand, and walk towards it until it comes to the ground and there take the batons out and fold the head together and wrap the body around it and hide it. It is also advisable, when you are controlling it with the string, that you should have an assistant with you who may walk directly under the kite, wherever it moves, so that if the string should break he may see where the kite comes to earth, so that it may not be lost. When the kite comes down it falls immediately under where it is flying; it does not fall more than one or two pike-lengths away, and so is not lost by that assistant. And it is good to have the assistant there so that many people may imagine that it is he who is controlling the kite, and thus he who is controlling it attracts less attention. If you want the kite to move down at particular places as if it were diving at the earth or at people, that also you may perform by skilful handling. Note too that with some care you can arrange that four or six smaller and larger kites fly together, as if the young ones were flying with the old one; and you can arrange that they fly one above the other, and are nevertheless controlled by a single string or line. Note also that following the preceding directions you may make the kite very big indeed, so as to create great astonishment.[1]

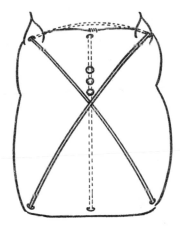

Fig. 14. Structure of the head of the pennon kite
in Vienna codex 3064.
The optional sticks are shown dotted

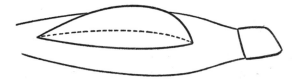

Fig. 15. Insertion of extra fulness for the body of
the pennon kite

The details of the structure are redrawn in Fig. 14, and the additional fulness for the body is shown in Fig. 15. A reproduction of the kite, which flies well, is shown in Plate 33. The head (18 in. × 24 in.) is of parchment, the body and tail of light

[1] Vienna, Österreichische Nationalbibliothek, codex 3064, ff. 4ᵛ–7ʳ.

cotton. The extra piece of cloth has been inserted in the back, and an attempt has been made to follow the instructions about the 'billowing and winglike' projections, which the writer suggests adding to the body to make it more lifelike. While it is plain that no rigid, aerodynamically supporting surfaces are intended, ornamental projections of the kind described may have been the origin of the probably imaginary wings found on so many of the copies of the Kyeser *draco*. The writer seems to have had in mind appendages such as are shown behind the creature's head in Plate 9.

The prescribed method of landing by pressing down the line and walking towards the kite, now known as 'underrunning', was independently developed by fliers of meteorological kites in the late nineteenth and early twentieth centuries. The method is especially useful for landing in a high wind (Plate 34).

The instructions regarding the three loops, or rings, for flying in varying wind strengths, are in conformity with the performance to be expected from kites of this type, though the method of attachment is much less satisfactory than the use of a bridle, as specified in Kyeser's text. None of the miniaturists who depicted Kyeser's *draco* fully understood the passage about the *tripla zona*, and the only one to have drawn it at all (see Plate 21) showed it attached in an impossible way, but there is little doubt that what was intended was something like Fig. 16.

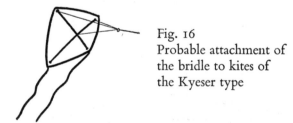

Fig. 16
Probable attachment of
the bridle to kites of
the Kyeser type

Apart from the Kyeser series, I know of only two other representations of mediaeval kites showing a general similarity to the one in Vienna codex 3064. These are the Milemete kite (1326/7) and a military standard in a Russian icon, also of the fourteenth century (Plate 35), which is probably a pennon kite of the same general configuration. The icon, from St Nicholas' Church in Nizhni-Novgorod, celebrates a battle between the Novgorodians and the invading Suzdalians, who remained in possession of the city during the thirteenth and fourteenth centuries. The shape of the kite, if it is indeed one, gives further support to the possibility that such kites were of eastern origin. It is also possible, as Duhem suggests,[1] that this banner bears some historical relationship to the fire-breathing *draco* standard used by the Mongols at Wahlstatt, as described by Długosz.

Nothing from the period can be found to compare with the text of Vienna codex 3064. No such description of a kite and its manipulation is, indeed, to be seen again before modern times, and no other unequivocal description of any sort appears before 1558. During this period of over a hundred years there appear, however, at least four other accounts, of a somewhat doubtful nature, which may refer to kite-flying. The first concerns the talented German mathematician and astronomer Johannes Müller von Königsberg, who was better known under his Latinised pseudonym Regiomontanus. He was born in Königsberg on 6 June 1436, but left his home town in adolescence and travelled widely. In 1450 he was in Vienna, where he matriculated at the university. He was in Italy in 1461, and in Hungary in 1467. In the spring of 1471 he travelled to Nürnberg, where he settled, and with which city he is most commonly associated. There he stayed until 28 July, 1475, when he left to visit Rome, where he was assassinated, at the age of 40, on 6 July, 1476.[2] One of the many stories about Regiomontanus which circulated in the sixteenth, seventeenth, and eighteenth centuries tells of his having built, while at Nürnberg, both an artificial eagle and an iron fly. As far as I can determine, the earliest printed account, which seems to be the ultimate source of all the later ones, is to be found in Peter Ramus' *Scholarum mathematicarum libri unus et triginta:*[3]

> ... among the artful curiosities of Regiomontanus, one of the inventors of Nürnberg, was the device of allowing an iron fly, as if released from the hand of the artificer, to flutter around the guests, and then as if tired to return to the hand of its master; and of sending forth from the city, high into the air, an eagle to greet the Emperor on his arrival and accompany him to the city gates. After Nürnberg's revelation of the fly and of the eagle with geometrical wings, we cease to be amazed at Archytas' dove.

The 'emperor' mentioned here was, of course, the Holy Roman Emperor of the day, Frederick III (1452–93). Some later reports anachronistically name Maximilian I (1493–1519) or even Charles V (1519–58). Frederick did in fact visit Nürnberg in February and March 1473/4, when the flight of the eagle, if it is more than legend, must have taken place.

[1] J. Duhem, *Histoire des idées aéronautiques avant Montgolfier*, Paris, 1943, p. 195.
[2] For biographical details of Regiomontanus, see E. Zinner, *Leben und Wirken des Joh. Müller von Königsberg genannt Regiomontanus*, rev. edn., Osnabrück, 1968.
[3] Basileae, 1569, lib. II, p. 65.

Regiomontanus' iron fly, which may have created at least the illusion of free flight, is discussed in Chapter Five, where I deal with mechanical birds, but while the eagle might also, perhaps, be interpreted as some form of free-flying automaton, I think it more likely that a kite is here being described, though in somewhat garbled fashion. A kite of the pennon shape, and perhaps equipped with wings, might readily be given the appearance of an eagle rather than of the by then traditional dragon. Partly owing to the misinterpretation of the so-called 'semi-kites', it has been assumed until recently that before the mid-sixteenth century kites were probably unknown or at least exceedingly rare in Europe. As the kite explanation did not offer itself, the story of Regiomontanus' eagle was usually taken to be fanciful. A quite searching investigation of the tradition, contained in a thesis by J. W. Baier and J. A. Bühel[1] which was presented at the university of Altdorf on 29 January 1707, concludes with the view that no such flight took place and that the story of the eagle was merely an exaggerated description of a large mechanical bird, with a hinged head, placed over the city gate. Zinner, who agrees with this interpretation, points out that the bird was first erected in 1541, for a visit by Charles V, an event which may help to explain the anachronism in those accounts which associate Charles V and Regiomontanus. In support of the many doubters of the truth of the story,[2] one must point to the very suspicious omission, from the meticulous and sober contemporary chronicles of the city of Nürnberg, of any mention of the flight.[3]

Indirect evidence to support the idea that the eagle may have existed in the form of a kite is found in a comparatively little known book, published in 1530, which describes a visit of Charles V to Munich in that year.[4] Charles, who was returning from coronation in Bologna, was met with great ceremony. Among the spectacles arranged in his honour was a flying dragon which welcomed him as he entered the city: 'When things had begun as indicated, His Majesty turned towards the town and his entry into it, and over the middle of his path there hung a flying dragon, most amazingly controlled, which hovered long in the air until the pro-

[1] *De aquila et musca ferrea, quæ mechanico artificio apud Noribergenses quondam volitasse feruntur*, Altorfiae, 1707.

[2] J. Duhem, *Histoire des idées aéronautiques avant Montgolfier*, Paris, 1943, pp. 128–30.

[3] H. Schedel, *Registrum hujus operis libri cronicarum . . .*, Nuremberge, 1493, f. cclv[r]; Zinner, *Leben und Wirken*, pp. 214–5.

[4] *Ain kurtze anzaygung und beschreybung . . .*, [Munich], 1530, [A4[r]]. The visit took place on 10 June 1530.

Fig. 17. Detail from the Meldemann woodcut, showing the flying
dragon which welcomed Charles V into Munich in 1530.

cession had passed.' Fortunately this dragon is represented in a large woodcut,
also dated 1530, by Nikolaus Meldemann, which celebrates the same scene (Plate 36
and Fig. 17). The dragon is there drawn with the same imaginative freedom that
one finds in the copies of Kyeser's *draco*, and although no retaining line is shown,
it seems probable that it was a kite. The anonymous writer's words, 'most amazingly

controlled' (*vast wercklich zugericht*), suggest some kind of manipulation from the ground. Such a spectacle would certainly have been a practical possibility at the time, while the relative unfamiliarity of kites would easily explain the misrepresentation of the woodcut. The dragon is emitting fire and smoke, as do many of those in earlier illustrations, a detail which led von Bassermann-Jordan to make the assumption, reasonable enough when he was writing, that a hot-air 'semi-kite' was intended.[1] It is worth noting, however, that the description of the scene says nothing about fire, nor anything which might be taken to refer to rocket-propulsion, which suggests once again that the dragon was a kite. It seems likely that, together with the ceremonial use of the mechanical eagle in 1541, some conflation of this scene with the popular story of Regiomontanus' activities may have contributed to the confusion over the identity of the emperor, especially since another story connected with Charles V (see Chapter Five) forms a parallel with the account of the iron fly.

The third possible allusion to a kite between 1430 and 1558 is contained in a story about Leonardo, which I discuss in Chapter Eight. The last, and slightest, of the four is a comment in Cardano's discussion of Archytas' dove, from which I have quoted in the previous chapter. His words 'And also a flying bird, but with a cord attached' suggest that he had once seen a kite, but it is clear that, if he did so, he was unfamiliar with such things.

While it is quite possible that European kites prior to the sixteenth century arose independently of eastern designs, a diffusionist approach becomes inescapable from at least as early as the mid-sixteenth century. Regular sea-going contacts with south-east Asia, and especially those formed by the Dutch trade routes, were almost certainly responsible for the appearance of a number of kites of various shapes, which rapidly displaced the pennon kites of the previous two centuries. By the end of the sixteenth century the dragon kite had almost totally disappeared. (For an exceptional late illustration, see Fig. 18.) Kites of the lozenge or arch-top kind, still common in Europe today, have for centuries been familiar in south-east Asia, and probably because of their relative ease of construction became more popular in Europe than the old pennon kites had ever been.

The date at which these eastern kites began to be imported is unclear. The first illustration of the new form appears in Jacob Cats' *Alcibiadis*, of 1618 (Plate 37), but a description of a kite of fundamentally similar type is found sixty years earlier

[1] E. von Bassermann-Jordan, *Alte Uhren und ihre Meister*, Leipzig, 1926, pp. 64–6.

Fig. 18. Seventeenth-century dragon kite. Conrad Meyer, *Sechs und Zwanzig nichtige Kinderspiel*, Zürich, [*ca.* 1650], plate 12.

in della Porta's *Magia naturalis*,[1] written in 1558, when he was only 22 or 23 years old. Della Porta (1535–1615) was a man of remarkably inquisitive, if also rather gullible, mind. The *Magia naturalis*, reissued in 1589 in greatly expanded form, became one of the best known of the many collections of 'natural wonders' which were so popular in Renaissance times. The description of the kite is somewhat ambiguous, but it is clear that a design in the eastern style, rather than a pennon, is intended. The passage served as the basis for most of what was written about kites for the next hundred years or more:

The Flying Dragon

Also called a comet. Whose construction is as follows: A rectangle should be constructed from very thin rods such that the proportion of length to width is one and a half to one. Two cross pieces are placed within it, either from side to side or from the corners. At their point of intersection a string is attached, and is joined to two others of the same length coming from the ends of the machine. This should be covered with paper or fine linen; and let there be nothing heavy in it. Then from

[1] G. B. della Porta, *Magiae naturalis . . . libri iiii*, Neapoli, 1558, pp. 69–70.

towers, hills, or a high slope, entrust it to the wind when it is blowing evenly and uniformly, not too strongly, which might break the machine, nor too lightly, for if the air is quite calm it will not raise the machine and the stillness of the air renders the labour vain. It should not fly straight, but at an angle, which is effected by pulling on [? *i.e.*, shortening] the string from one end [*i.e.*, the top] and from the other there should be a long tail made of parallel cords with papers tied at regular intervals. When it is sent up with a gentle tug, the artificer to whose hands it is entrusted should not pull it sluggishly or lazily, but powerfully, and thus the flying sail will move up into the air. When it is a little way up (out of the turbulence in the wind caused by the houses) it may be controlled and governed by the hands. Some attach a lantern to it, so that it may look like a comet, while others attach squibs filled with gunpowder, and when it is stationary in the air, a match is sent up the line by means of a ring or some other slippery thing. And this, moving straight up to the sail, sets fire to its mouth, and the machine breaks into many pieces with a great roar, and falls to the ground. Some tie on a kitten or pup and listen to its cries when it has been sent into the air. From this an ingenious man may discover by what means a man might fly with large wings attached to his arms and chest, and little by little from childhood might accustom himself to beating them, from ever higher places. And if anyone should think this extraordinary, let him consider what Archytas the Pythagorean is said to have devised and performed . . .

The description is rather vague, and there is some ambiguity in the wording of the passage about the bridle. The general form of the construction was probably as shown in Figs. 19 and 20, while the bridle was presumably to be attached as in Fig. 21. An inaccurate translation, published in English in 1658,[1] does not use the word kite, but gives the literal equivalents of della Porta's terms: 'flying dragon',

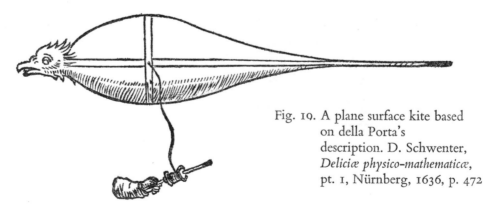

Fig. 19. A plane surface kite based on della Porta's description. D. Schwenter, *Deliciæ physico-mathematicæ*, pt. 1, Nürnberg, 1636, p. 472

[1] *Natural Magick . . . in twenty books*, trans. T. Young and S. Speed, London, 1658, p. 409.

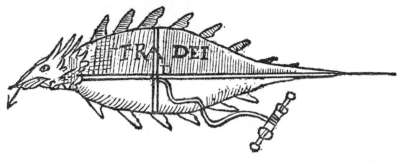

Fig. 20. Another version of della Porta's design. Athanasius Kircher,
Ars magna, Romae, 1646, pt. 2, p. 826

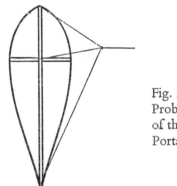

Fig. 21.
Probable attachment
of the bridle on della
Porta's kite

'Comet' and 'flying Sayle'. The inaccuracies are mainly attributable to the
translators' obvious bafflement as to the nature of the object intended. It is unfortunate that della Porta says nothing about the origin of his *draco volans*, which
appears still to have been a somewhat unusual sight in the mid-sixteenth century.
Johannes Schmidlap, in his manual on the manufacture and use of fireworks,[1]
dated in the Foreword 'New Year's Day, 1560', alludes to the unfamiliarity of kites
when he promises to expand his book for a future edition and to include in it a
description of a *fliegender Trachen*, which, he says, 'the inexperienced think to be
an impossibility'. The association of the kite with fireworks displays, which continues
well into the seventeenth century, suggests, of course, some direct link with the
old idea of putting fire into the windsock standards. In the sixteenth century most

[1] J. Schmidlap, *Künstliche vnd rechtschaffene Fewerwerck zum Schimpff*, Nürnberg, 1564,
A5ᵛ–A6ʳ. (Written about 1560.)

kites seem to have been flown by adults for such purposes, and it was not until somewhat later that they became the common plaything of children. Brueghel's famous picture of children at play (1569) contains no kite. The 219th game in the list of 223 in Chapter 22 of *Gargantua*, 'à la grue', may perhaps refer to kite-flying, a possibility which is supported by the similarity of the Languedoc word *gruo*, 'kite', but no kite appears in the 311 games of Fischart's *Gargantua*, of 1575,[1] and the earliest certain evidence of its use as a plaything in Europe is, once again, the 1618 woodcut in Cats.

As it is now clear that kites have been known in Europe for rather longer than was once thought to have been the case, one may well ask whether at any time they were considered as a potential means of human flight. Man-lifting kites, which were developed by nineteenth-century inventors for a variety of applications, had long been known in the east. Were they used in mediaeval or Renaissance Europe? In 1646, Kircher suggested that kites could lift a man; in 1558 they had made della Porta think of winged flight; and in the fifteenth century both the kites flown by the writer of Vienna codex 3064 and the *dracones* brandished by Kyeser's knights must have exerted a pull sufficient to suggest man-lifting possibilities. Despite these hints, there appear to be no reports of man-lifters, either real or imaginary, before modern times. Marco Polo, it is true, had mentioned seeing them in use on the Chinese coast, but as kites were unfamiliar to him he described them imprecisely, and in ambiguous terms, while, since the rare 'Z' manuscript in which the passage occurs was little known, Polo's description had no discernible influence.[2]

During the late sixteenth and seventeenth centuries the passage from della Porta was frequently quoted and paraphrased, but the idea that the kite might be used as the basis of a flying machine never seems to have caught the imagination of experimenters or theoreticians. Not only are there no reports of man-lifters, but important books like Flayder's *De arte volandi*[3] and Wilkins' *Mathematicall Magick*[4] ignore the kite entirely. In view of its many potentialities, the neglect of the kite in the seventeenth century is especially unfortunate, but as the increase in its

[1] H. A. Rausch, 'Die Spiele der Jugend aus Fischarts Gargantua,' *Jahrbuch für Geschichte, Sprache, und Literatur Elsass-Lothringens*, vol. 24, 1908, pp. 53ff.

[2] Marco Polo, *The Description of the World*, ed. A. C. Moule and P. Pelliot, 2 vols., London, 1938, vol. 1, pp. 356–7.

[3] F. H. Flayder, *De arte volandi* . . ., [Tübingen,] 1627.

[4] J. Wilkins, *Mathematicall Magick; or, the wonders that may be performed by mechanicall geometry*, London, 1648, pp. 191–223.

familiarity coincided with its relegation to the status of a toy, such a failure of response among the scientists and technicians was probably inevitable. Not until Cayley made his little glider in 1804 did the kite re-assume its important role in aeronautics.

5

MECHANICAL BIRDS

Men have always been greatly fascinated by the possibilities inherent in the idea of self-regulating machines, or 'automata', especially when these may be made to simulate the movements of human or animal life. Such machines were certainly known in antiquity, and they were the subject of much discussion by mediaeval and Renaissance writers.[1] Their interest arises only partly from their potential usefulness, springing in a more profound sense from their symbolic value as indicators of man's power to create coherent and orderly systems which will function without subsequent intervention. Such an assumption of god-like powers left the practitioners of this form of 'natural magic' open to charges of something approaching immoral or satanic behaviour, an attitude which is typified in the well-known story of how Saint Thomas Aquinas smashed the mechanical door-attendant said to have been built by his teacher Albertus Magnus, and which is seen again in the suspicions aroused by Torriano's wooden birds, discussed below. Despite these moral and religious doubts, many ingenious mechanicians of the Renaissance considered the possibility of building examples of that especially challenging sub-class, the 'volant automata'. Although Archytas' much-discussed dove, said to have been the earliest European invention of its kind, may have been made to fly by some form of jet propulsion, I am concerned in this chapter with the possibility that both the dove and some later constructions inspired by it were powered by a mechanism which flapped a pair of artificial wings. With such mechanical birds we move closer to the idea of sustained and con-trolled flight; consciously or unconsciously, those who contemplated building

[1] For automata in general, see A. Chapuis and E. Gélis, *Le monde des automates, étude historique et technique*, 2 vols., Paris, 1928; and A. Chapuis and E. Droz, *Les automates*, Neuchâtel, 1949.

them were taking a step towards the creation of the man-carrying ornithopter.

For centuries, non-flying simulacra of birds had been familiar, and by the later Middle Ages earth-bound models with moving parts had grown comparatively common. While it is probable that many of the reports are exaggerated, there is no doubt that life-like representations of birds were so constructed as to be able to move their heads and wings, and even to sing. According to Constantine Manasses (*d.* 1187) they were used in ninth-century Byzantium; Cassiodorus (*ca.* 485–580) mentions them in a letter to Boethius written during the reign of Theodoric (*d.* 526); and there is some reason to believe that they may have been known still earlier.[1] In the Middle Ages they became especially favoured by the makers of lavishly decorated pulpits and ecclesiastical lecterns which were sometimes adorned with eagles capable of bowing their heads to the word of God. A hurried sketch of a simple mechanism for producing such an effect is to be found in the album (Fig. 22) of Villard de Honnecourt (*fl.* 1235) and, as mentioned in the

Fig. 22. Non-flying eagle automaton. Paris, Bibliothèque Nationale, MS 1104, f. 22ᵛ, Villard de Honnecourt, Album, *ca.* 1235

previous chapter, the gates of Nürnberg displayed a large version of the same device. The general mode of construction of the decorative singing birds, built as expensive toys to amuse the wealthy, is depicted in a number of Renaissance books on mechanics, a good example being that in Ramelli (Plate 38).

Ambulant automata, sometimes winged, were also well known to the

---

[1] Constantine Manasses, Συνοψις Ἱστορικη, lines 4798 ff. (Migne, Series Gr., vol. 127, col. 400); Cassiodorus, *Epistola* xlv: *Metalla mugiunt, Diomedis in ære grues buccinant, æneus anguis insibilat, aves simulatæ fritiniunt; et quæ propriam vocem nesciunt habere, dulcedinem probantur emittere cantilenæ* (Migne, Series Lat., vol. 69, col. 540); and see Thorndike, *A History of Magic and Experimental Science*, vol. 1, p. 266.

constructors of artifices, the basic structure and general appearance of one such being sketched in Fontana's *Bellicorum instrumentorum liber* (Plate 39). With the example of Archytas' success in mind, inventors tried to make such creatures simulate real flight. What is perhaps most surprising, in view of the comparative ease with which one may build an artificial bird which will glide, if only for a short distance, is that there are so few reports of any such achievements. Nowhere, as far as I know, does anyone speak of simple paper gliders, and the total number of flying models of all sorts is very much smaller than the number of kites and windsocks. As in the case of the attempts at winged human flight, the explanation is certainly the concentration on feathers and flapping. The familiarity today of construction based on a distinction between the systems of sustentation and propulsion, that is, the use of fixed wings and of some separate motor power to push the wing through the air, may lead us to forget that the desirability of such a distinction was by no means always obvious. Although the separation is to be found in such hypothetical machines as Lana's airship and Gusmão's Passarola,[1] and while it is implicit in Fontana's rocket bird (if the wings produced any real sustentation), it was not the most obviously direct experimental procedure and was in fact a negation of the organic nature of flight.

After Archytas, Regiomontanus was the first and most frequently discussed inventor of what were said to be flying automata. The latter was the 'modern' representative of his 'classical' forerunner, the two making a natural pair. Ramus, and others after him, attributed to Regiomontanus the creation not only of the eagle, but also of the still more intricate, and perhaps more impressive, iron fly, which could be made to circle the table at dinner to amuse the guests. While there can be little doubt that in the fifteenth century a small, free-flying iron model was a technological impossibility (as it virtually is today) it is not only possible but even probable that a simulacrum of a fly was built and, by some means, whether or not including sleight of hand, given the appearance of flight. Duhem ingeniously suggests that Regiomontanus may have attached to his model a slender thread suspended from the ceiling, the fly being propelled in an ellipse around the table by a thrust from the maker's hand and being recaptured with certainty by means of a powerful magnet concealed in his palm.[2] While this explanation may

---

[1] C. H. Gibbs-Smith, *Aviation: An Historical Survey from its Origins to the end of World War II*, London, 1970, pp. 1, 12, 14.

[2] J. Duhem, *Histoire des idées aéronautiques avant Montgolfier*, Paris, 1943, p. 130.

perhaps seem rather fanciful, and although the hard-headed Baier and Bühel dismiss the fly as still less worthy of attention than the eagle in which they refuse to believe, some such device could indeed have been produced by the artisans of the time. The surprising smallness and intricacy of many of the early automata have been amply demonstrated by the researches of Chapuis and others, and it is even possible that the fly may have included some mechanism for simulating the movements of wings.

Although as late as the middle of the sixteenth century Archytas and Regiomontanus were virtually the only inventors reputed to have constructed flying models, the possibility of making such things was widely discussed. One of the most interesting, as well as most rational, of comments on mechanical birds is that by Cardano, who had seen artificial birds flying at the end of a string (*i.e.*, kites), but who confessed that he had never come across a free-flying mechanical model:

> . . . that it should rise of its own accord is hardly possible, since it is necessary that there should be strong cords to move it, which will be heavier than cords which move by their own power. It may nevertheless fly if it is moved in the first place by a thrust and then by the blowing of the strong wind caused by the size of the wings and the power of the wheels which makes them function. The dove may certainly fly properly if the lightness of the body, the size of the wings, the strength of the wheels, and assistance provided by the wind (which geese and other heavy birds do not ignore), are sufficient.[1]

Given a sufficient *impetus*, the bird will fly if the wings, operated by a gear system, can produce enough energy to compensate for the losses of *impetus* arising from movement through the air. As Cardano realises, the whole thing will, nevertheless, be rather heavy. (The cords which he mentions will be those attached to the wings to pull them down against the air.) In speaking of the blowing of a strong wind, caused by the wings, Cardano may have had in mind the old belief about the 'wind-gathering' capacity of feathers. The lifting force of the wind which is created by the flapping of the wings would be 'gathered' by the model, just as geese and other large birds are careful to absorb the energy of the air currents, the only difference in this case being that the wind must first be created by the model itself.

The learned but irascible J. C. Scaliger (1484–1558), scornful of Cardano's hesitancy over Archytas' dove, claimed that it was all very easy:

[1] G. Cardano, *De rerum varietate libri xvii*, Basileae, 1557, p. 440.

I should have no difficulty in making a model of a ship which would move of its own accord, setting its own oars in motion, and the same principle may be used for the bird. The readily procurable materials will be the pith of reeds, covered with bladders or the membranes used by goldbeaters and book-binders . . . , and reinforced with thin cords. When a semicircular gear has set one wheel turning, this will communicate its movement to the others, by means of which the wings will be flapped.[1]

The interesting suggestion for the use of goldbeaters' skin, which was to become so important a commodity in the early days of the hydrogen balloon, has several times been remarked upon. A structure such as Scaliger proposes would probably be the lightest that could be achieved using sixteenth-century materials. The mechanism for moving the wings is, however, so vaguely described as to suggest to Venturini that Scaliger, intent above all on attacking Cardano, had no real idea as to how it could have been done, and was merely attempting to score over his adversary.[2] Although, given Scaliger's character, this is far from impossible, the general sense of the passage is fairly clear. A semicircular gear has often been used to produce reciprocating or reversing motion, the gear turning another (or a rack) against some form of tension (*e.g.*, a spring), which is released during that part of the cycle when the teeth are not engaged. If Scaliger's wings were so arranged that they could be pulled down, against spring tension, by turning an axle around which cords were wound, this axle could be alternately turned and released by just such a semicircular gear.

In sixteenth- and seventeenth-century books there are one or two reports of experiments with flying models which are more or less entirely independent of the Archytas-Regiomontanus tradition. It is no doubt fitting that one of these should be associated with that political high-flier, Charles V of Spain. According to the voluminous but not always reliable accounts of his life during retirement,[3] the ceremonial entry into Munich in 1530 was not the only occasion on which he was entertained by an exhibition of artificial flight. During his two years of retreat near the monastery of St Yuste, he is said to have been amused by automata flown by Giovanni Torriano, his clock-maker:

[1] J. C. Scaliger, *Exotericarum exercitationum liber*, Lutetiae, 1557, f. 444ᵛ.

[2] G. Venturini, *Da Icaro a Montgolfier*, 2 vols., Roma, 1928, vol. 1, pp. 116–7.

[3] For Charles' life in the monastery, see L. P. Gachard, *Retraite et mort de Charles-Quint au monastère de Juste*, 3 vols., Bruxelles, 1854, 1855.

Sometimes he sent wooden sparrows out of his chamber into the Emperours Dining-room, that would flie round, and back again; the Superiour of the Monastery, who came in by accident, suspecting him for a Conjurer.[1]

Torriano was born in Cremona at the end of the fifteenth or early in the sixteenth century. In 1529 he was called upon, along with some others, to examine a clock which had been presented to Charles V at his coronation in Bologna but which now failed to work. Among those who had been summoned, only Torriano under-stood the function of the clock, but he suggested that he would achieve more satisfactory results by building another of the same design, rather than by repairing the original. He was accordingly taken into Charles' service, and followed him to Spain. Torriano managed to spend the next 29 years working on the clock, for which he planned many improvements.[2]

Although he has sometimes been unjustly denounced as a charlatan, Torriano was in fact a skilled and imaginative engineer. As to the 'wooden sparrows', how-ever, further details are lacking and one can only speculate on their nature. If he did indeed manage to make something fly, it may be that the sparrows were no more than gliders constructed, perhaps, like the rocket bird in Vienna codex 3064,[3] from a wooden frame covered with paper. Such gliders could well be made to follow a curving path; indeed, if they flew at all they would almost certainly have curved to one side or the other, thus providing the seeds of the statement that they flew around the room and back again.

At the end of his *Inuentions or Deuises*,[4] that extraordinary self-taught mechanical genius William Bourne discusses a number of automata and allows the possibility of making artificial birds. He does not claim to have tried any in practice, nor does he suggest that he has seen any, and the words 'it may flie', which he uses towards the end of the passage quoted below, suggest that the whole thing is speculation as far as Bourne is concerned. On the other hand his earlier statement 'some have thought that it hath bene done by inchantment' is equally suggestive of his having

[1] F. Strada, *De bello belgico decas prima*, Romae, 1632, p. 8: *Interdum ligneos Passerculos emisit cubiculo volantes reuolantesque: Cœnobiarcha, qui tum fortè aderat, præstigias subverente*. The translation is from the version by Sir Robt. Stapylton, *De bello belgico: the History of the Low-Countrey Warres*, London, z650, p. 7. Earlier accounts of Torriano mention only non-flying automata.

[2] Th. Beck, *Beiträge zur Geschichte des Maschinenbaues*, 2nd edn., Berlin, 1900, pp. 365–90.

[3] See p. 59.

[4] London, [1578,] pp. 98–9.

heard of the existence of such birds. The possibilities are set down with Bourne's characteristic semi-articulate enthusiasm:

> As touchyng the makyng of any strange workes that the world hath maruayled at, as . . . a Doue of woodde for to flie: or an Eagle made by arte of woode and other mettall to flie: and byrdes made of brasse, tinne or other mettall to sing sweetely, and such other lyke Deuises, some haue thought that it hath bene done by inchantment, which is no such thing, but that it hath bene done by wheeles, as you may see by clockes, that doo keepe tyme, some goyng with plummets, and some with springs, as those small clockes that be vsed in tablets to hang about mens neckes . . . And for to make a bird or foule made of wood & mettall, with other things made by arte, to flye, it is to bee done to goe with springs, and so to beate the ayre with the wings as other birds or fowles doe, being of a reasonable lightnes, it may flie: . . . and also the birds [may be] made to flie by Arte, to flie circularly, as it shall please the inuenter, by the placing of the wheeles and springs, and such other like inuentions, which the common people would maruell at, thinking that it is done by Inchantment, and yet is done by no other meanes, but by good Artes and lawfull.

If this passage arose as a direct response to reports of artificial birds, it may be that the birds were in fact paper kites which, before the end of the sixteenth century, appear to have been very rare in England. Mechanical birds must, however, have been still rarer, and although volant automata were discussed by a number of later writers, including Wilkins and Leybourn,[1] the only British claim to have built and flown one before the end of the seventeenth century was, as far as I am aware, made by Robert Hooke, whose interest in flight is well known:

> I . . . made a Module, which, by the help of Springs and Wings, rais'd and sustain'd it self in the Air; . . .[2]

Until we have an adequate study—long awaited—of the aeronautical material in Hooke's papers, it will not be possible to say more about this interesting assertion.

An amusing but wholly unsubstantiated and much more doubtful claim of a similar kind is to be found in the Earl of Worcester's famous little book *A Century of the Names and Scantlings of such Inventions as at present I can call to mind to have tried and perfected* . . .,[3] in which he says that he knows

---

[1] J. Wilkins, *Mathematicall Magick*, London, 1648, pp. 191–9; W. Leybourn, *Pleasure with Profit: Consisting of Recreations of Divers Kinds* . . ., London, 1694, pt. 3, pp. 19, 24–5.

[2] R. Waller, 'The Life of Dr. Robert Hooke,' in *The Posthumous Works of Robert Hooke*, London, 1705, p. iv.

[3] London, 1663, p. 31.

How to make an artificial Bird to fly which way and as long as one pleaseth, by or against the wind, sometimes chirping, other times hovering, still tending the way it is designed for.

A briefer statement of essentially the same claim is found in a manuscript by Worcester, now in the British Museum: 'By this I can make an Artificiall Bird to fly wch way & as long as I please.'[1] There is little reason to doubt that this is only a velleity. Some, especially Dircks,[2] have taken the Earl's claims seriously, and his description of a sort of proto-steam engine has aroused a good deal of comment, but the manifest impossibility of many of his 'inventions' throws doubt on everything.

Worcester's assertions about the lifelike qualities of his model may bring to mind a related pastime less pleasing to modern sensibilities. Rather than bother themselves with the very nearly impossible construction of flying models, children made a common practice of keeping a bird captive by tying a light line to one of its legs and letting it flutter around their heads at the end of the string. This amusement is to be found illustrated in many of the emblem books, and elsewhere. A typical example is reproduced in Plate 40. A similar practice involving bees or other insects, still occasionally seen today, dates back at least to the first quarter of the fourteenth century. In one of the lower margins of 'Queen Mary's Psalter', men are seen flying insects at the ends of threads (Plate 41). A further and most ingenious use of tethered birds is mentioned by Athanasius Kircher, who suggested that the movement of large ornamental kites might be controlled by tying trained birds to them.[3]

Compared to the accounts of kites, rocket-dragons, and even winged men, the reports of mechanical birds are sparse and very tentative, suggesting that little success was achieved in this field. Given the quite high degree of sophistication reached in the construction of Renaissance clockwork machinery, it is nevertheless likely that clockwork wings were at least attempted. It is, of course, highly improbable that any such model could have done more than reduce the rate of its fall, or perhaps raise itself very briefly into the air before fluttering down again, but this may have been the achievement of Robert Hooke, who is seldom found

[1] MS Birch 4459, f. 11r, item 3.
[2] H. Dircks, *The Life, Times, and Scientific Labours of the Second Marquis of Worcester*, London, 1865, especially pp. 440–3, 556.
[3] A. Kircher, *Ars magna lucis et umbrae*, Romae, 1646, pt. 2, p. 826.

making wild claims. In any case, if the iron fly of Nürnberg ever managed to raise itself even momentarily, we should have to concur with the judgement implied in Sir Thomas Browne's question: 'Who admires not Regiomontanus, his fly, beyond his eagle?'

6

WINGED MEN

Among the many possible methods of achieving human flight, the direct imitation of birds has always captivated most completely the imaginations of inventors and speculators. Despite the flamboyant potentialities of airborne chariots powered by tame birds or by mysteriously harnessed supernatural forces, the relatively remote control which one might exercise over such a vehicle seems to have been found less exciting than the possibility of a close organic relationship between the body and a pair of finely wrought wings.

It seems highly probable that many men of whom nothing is now known flapped feathered arms in vain attempts to rise from the ground, and some may even have met with partial success. Just as, in the years preceding and following the successful flights of the Wright brothers, several experimenters managed to build machines which could achieve powered 'hops' of a few yards or more, so in previous centuries many enthusiasts less enterprising than Eilmer, Danti, and Guidotti, and perhaps less successful, must have made wings with which, after running vigorously along the ground, they were able to glide briefly through the air. Wilkins mentions one such nameless experimenter:

Though the truth is, most of these Artists did unfotunately [sic] miscarry by falling down and breaking their arms or legs, yet that may be imputed to their want of experience, and too much fear, which must needs possesse men in such dangerous and strange attempts. Those things that seem very difficult and fearfull at the first, may grow very facil after frequent triall and exercise. And therefore he that would effect any thing in this kind, must be brought up to the constant practise of it from his youth. Trying first only to use his wings in running on the ground, as an Estrich or tame Geese will doe, touching the earth with his toes; and so by degrees learn to rise higher, till hee shall attain unto skill and confidence. I have heard it from credible testimony, that one of our own Nation hath proceeded so far in this experiment, that he was able by the help of wings in such a running pace to step constantly ten yards at a time.[1]

There seems to be no good reason to doubt the truth of this report, which is certainly within the bounds of possibility.

Such hops were obviously much less exciting than attempts at flight of a more spectacular kind, and it is not at all surprising that most of the surviving stories tell of foolhardy men who launched themselves into the air from towers or other eminences, sometimes with fatal results. In view of the obviousness of the danger, it is perhaps curious that no one is reported to have tried a pair of wings in ballast. As with ground-level flappers it may simply be that such attempts, if made, were not sufficiently interesting to be recorded, but a more likely reason is the dominance of the concept of organic flight. As flapping and immediate control over movement through the air were thought to be necessary, it might have been argued that nothing would be gained by inconclusive experiments using rigid wings attached to ballast.

The legend of Daedalus, often taken to refer to a real but lost art, inspired attempts at flight throughout Europe, and nowhere more often than in Rome. Dio Chrysostom (*ca.* A.D. 40–112), speaking of Nero's claim to absolute power even in ordering the performance of the apparently impossible, uses the example of human flight:

> . . . no one contradicted him in anything, whatever he said, or affirmed that anything he commanded was impossible to perform, so that even if he ordered anyone to fly, the man promised that too and for a considerable time he would be maintained in the imperial household in the belief that he would fly.[2]

This is not the only allusion to such enforced attempts at flight. I know of no accounts which suggest that the result was ever more than an empty, though often violent, spectacle, but the unfortunate participants no doubt did their best to provide themselves with wings large enough to help break their fall. That the Roman attempts were wholly unsuccessful seems clear from Suetonius' brief mention of one such flight at a Neronian feast: 'Icarus at his very first attempt

---

[1] J. Wilkins, *Mathematicall Magick*, London, 1648, pp. 204–5.
[2] Dio Chrysostom, *Discourses*, 21. 9. (Loeb, vol. 2, pp. 280, 281.)

fell close by the imperial couch and bespattered the emperor with his blood.'[1] Martial is more sarcastic: 'Daedalus, now thou art being so mangled by a Lucanian boar, how wouldst thou wish thou hadst now thy wings!'[2]

To these spectacles should perhaps be added some enforced 'flights' of a slightly different kind, those made by the criminals hurled from the famous 'Leap' at Leucas. Strabo describes the annual event:

> It was an ancestral custom among the Leucadians, every year at the sacrifice performed in honour of Apollo, for some criminal to be flung from this rocky look-out for the sake of averting evil, wings and birds of all kinds being fastened to him, since by their fluttering they could lighten the leap, and also for a number of men, stationed all round below the rock in small fishing-boats, to take the victim in, and, when he had been taken on board, to do all in their power to get him safely outside their borders.[3]

As was, perhaps, inevitable, the early reports of theatrical simulation later came to be interpreted as fully successful flights. Sabellicus (*ca.* 1436–1506) says that among the spectacles to be seen in Rome at the time of the Caesars was a man simulating the flights of birds and rising to some height from the ground,[4] but this can be little more than an imaginative exaggeration of such displays as those seen by Suetonius and Martial.

For nearly a thousand years after the Roman simulations nothing more is heard of bird-men in Europe, but after about A.D. 1000 reports become increasingly frequent. From Britain to Italy, from Spain to Constantinople, hazardous trials were undertaken by men of the most diverse types. The stories which I recount in the remainder of this chapter concern, among others, a physician, a monk, a mathematician, a court adventurer, an old church cantor, and a painter. Scholarship appears to have been no guarantee of success: the monk and the mathematician fared no better than did the adventurer.

The increasing interest in experimental aeronautics coincides, of course, with the growth of European technology, and it may be that, as with some other aspects of that technology, Islamic influences must be taken into account. Bird-men everywhere must have provided a sufficiently astonishing sight to give rise to

[1] *De vita Caesarum*, VI. XII. 2: *Icarus primo statim conatu iuxta cubiculum eius decidit ipsumque cruore respersit.* (Loeb, vol. 2, pp. 104, 105.)

[2] *On the Spectacles*, VIII: *Daedale, Lucano cum sic lacereris ab urso,/quam cuperes pinnas nunc habuisse tuas!* (Loeb, vol. 1, pp. 8, 9.)

[3] Strabo, *Geography*, X. 2. 9. (Loeb, vol. 5, pp. 34, 35.)

[4] Sabellicus (Marcus Antonius Coccius), *Exemplorum libri decem*, X. 9, Argentoraci, 1509, f. 98ʳ.

stories which would circulate widely, and it may not be entirely accidental that the upsurge of attempted European flights was preceded by reports of a number of similar attempts in the Near East.

A story handed down by the Arabic geographer Ibn al-Faḳīh (ninth century) tells of an architect who built, in Hamadhān, a tower for King Shapur I of Persia (A.D. 241–272):

> The jealous king decided to leave the master-builder on the top of the tower, as he did not want any one else to profit by his genius. The architect consented, but asked one favour of the king; he was permitted to erect a wooden hut on the tower to protect his corpse from the attack of vultures. The king granted the request and ordered to supply him with as much timber as he needed. Then the architect was abandoned to his fate. He took up his tools, made a pair of wings from the wood left with him, and fastened them to his body. Driven by the wind he rose into the air and landed unscathed at a safe place, where he kept in hiding.[1]

As Laufer points out, this story, hardly more than legend, bears a striking similarity to the story of Daedalus. More credit may, perhaps, be given to an account from Moorish Spain. According to the historian al-Maḳḳarī (d. 1632), an attempt at flight was made in Andalusia in about A.D. 875. The story concerns Abu'l-Ḳāsim 'Abbas b. Firnās, the physician. Al-Maḳḳarī says that he

> was the first who made glass out of clay, and who established fabrics of it in Andalus . . . Among other very curious experiments which he made, one is his trying to fly. He covered himself with feathers for the purpose, attached a couple of wings to his body, and, getting on an eminence, flung himself down into the air, when, according to the testimony of several trustworthy writers who witnessed the performance, he flew to a considerable distance, as if he had been a bird, but in alighting again on the place whence he had started his back was very much hurt, for not knowing that birds when they alight come down upon their tails, he forgot to provide himself with one. Múmen Ibn Sa'íd has said, in a verse alluding to this extraordinary man,—
>
> > He flew faster than the phoenix in his flight when he dressed his body in the feathers of a vulture.[2]

[1] B. Laufer, *The Prehistory of Aviation*, Chicago, 1928, p. 66.

[2] al-Maḳḳarī, *The History of the Mohammedan Dynasties in Spain*, trans. P. de Gayangos, 2 vols., London, 1840, 1843, vol. I, p. 148. The verses by Mūmen, mistranslated by de Gayangos in the most extraordinary fashion as 'He surpassed in velocity the flight of the ostrich, but he neglected to arm his body with the strength of the vulture', are given here in the translation published by Lynn White, Jr., in 'Eilmer of Malmesbury, an Eleventh Century Aviator,' *Technology and Culture*, vol. 2, 1961, p. 101. See also A. Zéki Pacha, 'L'Aviation chez les Arabes,' *Bulletin de l'Institut Egyptien*, 5th series, vol. 5, 1911, pp. 92–101.

Although 'Abbas b. Firnās may have managed to glide for some distance, he cannot have alighted again 'on the place whence he started', as this would imply that he was able to sustain himself at a constant height in the air. The most interesting passage, however, is that which mentions the unfulfilled need for a tail, a detail which appears again in the story of Eilmer of Malmesbury. Al-Makkarī's comment on the function of the tail is absurd, and may have been garbled in transmission, but following their unfortunate experiences with the instability of a single wing surface, both 'Abbas b. Firnās and Eilmer seem to have had some dim understanding of its aerodynamic importance.

The great lexicographer Abū Naṣr Ismā'īl b. Ḥammād, better known as al-Djawharī, was born in Fārāb (later called Otrār) in Turkestan, the date of his birth being unknown. After completing his education in Baghdad he travelled widely among the desert people, gathering material for his lexicographical studies. He became a scholar, theologian and philosopher of note, and was reputed to be one of the finest calligraphers in Islam. After his wanderings he settled in Nīsābūr, where he worked and taught in the mosque. His death is reported to have occurred either as early as 1002–3 or perhaps as late as 1009–10; authorities appear still to be divided on this matter. Perhaps in a fit of madness, al-Djawharī stood on the roof of the mosque and addressed the people, claiming that he would astonish posterity with a deed never before performed. Having attached two large wooden wings to his body, he then threw himself into the air only to fall immediately to the ground, where he died instantly. L. Kopf has made the interesting suggestion that the wooden wings may have been the 'wings' of a door, which would certainly have resulted in al-Djawharī's falling vertically downwards. Whatever actually happened, this is one of the very few accounts of attempted flights which make no claim whatever to success.[1]

A younger contemporary of al-Djawharī fared rather better. At the Abbey of Malmesbury an Anglo-Saxon Benedictine monk called Eilmer, who had probably not heard of the death of the lexicographer, launched himself into what may have been the first substantial glide in the history of flight. In his *Chronicle* William of Malmesbury writes:

A comet, a star foretelling, they say, change in kingdoms, appeared trailing its

[1] A. Zéki Pacha, 'L'Aviation chez les Arabes.' See also 'al-Djawharī', by L. Kopf, in H. A. R. Gibb, *et al.*, *The Encyclopedia of Islam, new edition*, Leiden and London, 1960, etc., and Lynn White, Jr., 'Eilmer of Malmesbury,' p. 100.

long and fiery tail across the sky. Wherefore a certain monk of our monastery, Eilmer by name, bowed down with terror at the sight of the brilliant star, sagely cried 'Thou art come! A cause of grief to many a mother art thou come; I have seen thee before, but now I behold thee much more terrible, threatening to hurl destruction on this land.'

He was a man learned for those times, of ripe old age, and in his early youth had hazarded a deed of remarkable boldness. He had by some means, I scarcely know what, fastened wings to his hands and feet so that, mistaking fable for truth, he might fly like Daedalus, and, collecting the breeze on the summit of a tower, he flew for more than the distance of a furlong. But, agitated by the violence of the wind and the swirling of air, as well as by awareness of his rashness, he fell, broke his legs, and was lame ever after. He himself used to say that the cause of his failure was his forgetting to put a tail on the back part.[1]

As Lynn White points out in his authoritative study of Eilmer, William of Malmesbury was sufficiently close to the events to have known monks who had known Eilmer, while William's reputation for learning and accuracy suggest that his report should be considered as fairly reliable. White also points out that Eilmer lived in an environment conducive to comparatively advanced thinking in technological matters. Whatever the reason for his partial success, in later mediaeval and Renaissance times Eilmer (whose name, owing to a misreading, is sometimes rendered as 'Oliver') was frequently celebrated as the first man to have flown in Europe. If the distance covered was, as William claims, more than a furlong (*spatio stadii et plus*) the flight was indeed a remarkable one, even though it can have been no more than a relatively uncontrolled and lucky glide.

The date of Eilmer's flight would appear to have been *ca.* 1000–1010. The comet which he saw was, of course, Halley's, at its appearance just prior to the Norman invasion in 1066. If, in 1066, he was an old man of 80 or more, Eilmer could indeed have seen the same comet at its previous passage in 989. This would suggest the first decade of the millennium as the probable date for a flight said to have been undertaken *prima juventute*.

A much less successful attempt, and one which produced still more crippling results, is said to have taken place in Constantinople in the twelfth century. In 1161 Manuel Comnenus had carried out a successful campaign in the Meander

---

[1] William of Malmesbury, *De gestis regum anglorum libri quinque*, 2 vols., ed. W. Stubbs, London, 1887, 1889, vol. 1, pp. 276–7. The translation is that given by Lynn White, Jr., in 'Eilmer of Malmesbury,' pp. 97–8.

valley, during which he removed any immediate threat from Kilij Arslan, the Seljuq Sultan of Rum. Following the treaty with Manuel, the Sultan visited Constantinople in 1162, where he was received with great festivities. The account of the attempted flight by one of the Sultan's followers which took place during that visit is remarkably reminiscent of the scenes in the Roman arena.[1] With the printing of Nicetas' history of the Turks,[2] written in about 1206, the story became fairly well known in the sixteenth century and may have had some influence on European flights. The following is the lively version given by Knolles, in his translation of 1603:

> Among other queint deuises of many, for the solemnizing of so great a triumph, there was an actiue Turke, who had openly giuen it out, that against an appointed time he would from the top of an high tower in the tilt-yeard, flie by the space of a furlong. The report whereof had filled the citie with a woonderfull expectation of so strange a noueltie. The time prefixed being come, and the people without number assembled; the Turke according to his promise, vpon the top of the high tower shewed himselfe, girt in a long and large white garment, gathered into many plites and foldings, made of purpose for the gathering of the wind: wherewith the foolish man had vainely persuaded himselfe to haue houered in the aire, as do birds vpon their wings, or to haue guided himselfe as are ships with their sailes. Standing thus houering a great while, as readie to take his flight; the beholders still laughing, and crying out, Flie Turke, flie, how long shall we expect thy flight? The emperour in the meane time dissuading him from so desperat an attempt: and the Sultan betwixt feare and hope hanging in doubtfull suspence what might happen to his countrieman. The Turke, after he had a great while houered with his armes abroad (the better to haue gathered the wind, as birds do with their wings) and long deluded the expectation of the beholders: at length finding the wind fit, as he thought for his purpose, committed himselfe with his vaine hope vnto the aire: But in steed of mounting aloft, this foolish *Icarus* came tumbling downe headlong with such violence, that he brake his necke, his armes and legs, with almost all the bones of his bodie. This foolish flight of the Turke gaue such occasion of sport and laughter vnto the vulgar people, alwaies readie to scoffe and jest at such ridiculous matters, that the Turks attending vpon the Sultan, could not walke in the streets vnderided; the artificers in their shops shaking their armes with their tooles in their hands, as did the Turke, and still crying out Flie Turke, flie: whereof the emperour hearing, although he

[1] For the date and historical context of the flight, see *The Cambridge Medieval History*, IV. 1, Cambridge, 1966, p. 236.

[2] Nicetas Choniates, *Nicetae Acominati Choniatae LXXXVI annorum historia . . .*, Basileae, 1557, p. 60.

could not chuse but thereat smile himselfe, as not ignorant of the scoffes and taunts of the vulgar people; yet in fauour of the Sultan, who was not a little grieued therewith, he commanded such their insolencie to be restrained.[1]

Of the several further reports of attempts to fly during the Middle Ages and Renaissance, only two or three are written in such a manner as to carry any kind of conviction. Several writers are openly derisive, and most are sceptical. The attempts fall into two general categories: first, flights staged as public spectacles, and, second, genuine aerodynamic experiments, undertaken for their own sake. It is strange that in only one case, that of John Damian, whose adventure otherwise falls into the first category, is there any question of the use of the putative power of flight for an immediate practical purpose.

While many bones appear to have been broken in the cause of public entertainment, there is at least one report, which seems genuine enough, of a flight abandoned at the last minute despite the scorn which was provoked by such a policy of safety first. In his *Chronicle* Salimbene (1221–*ca.* 1287) writes of the Florentine charlatan Buoncompagno, who was in Bologna at the same time as friar Giovanni of Vicenza. Giovanni, who had been making allegedly supernatural predictions, was widely gaining a reputation for being a miracle worker. In order to attract the public's attention away from Giovanni and towards himself, Buoncompagno announced that he would fly. The news was given out and, on the day set down for the flight, the whole city, men and women, the children and the aged, gathered together at the foot of a hill. Buoncompagno, who had made wings for himself, stood at the top of the eminence looking at the people. After they had stared at each other for some time, he addressed them, saying 'Depart with divine benediction, and let it suffice that you have looked upon the face of Buoncompagno'. The people did indeed depart, in derision. This act of prudence, or cowardice, as one wishes, occurred in 1232 or 1233.[2]

Another passage about an unrealised flight, and one which may occasion more regret than does Buoncompagno's failure of nerve, is found in the *Metrologum* of Giovanni da Fontana, whose detailed advice on rocket birds I have already quoted. This imaginative technician also considered the problem of the bird-man, but, unfortunately for us, was too busy to do anything about it:

According to the poets, Daedalus, . . . using wax and a few feathers, made for

[1] R. Knolles, *The Generall Historie of the Turkes*, London, 1603, p. 37.
[2] Salimbene de Adam, *Cronica*, 2 vols., ed. G. Scalia, Bari, 1966, vol. I, pp. 109–10.

himself wings which he is said to have flapped by the use of his own strength and thus he is said to have flown up to the region of the air and to have crossed the Icarian sea.

I, indeed, have no doubt that it is possible to attach to a man wings which may be artificially moved, by means of which he will be able to raise himself into the air and move from place to place and climb towers and cross water, on which subject I some time ago began to write and set forth my ideas, but being distracted by other activities I never completed the work. Many others have risen by means of cords and ladders and suchlike apparatus. But the discussion of these things I shall put aside until I have a better opportunity at another time.[1]

Perhaps the most celebrated would-be aviator of the early Renaissance, and certainly the one to have received the most careful attention of the later commentators, was Giovanni Battista Danti (*ca.* 1477–1517). The real family name was Rainaldi, but Pietro Vincenzo Rainaldi (*d.* 1512), an admirer of the poet, changed it to Dante, or Danti. Of the four early accounts of Danti's flight, two, those by Cesare Alessi, in the second Century of his *Elogia civium perusinorum*,[2] and Cesare Crispolti, in his *Perugia augusta*,[3] have special value as sources. Of the two, Alessi's was published second, in 1652, but for various reasons discussed below it is probably the better. Alessi, a Perugian himself, died in 1649, having previously published the first Century of the *Elogia* in 1635. The following is his version of the story:

A man to induce astonished admiration was Giovanni Battista Danti, the Daedalus of Perugia, who, after he had worked hard at mathematical studies, made, among many other such things of his own devising, a pair of wings, properly proportioned to his body, which he fixed to himself with the skill of a man of the greatest mechanical genius. Having arranged these so as to produce effective flight, he several times tried them over lake Trasimeno. As soon as they responded perfectly to his control, he decided to try them publicly in Perugia. And when in that town a great gathering of eminent people was assembled for the nuptials of the sister of Giampaolo Baglioni, who was being given in marriage to the most valiant duke Bartholommeo Alviano, and when a crowd of people were gathered in the great square for jousting, behold, suddenly there was Danti, flying through the air from a high part of our city with a great rushing sound, enveloped in various kinds of feathers, crossing from one side to the other of the square with his great pair of wings, so astonishing everyone, and indeed terrifying quite a few, that they thought they were witness to some great and

[1] Giovanni da Fontana, *Metrologum de pisce cane et volucre*, Bologna, Biblioteca Universitaria, MS 2705, f. 97ʳ⁻ᵛ.

[2] Romae, 1652, pp. 204–7.

[3] Perugia, 1648, pp. 360–1.

portentous monster. But when, having left the low earth behind, he was trying with his proud limbs to attain through the high air the summit of his genius, envious Fortune, indignant at so much audacity, broke the iron bar which controlled the left wing, and as Danti could not sustain the weight of his body with the help of the other wing alone, he fell heavily on to the roof of the church of St Mary, and to his great distress, and that of everyone, hurt his leg. After he had recovered, Giampaolo Baglioni took him to Venice as his mathematician, distinguishing him both with honours and with a large stipend. There he was pointed out by everyone, just as Demosthenes had once been, and was revered by all as a man worthy of the greatest respect, who by the subtlety of his genius had taught men how they might fly. But when still not forty, he was attacked by a severe fever and passed away on the wings of his virtue (more safely than he had flown on counterfeit wings while living) to heaven, as one may hope, in the year 1517.

The version by Crispolti (also a Perugian) published in 1648, may have priority in the writing. Crispolti died in 1606, and his book was subsequently edited by a nephew. As that part of it which contains the story of Danti was prepared from Crispolti's incomplete notes, which have not survived, there is no means of telling how close the published version may be to what the author wrote. Again, Alessi speaks of having used old manuscripts, no longer extant, manuscripts which may also, perhaps, have been available to Crispolti. In any case the only substantial difference between these two accounts concerns the nuptial celebrations, which in Crispolti are said to have been for the marriage of Giampaolo himself. In so far as one of the reports may contain an error of oversight or transcription, it is more likely to be that by Crispolti, the simpler version, which might easily arise as a corruption of the details given by Alessi. If we assume that Alessi is right, the date of the flight must be 1498/9. The marriage of Bartolommeo Alviano to Giampaolo's daughter Pantasilea, which was the Duke's second, appears to have taken place in the first two or three months of that year, for a surviving document speaks of a gathering of the commune of Todi which was held on 12 January to consider an invitation to the wedding.[1] Despite his feathered apparel, Danti must have felt bitterly cold as he flew through the winter air. No further information is to be found in contemporary or seventeenth-century histories of Perugia, none of which mentions Danti's flight or gives a date for the celebrations. The omission from such a book as Pompeo Pellini's three-volume *Historia di Perugia*[2] of any

[1] L. Leônij, *Vita di Bartolommeo di Alviano*, Todi, 1858, pp. 48–9, 152.
[2] P. Pellini, *Dell'Historia di Perugia*, 3 pts., Venetia, 1664.

mention of Danti's flight has, of course, led to doubts about the truth of the story, but Venturini,[1] in his thorough investigation of the matter, points out that contemporary historians would have been at pains to play down the Baglioni family, which, largely owing to the dealings of the infamous Malatesta, had fallen into particularly ill repute. Whether this provides sufficient explanation for a delay of more than a hundred years in the reporting of so spectacular and exciting an event in the city's history may well seem unlikely and the whole account is perhaps no more than a seventeenth-century fabrication.

There is, however, no reason whatever to doubt that an attempt was made in Scotland only a few years after the supposed events in Perugia. John Damian, an Italian charlatan, had managed early in the sixteenth century to ingratiate himself with King James IV of Scotland, who was pleased by the man's merry, jesting nature. John Lesley[2] comments that Damian's only real purpose was to 'milk purses' in the court, but he was so successful in cultivating a reputation as surgeon, apothecary, and alchemist as to beguile the King into making him, in 1504, Abbot of Tungland. Seeing his personality only too well understood by the courtiers who hated him to a man, and having after some time been unable to achieve anything of what he had promised in alchemy, Damian apparently thought to try something new. On 27 September, 1507, the King had sent ambassadors to France, together with the Archbishop of St Andrews and the Earl of Arran:

> This Abbott tuik in hand to flie with wingis, and to be in Fraunce befoir the saidis ambassadouris; and to that effect he causet mak ane pair of wingis of fedderis, quhilkis beand fessinit apoun him, he flew of the castell wall of Striveling, bot shortlie he fell to the ground and brak his thee bane; bot the wyt thairof he asscryvit to that thair was sum hen fedderis in the wingis, quhilk yarnit and covet the mydding and not the skyis. In this doinge he preissit to conterfute ane King of Yngland callit Bladud, quha, as thair histories mentiones, decked him self in fedderis, and presumed to flie in the aire as he did, bot falling on the tempell of Appollo, brak his neck.

Despite this blow to his reputation, Damian appears to have continued in the King's favour. During the following year there are records of the two playing at cards and dice, while in 1508 Damian received a licence to pass out of the realm,

[1] G. Venturini, *Da Icaro a Montgolfier*, 2 vols., Roma, 1928, vol. 1, pp. 69–77.
[2] *The Historie of Scotland*, Edinburgh, 1830, p. 76. (Written 1568–70.) The later Latin version was published as *De origine moribus, et rebus gestis scotorum libri decem*, Romae, 1578, p. 346.

7

and return, without hindrance. He did, in fact, leave for almost five years, returning, as Mackay says, 'like a bird of ill omen' in the year before Flodden.[1]

While Damian's ironic comment on the reason for his failure is certainly consistent with what else we know of his character, it is also consistent with contemporary attitudes to reality. Anyone who made wings using the readily available
hen feathers instead of seeking out the rarer feathers of the eagle would have been
thought to court disaster. In the sixteenth century 'natural affinities' were still
an important element in explanations of physical phenomena, and it was indeed
held to be true that the feathers of the largely earth-bound domestic hen would
be drawn more to the midden than to the skies. The moral for John Lesley's
generation was even sharper than it is for ours: although Damian tried to cut
corners, to do things the easy way, nature was not to be fooled and the man's
charlatanry was finally revealed to all. It was revealed in particular, one might add,
to the poet William Dunbar, who saw his own hopes of ecclesiastical preferment
from the King prejudiced by the favour shown to Damian. Dunbar relieved his
feelings by writing two satires in which he called Damian by many unflattering
names, including 'Turk of Tartary' and 'homecyd' (alluding to his medical pre-
tensions). The poems are quoted in full in Appendix D.

It is possible that Danti and Damian are the two aeronauts to whom Cardano
alludes in a brief discussion of flight in his *De subtilitate*.[2] He speaks there of 'the
invention of flying, which was recently attempted by two men who, however,
fared badly in the matter,' and he goes on to mention Leonardo, who, he says,
'tried, but in vain'. If the attempts of Danti and Damian, which had been made
about half a century before, were already too old to qualify for Cardano's 'recently'
(*nuper*), it may be that he was referring to my next two aeronauts, about whom
very little is known.

Johannes Sturm (1507–89) speaks of a man making wings for himself and jumping from the tower of St Mark's in Venice. As the passage occurs in a discussion
of rhetoric and methods of argument, for which it provides one of the examples,

---

[1] M. Livingstone (ed.), *The Register of the Privy Seal of Scotland. Vol. I. A.D. 1488–1529*,
Edinburgh, 1908, pp. 259–60; Sir J. B. Paul (ed.), *Accounts of the Lord High Treasurer of Scotland.
Vol. IV. A.D. 1507–13*, Edinburgh, 1902, pp. 83, 89, etc. For a general discussion of Damian's
life and character, see Ae. J. G. Mackay, *William Dunbar 1460–1520: a Study in the Poetry and
History of Scotland*, Edinburgh, 1889, pp. xlvi–xlvii, cxvii–cxix, ccxiv–ccxvi.

[2] *De subtilitate libri xxi*, Norimbergae, 1550, p. 318: *Sunt autem quæ latent . . . uolandi inuentum,
quod nuper tentatum à duobus illis pessimè cessit: Vincius . . . tentauit & frustra: hic pictor fuit egregius.*

it may be no more than an illustration imagined for the occasion. Although the supposed event was quoted by a number of later writers, including Wilkins, there appears to be no further contemporary evidence to support the story.[1]

A single report of an undated (probably sixteenth century) flight tells of an old Nürnberg cantor who 'having risen into the air by the help of wings, or by means of some beating arrangement, flew here and there, and then, like a bird of omen, descended once more. But even so, having fallen at last owing to some error (which caused the little wheels, of what kind I do not know, to which the wings were fixed and which made the flight possible, to become either distorted or improperly applied, and rendered powerless) he, having been thrown to the ground, broke his arms and legs.' Burggravius, to whom we owe this account, does not say where the flight took place, but one may safely assume that it was in Nürnberg itself.[2] After repeating the story in his 'book of secrets,' the seventeenth-century German lawyer and chemist Johann Staricius goes on to make one of the earliest suggestions for the establishment of a military air-force:

> Let us here remember & consider a little: if a Generall of an armée had some such Engeniers about him, who could shew themselves in a dark night in the ayre about a Fort, being tyed about with burning lampes, which by wind & water could not be extinguished, what manner of affrightments could be infused on those in the Fort, to force them to a surrendre, which they were not resolved on![3]

Still less is known of another sixteenth-century attempt, this time by an Italian who had obtained a pair of wings with which he said he would fly 'like a turtle-dove'. The only source for this account is a passage by the sixteenth-century Provençal poet Augié Gaillard (*ca.* 1530–92), who is profoundly scornful of the whole enterprise. He says that before a crowd of five hundred thousand people or more, the 'dolt of an Italian' took flight from the Tour de Nesles, but dropped 'like a pig' close by its base, and broke his neck.[4] Gaillard has no doubt that this

---

[1] J. Sturm, *Lingvae latinæ resoluendæ ratio*, Argentorati, 1581, p. 40: *Alius quidam dixit, se velle se demittere ex turre D. Marci Venetiis: fecit itaque se alatum, & dimisit se: tunc alter dixit, & ego hoc fecissem, si dixisses, te velle alis vti. respondit is, cur igitur non fecisti.* J. Wilkins, *Mathematicall Magick*, London, 1648, p. 204.

[2] J. E. Burggravius, *Achilles πάνοπλος redivivus*, Amsterodami, [1612], p. 52.

[3] *Ernewerter und Künstlicher HeldenSchatz*, n.p., 1616, Biiiʳ⁻ᵛ. The book seems never to have been published in English. The passage which I have quoted is taken from a complete manuscript translation in the Wellcome Historical Medical Library, MS 763, f. 5ᵛ.

[4] A. Gaillard, *Lou banquet d'Augié Gailliard*, Paris, 1583. Edn. used: *Lou banquet d'Augie Galliard* [sic], Paris, 1584, f. 17ʳ⁻ᵛ. The passage in question was written *ca.* 1581–3.

was a genuine, if misguided, attempt to fly, but Henri Sauval, referring to Gaillard's account in his *Histoire et recherches*,[1] is unwilling to credit even the attempt, preferring to interpret it as an exaggerated description of an accident to a tight-rope walker trying to cross from the Tour de Nesles to the Tour du Grand Prévôt. The truth may conceivably have been a combination of the two interpretations. Wings to help provide steadying forces, seen occasionally in use by the acrobats of today, were known at least as early as the seventeenth century, and may have been common even earlier. Wilkins says that

> It is a usuall practise in these times, for our *Funambulones*, or Dancers on the Rope, to attempt somewhat like to flying, when they will with their heads forwards slide downe a long cord extended; being fastned at one end on the top of some high Tower, and the other at some distance on the ground, with wings fixed to their shoulders, by the shaking of which they will break the force of their descent.[2]

It seems probable that wings of the same kind were used by the funambulists mentioned by Boaistuau (1500–66) in the mid-sixteenth century. Writing hopefully about man's future conquest of the air, he speaks of Leonardo, who almost succeeded in achieving that aim, and goes on to discuss 'those actors we have seen in our time flying through the air on a rope, with such dexterity and danger that the Princes and Lords who were present could not bear to watch.'[3]

Wilkins' words 'by the shaking of which' are vague and ambiguous. The steadying force is provided by twisting the wings in order to achieve control in roll. While no flapping is involved it is, of course, possible that the experience of the small lifting force which the wings would provide, if well made, induced adventurous acrobats such as Gaillard's Italian may have been, to attempt free flight. This reconstruction of events is, however, unlikely to have any relevance to our understanding of the flights of al-Djawharī, the great scholar, or of Eilmer, the monk. While the date of the story of the Italian's adventure in Paris is uncertain, the tone of Gaillard's poem, which was written in the early 1580s, suggests that the events may at that time have been recent. According to Gaillard, the wings with which the Italian equipped himself were made of cloth, which is at least an improvement on the all too frequent attempts to gain some lift from the

[1] H. Sauval, *Histoire et recherches des antiquités de la ville de Paris*, 3 vols., Paris 1724 vol. 2, p. 544.
[2] J. Wilkins, *Mathematicall Magick*, London, 1648, pp. 207–8.
[3] P. Boaistuau, *Bref discovrs de l'excellence et dignité de l'homme*, Paris, 1558, f. 20r.

use of feathers. Here, however, one must be careful, for it may be that Gaillard's *telo* (cloth) is no more than a guess giving him a convenient rime with *tour Denelo*.

A story which probably contains rather more substance attributes a partially successful flight to Paolo Guidotti, the painter, sculptor, and architect who was born in Lucca in 1569. In about 1582 he went as a student of the arts to Rome, where he soon achieved some success. He was a man of enquiring mind and of wide-ranging interests which, in the opinion of Baldinucci, kept him from a proper concentration on what should have been his principal concern, his painting. He was musician, poet, and doctor of laws, and was skilled in astrology and mathematics. His brilliant but rather flashy character may be judged from his megalomaniac plan to write a poem called *Gerusalemme destrutta*, every verse of every octave of which would end with the same words as those used by Tasso in the octaves of his *Gerusalemme liberata*. Owing to Guidotti's dilettantism and a certain degree of instability in his character, he has been accused of charlatanism by a number of later commentators. At all events, at some time probably around the turn of the century he decided to try to add human flight to his other achievements:

> Matteo Boselli, the Painter, . . . who had spent a long time in his school, reported that Paolo once took it into his head that he could discover how to fly, and that with great ingenuity and labour he made wings from whalebone covered with feathers, giving them curvature by means of springs. He fixed them under his arms so that he might also use them in raising the wings during the act of flight, and after he had made many trials he finally put himself to the test, throwing himself from a height and, with the help of the wings, carried himself forward for about a quarter of a mile, not, in my view, flying, but falling more slowly than he would have done without the wings . . . This, then, is what Guidotti did, who, finally tired with the fatigue of moving his arms, fell on to a roof, which broke, and he, dropping through the hole, found himself in the room beneath, gaining from his flight a broken thigh which left him in a sorry plight.
>
> The same Boselli also affirmed that he had seen with his own eyes the fragments of the apparatus, and the wings themselves, which the Master had used.[1]

Although neither the time nor the place of this adventure is known, the date is

[1] F. Baldinucci, *Notizie de' professori del disegno*, Firenze, 6 vols., 1681–1728, vol. 4 (1700), pp. 248–50.

unlikely to have been as late as 1628, as has been suggested by some. At 59, Guidotti would have been rather too old to undertake such strenuous activities. The date appears to have been proposed on the assumption that he died as a result of his injuries, but nothing in Boselli's account, which certainly sounds like a genuine eye-witness report, suggests that this was the case. There is, however, an aspect of the account which may lead to certain doubts. While Guidotti could well have jumped from a height and fallen through a roof, breaking his leg, these details are suspiciously similar to the circumstances of Danti's exploit and may well have been falsely transferred from the earlier descriptions of the flight in Perugia. The truth will probably remain unknown, but such a daring public spectacle would certainly seem to be in keeping with the man's personality, and we may perhaps credit the attempt, if not the length of the flight.

To conclude these accounts of flights by winged men we once again find, as at the beginning, a story of a flying monk. Kaspar Mohr, a Premonstrant at the monastery of Schussenried, in Württemberg, was born in 1575. In 1610 he left to study theology in Rome, where he took his doctorate in 1614. After his return home Mohr was celebrated as a universal genius, being especially well known for his mechanical skills. He was mathematician, organist, sculptor, painter, joiner, locksmith, turner, and clockmaker. Above all, however, he is remembered for his flying apparatus, which consisted of a pair of wings made from goose feathers held together with whipcord. He is said to have practised in secret until he was sufficiently proficient to offer to fly from the top of the three-storey dormitory of the monastery, but this he was forbidden to undertake, and the apparatus was confiscated. He died on 6 June 1625.

It is possible that while he was in Italy Mohr learned of the aeronautical work of Leonardo, and of the attempts by Danti and Guidotti. A later report claiming flights of two hours' duration is of course merely narrative embroidery.[1]

Reports of flights of the sort I have been considering are to be found in comparatively large numbers in books of the seventeenth and eighteenth centuries. Becher, for example, speaks of flights in France and in The Hague, of one by the celebrated but discredited inventor Hautsch, and of one by a cobbler in Augsburg.[2]

---

[1] B. Wilhelm, S.J., 'Schweikart und Mohr, zwei schwäbische Flieger aus alter Zeit,' *Illustrierte Aeronautische Mitteilungen*, vol. 13, 1909, pp. 441–5.

[2] J. J. Becher, *Närrische Weiszheit und weise Narrheit*, Franckfurt, 1682, pp. 164–68.

Agricola, who was scornful of all such tales, derisively imagines the cobbler fluttering clumsily around in the air with his last.[1]

How seriously may we take these reports? Of the attempts there can be no doubt, but what degree of success may we attribute to Eilmer, to Danti, or to Guidotti? The writers usually speak explicitly of a *pair* of wings, with the implication (clear in the case of Danti, for example) that these were capable of independent movement, and hence that, if joined, they were articulated. Flapping such a pair of wings can never have served to raise a man from the ground—it needs all the skill of modern technology and the use of modern materials to enable a man, even now, to raise himself briefly into the air without the aid of a prime mover. Gliding flight, of the sort which Lynn White proposes in the case of Eilmer, might have been possible, but to sustain one's full weight on one's outstretched arms even for a short period is extremely tiring and, as White points out, we should need to suppose that the articulated wings were so hinged as to be able to move downwards, but not upwards. Again, while it is just conceivable that a man might control a brief descent using a large, rigid pair of wings without the addition of a tail, the experiences of 'Abbas b. Firnās and Eilmer suggest that the lack of such a necessary independent stabilising surface was one of the most fundamental errors to delay significant achievement. Had the importance of a tail been fully appreciated, flights would still have been brief and highly dangerous, but a sufficient degree of success might perhaps have been won to encourage the development of controlled gliding before its very late beginning in the second half of the nineteenth century.

[1] G. A. Agricola, *Neu- und nie erhörter doch in der Natur und Vernunfft wohlgegründeter Versuch der Universalvermehrung aller Bäume, Stauden, und Blumen-Bewächse . . .*, 2 vols., Regenspurg & Leipzig, 1716–17, vol. 1, pp. 121–2.

7

FLYING CHARIOTS, PARACHUTES AND WINDMILLS

In his *Mathematicall Magick* John Wilkins distinguishes four principal means whereby flight 'hath beene or may be attempted':

1. By spirits or Angels.
2. By the help of fowls.
3. By wings fastned immediately to the body.
4. By a flying chariot.

Of the fourth, which concerns us here, he says that it seems to him 'altogether as probable, and much more usefull then any of the rest,' but despite this judgement he finds nothing of a practical nature to report.[1] It is, of course, readily understandable that there should have been so few attempts to build a real flying chariot, but one might, perhaps, have expected a little more speculation about the matter than is in fact to be found. Although throughout the Middle Ages Alexander's griffon-drawn basket remained an immensely popular legend, that exciting combination of Wilkins' second and fourth categories seems to have inspired very few projects for turning legend into reality. This may have been because the idea of flying ships of any sort inspired suspicion and terror in a good many people. Like the dragons seen hovering in the sky in troubled weather, flying ships seem to have been imagined by the observers of the more spectacular 'meteors'. In his *Contra insulsam vulgi opinionem de grandine et tonitruis*,[2] Agobard (*ca.* 769–840), Bishop of Lyons, says:

[1] J. Wilkins, *Mathematicall Magick*, London, 1648, pp. 200, 209.
[2] Saint Agobard, *Contra insulsam vulgi opinionem de grandine et tonitruis*, II. (Migne, Series Lat., vol. 104, col. 148.)

We have seen and heard many, so struck with madness, so crazed with stupidity, that they believe and say there is a place called Magonia, from which ships sail into the clouds and in these the crops knocked down by hail and ruined by storms are carried to that region, the aeronauts paying the gods of the tempests, and receiving in exchange the corn or other crops. We have seen several, so blinded by profound stupidity that they believe such things to be possible, exhibiting in an assembly four people, three men and a woman, who had been bound because they were thought to have fallen from such ships. These, having been kept prisoner for some days, were at last presented to the whole assembly of men, in our presence, as I have said, as people fit to be stoned.

In the annals of Geoffroi de Vigeois (*ca.* 1140–84) there is a more straightforward report of a flying chariot, or flying ship, which is said to have terrified the inhabitants of London at some time during the years 1122–24. The laconic description is presented, in the manner of so many legendary annals, without comment and with no hint of its possible unreality:

In England a ship was seen sailing through the air as if over the surface of the sea. When the anchor had been dropped in the middle of the city, the citizens of London would not let it go. One of the sailors was sent down to release the anchor, but, having been held back by several people, was thrown into the river and drowned. The sailors, crying out, sailed off once more, having cut the anchor rope.[1]

The origin of Geoffroi's story and its relationship to the real events of the time remain a mystery.

A most ingenious suggestion for finding a means of 'navigating the air' appears in Albert of Saxony's book of *Quaestiones* about Aristotle's *Physics*. The region of 'fire', consisting not of fire in the everyday sense, but of a highly tenuous and inflammable substance, was not necessarily dangerous to man. (Opinions were sharply divided on this subject.) Assuming that between the atmosphere and the region of fire there was a clearly defined boundary, analogous to that between water and air, Albert makes the following suggestion:

Fire is much subtler and more tenuous and lighter than is the air, for it is related to air as air is to water. Now air is much more tenuous and much subtler and lighter than is water; therefore the same is true of fire with respect to air. From this follows what may be readily demonstrated from the science of relative weights: that the

[1] Geoffroi de Vigeois (or, du Breuil), *Chronica Gaufredi cœnobitæ*, XL, 1584. In P. Labbe, *Novæ bibliothecæ manuscript. librorum*, 2 vols., Paris, 1657, vol. 2, pp. 299–300. (Written in the late twelfth century.)

upper air, where it is contiguous with fire, is navigable, just as the water is where it is contiguous with the air. Hence if a ship is placed on the upper surface of the air, filled, however, not with air but with fire, it will not sink through the air; but as soon as it is filled with air it will sink. Just as, if a ship is filled with air rather than with water, it will float on the water, and not sink; but when it is filled with water, it sinks.[1]

Albert has, of course, failed to take account of the need to build the aerial ship of materials of comparable lightness, but in view of the inadequate concepts of relative weight available to him, this oversight is hardly surprising.

The earliest mention of a flying chariot in a really practical context is to be found in a famous pair of passages by Roger Bacon (*ca.* 1220–92), in his *De mirabili potestate artis et naturae*:

It's possible to make Engines for flying, a man sitting in the midst whereof, by turning onely about an Instrument, which moves artificiall Wings made to beat the Aire, much after the fashion of a Birds flight.

A page later he goes on to speak of 'that instrument of flying, which I never saw or know any, who hath seen it, though I am exceedingly acquainted with a very prudent man, who hath invented the whole Artifice.'[2] While this does not say much, it might be thought sufficiently challenging to inspire attempts by later experimenters, many of whom took very seriously any claim advanced by Roger Bacon. If such attempts were indeed made, they remained, however, unrecorded. Except for some suggestions by Leonardo, very little is heard of flying machines before the seventeenth century, when reports, all more or less fantastic, begin to be found in large numbers. In 1604 Magnus Pegel, who mentioned that he also knew how to make a kite (*alligatum volantem dictum Draconem*), claimed to be able to build a *navigium aerium*. The tone of the passage recalls Scaliger's scornful comments over the matter of Archytas' dove: 'On a first consideration it may seem, to those who are ignorant of the means, an extraordinary, dangerous, and impossible thing to do. But that which is criticised, jeered at, and treated with scorn, can be performed by anyone, even by the most obtuse and stupid.'[3]

---

[1] Albert of Saxony, *Questiones . . . in octo libros Physicorum Aristotelis*, IV. vi. 2. 3, Parisiis, 1516, f. 47ʳ.

[2] R. Bacon, *De mirabili potestate artis et naturae*, Lutetiae Parisiorum, 1542, f. 42ʳ⁻ᵛ. (Written *ca.* 1260.) English translation published as *Frier Bacon, his Discovery of the Miracles of Art, Nature, and Magick . . .*, London, 1659, pp. 17–19.

[3] M. Pegel, *Thesavrvs rervm*, 1604, p. 123.

Among my favourites from the later reports is one by Becher, mentioning a chariot made from straw by the Italian engineer Burattini, who lived for a time at the Polish court.[1] Becher says that this machine raised its inventor three times from the ground, with limited success, sustained flights never being achieved. While this sounds highly ridiculous, such an unlikely account may have had some slight basis in reality. A man seeking lightness combined with strength might first have constructed a basket from woven straw, and then have conceived of making wings from the same material, which, with some rigid frame members as a base, could be lashed into a cambered shape similiar to that of a bird's wing. While such a structure would inevitably have fallen to pieces almost immediately, an enthusiastic experimenter might well have tried launching himself in it two or three times from a wall or small hill before the failure became manifest. Becher's story is, nevertheless, very likely apocryphal. Other and better informed accounts of Burattini speak only of a model which was probably some kind of kite with

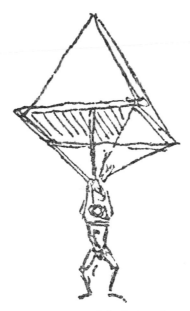

Fig. 23. Leonardo's design for a parachute.
Milan, Biblioteca Ambrosiana,
Codice Atlantico,
f. 381v–a, *ca.* 1485

[1] J. J. Becher, *Närrische Weiszheit und weise Narrheit*, Franckfurt, 1682, pp. 165–6.

moving wings, and with a passive windmill attached to the body. A project for building a full-scale machine appears to have remained unrealised.[1]

Until recently it had been universally believed that the first parachute was designed and sketched by Leonardo (Fig. 23).[2] Two drawings in British Museum Add. MS 34113 cast some doubt, however, on this belief. The manuscript, the bulk of which is a collection of machine drawings and instructions in the art of warfare, contains recipes for various destructive fires, designs for assault weapons, and sketches for fortifications similar to those found in many such manuscripts of the fifteenth and sixteenth centuries. It is neither so well ordered as the best treatises on warfare, such as Kyeser's *Bellifortis*, nor so heterogeneous as one might expect a raw notebook to be. While its authorship is unknown, some of it draws on Taccola, and the section which concerns us suggests that the manuscript is probably the work of a Siennese engineer who had some association with the great Francesco di Giorgio. The exact date of the notebook is also in doubt, but it appears to be no later than the 1470s or early 1480s.[3] The parachute (Plate 44) would therefore just antedate Leonardo's, placed at *ca.* 1485 by Carlo Pedretti.[4]

The first of the drawings (Plate 43), which appears to be unique among mediaeval illustrations of aeronautical devices, is not a parachute in the usual sense of the word, but the raised skirts of the tunic show that the figure, almost identical with that of Plate 44, is certainly falling. The man is apparently attempting to break his fall by means of the two wholly flexible surfaces which are reefed to batons in the style frequently seen in contemporary illustrations of banners and sails. It is unclear whether this is merely a crude and somewhat puzzling attempt at a parachute, or whether some equally futile ornithoptering effect is also intended. It is difficult to believe that anyone, even in those days of sometimes strange aeronautical assumptions, could have supposed the two broad ribbons of cloth to have had any decelerating effect on a man's fall. Although the ends of the ribbons run off the

[1] An excellent discussion of Burattini's machine may be found in C. von Klinckowstroem, 'Tito Livio Burattini, ein Flugtechniker des 17. Jahrhunderts,' *Prometheus*, no. 1100, 26 November 1910, pp. 117–20.

[2] C. H. Gibbs-Smith, *Leonardo da Vinci's Aeronautics*, London, 1967, p. 29.

[3] Lynn White, Jr., 'The Invention of the Parachute,' *Technology and Culture*, vol. 9, no. 3, July, 1968, pp. 462–7.

[4] Milan, Biblioteca Ambrosiana, *Codice Atlantico*, f. 381[v-a]. C. Pedretti, *Studi Vinciani*, Genève, 1957, p. 285.

edge of the page of the manuscript as it is today, the drawing is clear and unambiguous, and would not appear to allow of alternative interpretations of the structural details. The two bands were never intended to meet over the man's head, nor was any part of them intended to be held rigid by frame members. What the designer thought he would achieve with this arrangement can only be guessed at.

The strange, mottled appearance of the mouth has been brilliantly elucidated by Lynn White. The artist has provided the parachutist, if that is what we should call him, with a sponge to grip between his jaws, presumably to ease the jarring effects of impact with the earth. The sponge reappears in Plate 44, where it is now attached to a tape which is tied behind the man's head, holding the sponge in place so that, as Lynn White says, 'if he cries out in terror he will not drop it'.[1]

There is no doubt at all about the draftsman's intentions in Plate 44, which shows a parachute strikingly similar to Leonardo's, and in some respects superior to it. The cone, whose panels are presumably of cloth, is aerodynamically more satisfactory than is Leonardo's pyramid; the cross-bars ensure rigidity; and the suspension, over which the parachutist would be able to exercise some control by varying his grip on the cross-bar, appears to have been thought out with care. (The dimensions of a parachute with a canopy large enough to be an effective decelerator would of course render this method of control impossible in practice.)

No notes accompany either of the illustrations, nor does the remainder of the manuscript provide any further hint as to the designer's sources or other aeronautical ideas. The most striking difference between the Siennese design and Leonardo's is of course in the fundamental shape, the one being conical, the other pyramidal. Despite this important distinction, it may be, as Dr A. G. Keller believes,[2] that Plate 44 is the source of the familiar later parachute of Faustio Veranzio (Plate 45)[3] which, although square-based like Leonardo's and differing from the Siennese one in many other important respects, shows a pronounced similarity in the rigging. Veranzio's parachute became quite well known after the publication of his book in 1615–16 and the design was reproduced several

---

[1] Lynn White, Jr., 'Medieval Uses of Air,' *Scientific American*, vol. 223, no. 2, August, 1970, p. 100.

[2] Private communication, dated 18 December 1968.

[3] F. Veranzio, *Machinae novae Fausti Verantii Siceni*, Venezia, [1615–16], plate 38. (Composed *ca.* 1595.)

times. Parachuting did not, however, catch on either as an idea or as a practical possibility. No other designs appeared until the eighteenth century, and it was not until 1797 that anyone, so far as is known, made a successful jump.[1]

It is possible that the Siennese parachute bears some relationship to another conical device discussed half a century earlier in Fontana's *Metrologum* which, as I have pointed out in Chapter Three, was known to other technological designers. After describing the construction of his rocket-propelled birds and dragons, Fontana examines the ideas of an unidentified predecessor who had conceived a plan for building a new kind of flying machine.

> There was one from among those who claim to be inventors and who reason badly, who said that it would be possible for a man to rise into the air by the use of some such artifice. And he conceived of making, from thick cloth and rings of wood, a pyramid of very great size whose point would be uppermost, and of firmly tying across the diameter of the circle at the base a bar of wood, on which a man might sit or ride, holding in his hands burning brands made of pitch and tallow or other material producing intense fire which is long-lasting and creates a great deal of thick smoke. He suggested that because of the fire the air enclosed within the pyramid would be made lighter and rarer, and consequently that as it would move upwards, and could not, of course, get out, the pyramid and the man sitting in it would be raised; in further support of which he suggested that the vapour from the brands, produced in the pyramid, being both enclosed and forced upwards, would rise. He said, however, that the experiment had not succeeded, either because the pyramid had been too small, or too heavy, or because it had had some leak in its cover, or because there had been too little fire, or because too little of the aforesaid vapour had been enclosed.
>
> But I was not a little astonished by this man's ideas, and more so than by those of him who proposed descending under the water with the use of a diving-bell. [A reference to another part of the text.] There are indeed many difficulties in this, not to say the greatest danger. In the first place one cannot tell how, in such rare and hot air and in such thick smoke, which should not be lacking from the machine but gather in great quantity, a man might breathe. Again it is to be feared that from so much uncovered fire the pyramid may be burned up, so causing the burning of the man, or his fall, since the air and smoke will have been able to escape through the burnt parts of the cloth.
>
> In the third place, if everything he has said up till now be true, one nevertheless wonders how the man may descend without harm and danger, since as long as the firebrands are burning the pyramid will rise, but when they have been consumed,

[1] Gibbs-Smith, *Leonardo da Vinci's Aeronautics*, p. 29.

with the failure of the motive and sustaining power, the pyramid will be turned back from the air and will rapidly fall downwards, just as things which have been carried up by a whirlwind fall back of their own weight when the wind drops.

I shall not deal with the remaining difficulties. This man, indeed, just like many who presume to begin that which they neither know how to, nor are able to finish, had not thought his idea out to the end, since as regards the ascent he gave insufficient attention to his reasons and arguments, which equally fail to specify the method of descent.[1]

If, as Fontana claims, such a pyramidal canopy was indeed constructed, its resistance to the air would probably have been noticed. Its form is in any case sufficiently similar to that of Plate 44 to suggest a possible source.

Equally interesting is the clear anticipation here of the hot-air balloon. The description involves the common assumption that the 'vapours' themselves, produced by the fire, are as important as the heated air in creating the lift. The misconception was not, of course, to be dispelled until more than three centuries later. In the 1780s it was still, for example, a part of the thinking of the Montgolfier brothers who experimented with various kinds of smoke-producing fuel for their balloons, including old shoes and rotting meat.[2]

The tone of Fontana's text suggests that a real attempt was made to fly in a 'balloon' of this kind. The inevitable failure, as with the fifteenth-century parachutes, was caused principally by an inadequate grasp of the matter of scale. There was a lack of awareness of how small is the difference in density between hot and cold air, and hence a failure to understand how large a machine would be required. However impractical in the details, this is, nevertheless, the first western description, and a remarkably complete one, of a hot-air balloon intended to carry a man. As with so many other bright ideas from the period, it was never followed up, and the inventor—despite Fontana's strictures, a man of some insight—remains anonymous.

While the windmill, whether active or passive, is of course among the most fundamental and useful of aerodynamic devices,[3] it was very rarely considered

[1] Giovanni da Fontana, *Metrologum de pisce cane et volucre*, Bologna, Biblioteca Universitaria, MS 2705, ff. 96ᵛ–97ʳ.
[2] L. T. C. Rolt, *The Aeronauts: a History of Ballooning 1783–1903*, London, 1966, pp. 28–9.
[3] For general surveys of windmills in Europe, see R. Wailes, 'A Note on Windmills', in *A History of Technology*, ed. Ch. Singer, *et al.*, vol. 2, Oxford, 1956, pp. 623–28, and J. Needham, *Science and Civilisation in China*, IV. 2, Cambridge, 1965, pp. 556–66.

by any experimenters earlier than Cayley to be a potential *aeronautical* device. In view of the widespread familiarity of windmills and toy helicopters in mediaeval Europe this may seem surprising. As early as the middle of the tenth century windmills were used in the region of Persia and Afghanistan, and may have been known still earlier. A description, *ca.* 950, of the province of Seistan mentions that 'strong winds prevail, so that, because of them, mills were built rotated by the wind'. These differed from the familiar European design in two fundamental respects. First, they were operated by vanes attached to a vertical shaft, the vanes being partially enclosed by the structure of the mill so that the prevailing wind could blow on only one side (Fig. 24). Second, the vanes were pushed forward

Fig. 24. European vertically shafted windmill. J. Besson, *Théâtre des instrumens mathématquies et méchaniques*, Lyon, 1578, plate 50

in the direction of the wind's motion, whereas the vanes on European wind-mills are set at an angle (either constant or varying in approximation to the segments of an Archimedian screw) and thus rotate in a plane at right angles to the direction of the wind. The vertically shafted mill was known in Europe at least as early as 1432/3, when it is shown in schematic form in a manuscript notebook by Taccola (Plate 46).[1] The date and manner of its introduction are unknown, and in any case it does not seem to have had any influence on the European horizontally shafted mill, which appears to have developed independently at some time during the twelfth century. The earliest mention of a European windmill (*molendinum uenti*) so far discovered is found in a manuscript dated *ca.* 1185. The

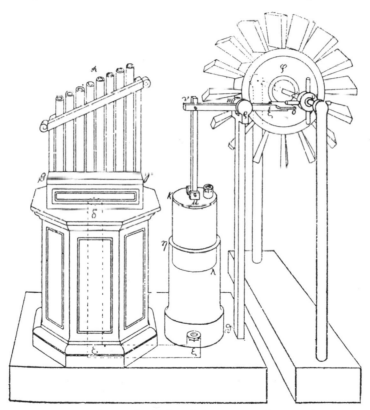

Fig. 25. Heron's windmill for playing a set of pipes, first
century A.D. Reconstruction by W. Schmidt, ed.,
Heronis Alexandrini opera, Lipsiae, 1899, vol. 1, p. 205

[1] For the date of this part of the manuscript, see L. Thorndike, 'Marianus Jacobus Taccola,'
Archives Internationales d'Histoire des Sciences, vol. 8, 1955, pp. 21ff.

mill to which the manuscript refers is thought to have stood in Weedley, in the East Riding of Yorkshire.[1]

A much disputed wind-operated machine 'that sounds a pipe when the wind blows' is found in the manuscripts of the *Pneumatica* of Heron of Alexandria.[2] A piston to produce wind for the pipes is to be driven by a trip mechanism consisting of a number of pins set around a drum and arranged so as to strike the end of a lever as the drum rotates. A second drum, mounted on the same axle as the first, is provided with a series of plates 'like weather vanes' set around its circumference and turned by the wind. There is no indication of partial housing of the sort used on the old vertically shafted mills of the east; on the contrary, the last sentence of Heron's description reads 'It is possible always to turn the frame carrying the axle

Fig. 26.
One of the original
sketches for Heron's
windmill, as redrawn
in Schmidt, vol. 1,
p. xxxix

towards the wind blowing, so that the turning becomes stronger and steadier.' His machine seems to have been intended to operate as a horizontally shafted mill on the screw principle. In his edition of the *Pneumatica* Schmidt redrew the machine from sketches in the manuscripts and, as may be seen from Fig. 25, showed the

[1] See B. A. Lees, ed., *Records of the Templars in England in the Twelfth Century: The Inquest of 1185*, London, 1935, p. 131.

[2] *Heronis Alexandrini opera qvae svpersvnt omnia*, 5 vols., ed. W. Schmidt, vol. 1, 'Pnevmatica et avtomata,' Lipsiae, 1899, pp. 202–7. For a discussion of the windmill see A. G. Drachmann, 'Heron's Windmill,' *Centaurus*, vol. 7, no. 2, 1961, pp. 145–51.

windmill part of the structure mounted on a separate base which might be turned to follow the wind. Heron's insight into the principle of the screw-windmill was an isolated flash of genius, perhaps too early for his time. It is not known whether the machine was ever built, but even if it was, no other writer mentioned it and it appears to have had no progeny.

The usefulness of the windmill proper, once invented, was immediately and strikingly apparent. Horizontally shafted mills were very soon widespread in Europe and are to be seen in manuscript illustrations as early as the thirteenth century (Plate 47).

The fundamental structure of these horizontal passive windmills (that is, mills whose vanes are turned by the impingement of a stream of air) soon found an ancillary application as a child's toy. A set of four or more inclined blades fixed to a spindle on the end of a stick—a toy still common today, especially on fairgrounds—is frequently to be seen in early illustrations of children at play (Fig. 27).

Fig. 27. The toy windmill as an emblem of childishness. Cesare Ripa, *Nova iconologia*, Padua, 1618, p. 400

A conceptual jump was needed before these passive objects could be turned into active airscrews capable of doing work against the air. Someone must one day have noticed that if a windmill is rotated by hand, it produces a force along the line of the axle. This is the basis of Leonardo's famous helical design for a flying machine, a primitive and rather inefficient helicopter.[1] With the exception of that design, which, like so much that Leonardo noted, remained buried in his manuscripts, the lifting power of the active airscrew seems, until the eighteenth century, to have inspired nothing more than another toy. Today children still play with a form of miniature helicopter consisting of a vertical axle with an airscrew fitted to the top, and a simple form of bearing below. The axle is made to rotate by means of a thread which is wound around it and then pulled sharply back, so that the airscrew (with or without the axle attached) flies upward. This form of toy may have been known in Europe as early as the fifteenth century, and possibly as early as the fourteenth. Plate 51, reproduced from a manuscript notebook by Taccola, appears to illustrate a toy helicopter. The diagram to the left gives a plan view of what may be a swastika-form airscrew, lying on top of the platter, while the platter, spindle, bearing, thread, and handle are clearly shown in elevation on the right. Assuming that the thick platter is meant to turn, it would provide efficient flywheel action to rotate the airscrew, which would then fly up. Taccola's note calls it *puerorum ludus*. It is not certain, however, that this interpretation of the toy is correct, and still more caution is needed when one considers a number of slightly different toys of the same general configuration, of which Plate 52 reproduces the earliest known example (*ca.* 1325). These toys, called *moulinets*, differ from Taccola's in having a (usually) cruciform set of vanes attached directly to the top of the spindle. Mr Gibbs-Smith and Dr Lynn White, among others, interpret them as helicopters.[2] As late as the nineteenth century, however, a non-aerodynamic form of the *moulinet* was known. This was merely a 'return-toy', working, like the yo-yo, on the momentum principle. The thread was pulled, to rotate the spindle; the momentum caused the thread to be wound in the reverse direction; it was again pulled, and so on, the vanes spinning backwards and forwards, and no doubt humming. While it may be that

[1] Gibbs-Smith, *Leonardo da Vinci's Aeronautics*, pp. 30–31.

[2] C. H. Gibbs-Smith, *Aviation: An Historical Survey from its Origins to the end of World War II*, London, 1970, p. 6; Lynn White, Jr., 'Medieval Uses of Air,' *Scientific American*, vol. 223, no. 2, August, 1970, pp. 96, 97.

these were degenerate examples of earlier and genuinely aerodynamic toys, Mr Patrick Murray, curator of the Edinburgh Museum of Childhood, points out with some cogency that none of the illustrations of the *moulinet* ever shows the vanes in flight, a fact which convinces him that they were never aerodynamic objects.[1] Most of them are found in indoor scenes, and the three-tier one in Brueghel's 'Children's Games' is held by a boy sitting closer to a wall than would seem appropriate to the operation of a flying toy. In sharp contrast to European windmills, however, they are almost invariably drawn with the shaft vertical and the vanes horizontal, which strongly supports the helicopter interpretation. (See Appendix B, page 146.)

Whether the cruciform *moulinets* were helicopters or return-toys, they were certainly inspired by the horizontally shafted windmills which had become so salient a feature of the European landscape. The vanes of the toy in Plate 52 and of many others in similar illustrations were clearly constructed in emulation of the sail-frames of the full-sized mills which they were in part intended to represent. If they were angled, as seems probable, a force would have been exerted along the line of the spindle and the *moulinets* would thus have been at least potentially aerodynamic devices.

Since, as we have seen, the would-be aeronauts of the Middle Ages and Renaissance were frequently endowed with far-reaching imaginations, one must seek some explanation of their apparent blindness to the practical possibilities of the active windmill. Even if those possibilities had been understood, any attempts to realise them in practice would, of course, have been vitiated by the lack of a prime mover, but the same is true of all the flying machines of the period, and the significant thing is that no early attempts to apply the airscrew for forward motion have been recorded. Mr Gibbs-Smith takes the question further in his notes on Leonardo's helicopter: 'It is ... strange—we being now wise in hind-sight—that he never seems to have thought of applying the Archimedean helicopter screw to work horizontally as an airscrew for a flying machine; but ornithopters ruled his mind.' And again, when writing of Leonardo's sketch for an airscrew-operated spit (Plate 64), he says 'It raises ... the problem of why Leonardo did not experiment further with the air or water screw; but they did not seem to interest him very much.'[2] Why did the airscrew not interest him very much? I

[1] Private communications from Mr Murray, November and December, 1970.
[2] *Leonardo da Vinci's Aeronautics*, pp. 31, 33.

believe Mr Gibbs-Smith's words 'ornithopters ruled his mind' are the key to the general neglect of the airscrew. Once again it is a matter of the insistence on an organic approach to the problem of flight. Rotary motion does not occur in nature; it seems to have nothing to do with birds, bats, or flying insects. The best way to fly was to imitate nature, and a whirling airscrew would not seem to be relevant. The power which this habit of thought may exert over the mind is emphasized in the example of Leonardo himself, who, having hit upon the fundamental idea for the man-carrying helicopter, immediately abandoned it, to return to his flappers.

Finally I must mention the application of the windmill in reverse, so to speak. In the Middle Ages it was well understood that a rotating set of fan blades could be used as an air brake to slow the turning of an axle. Such air brakes, used in the chiming mechanisms of clocks, may be seen today in some surviving examples. The principle also seems to have been applied, at least in theory, to slow the descent of a primitive lift which formed part of the equipment used for besieging castles and cities. In Kyeser's *Bellifortis* the word *ventilabrum* (flail, winnowing fork, or fan) is twice used in that sense. The assault engine, based on a double winch, is seen in Plate 53. While it is possible that the machine is to be so orientated that the windmills are turned by the wind, thus providing a source of power to lift the load, the main purpose of the construction seems to be to provide a safe descent. The man may raise himself by pulling on the endless rope wound over the two axles, and in order to come down again he may, to a limited extent, let himself go, the rotating vanes slowing his fall sufficiently to prevent his being hurt. Kyeser says that although some people build the machine with only two fans, it is 'safer, firmer, and more rapid' with four. By 'more rapid' he must mean that the greater decelerating force provided by four fans enables the man to let himself go, with safety, from a greater height.

8

LEONARDO

$$———$$

Among those who tried to fly, or who speculated on flight before 1600, only Leonardo (1452–1519), as far as I know, committed his designs to paper.[1] In recent decades we have learned to be a little more cautious than were some earlier commentators in praising Leonardo's remarkable genius. While his greatness is not in question, studies of the work of other engineers of the period have shown how distorted some of the appraisals have been, for lack of knowledge of the context in which Leonardo worked. The engineers of his day, of whom he was of course one, continually exchanged ideas, copied each other's designs, put old machines to new uses. In Europe there was a sort of engineering freemasonry rather different in tone from the present-day insistence on the ownership of ideas. Many of the machines drawn in Leonardo's manuscripts were conceived by others, while many more were so much the common property of engineers throughout Europe as to defy attribution.[2]

Leonardo's flying machines present, however, a special case. Most of his designs in this field seem to be without precedent. Apart from the two parachutes in B.M. Add. MS 34113 and the one in Veranzio, no sketches of anything to do with human flight are to be found in the numerous engineering and mechanical treatises of the late Middle Ages and Renaissance. Leonardo's designs are not only

---

[1] In this chapter I attempt only a general survey of how Leonardo thought human flight might be achieved. Readers wishing to pursue the functional details of his designs in greater depth should consult C. H. Gibbs-Smith, *Leonardo da Vinci's Aeronautics*, London, 1967, and R. Giacomelli, *Gli Scritti di Leonardo da Vinci sul Volo*, Roma, 1936.

[2] A useful introduction to comparative studies of workers in the field may be found in B. Gille, *The Renaissance Engineers*, London, 1966.

unique; they are also very thorough, comprising several complete sketches of highly complex machines which could certainly have been built and tested.

Many themes repeatedly recur in Leonardo's notebooks, but none more frequently than the idea of flight. While I believe it is untrue to say, as some have done, that he was obsessed with the question, it was certainly one of his favourite problems. To solve it he designed a remarkable variety of machines including several kinds of man-powered ornithopter, an ornithopter powered by a spring motor, a partial glider with flapping wing tips, a number of machines which fall more or less into the category of flying chariots, a helicopter (together, perhaps, with a self-powered model of one), and some ancillary apparatus for directional control, wing-testing, and the like. Owing to Leonardo's entirely natural acceptance of many of the contemporary misconceptions which are outlined in Chapter One and further discussed below, none of these machines was fully practical.

The period of Leonardo's most important work in aeronautics ran from about 1485 to 1499, during his years of service with Lodovico Sforza, Duke of Milan. Later, in 1505, he gathered together many of his notes on bird flight[1] to write a draft of the important but fundamentally incorrect treatise *Sul Volo degli Uccelli*,[2] most of the inadequacies of which arise from faulty notions of mechanics and dynamics. As he had the habit of making copious notes on anything that interested him, saying the same thing many times, often with subtle modifications, and frequently altering his opinions, it is not easy to summarise his beliefs, but some comments of a general nature can nevertheless be made. Two main groups of ideas are of special importance in the present context: those concerning momentum and movement through the air in general, and those concerning relative motion.

Leonardo could never quite decide on the nature of momentum. Even in the last years of his life he was still wavering between the *impetus* theory and the older,

---

[1] He subsequently made many further notes, especially in MS E, 1513–15. Professor Ladislao Reti tells me that the only passages of any aeronautical interest to be found in the recently recovered Madrid Codices are some pages on bird flight which are elaborations or drafts of material in MS K (1504–9) and in the *Codice sul Volo*.

[2] In quoting from this and from Leonardo's other notebooks, I have not thought it necessary to give full details of the original manuscripts, which are widely available in facsimile and transcription. The translations are based on those of E. MacCurdy, in his *The Notebooks of Leonardo da Vinci*, vol. 1, London, 1938, to which reference is made in the footnotes. At a number of points I have departed from MacCurdy's readings. Relevant facsimiles and transcriptions are listed in the bibliography.

Aristotelian concept of the role of the air in maintaining motion. The *impetus* theory is expressed with vigour in notes written *ca.* 1510–15:

> Impetus is the impression of movement transmitted by the mover to the movable thing.
>
> Impetus is a power impressed by the mover on the movable thing.[1]
>
> . . . if one were to say that the impetus which moves the movable thing is in the air that surrounds it from the middle backwards, one would deny this, because the air that follows the movable thing is drawn by the movable thing to fill the void left by it, and because also the air that is compressed in front of the movable thing escapes backwards in the opposite direction.
>
> . . . and if the air turns back it is a manifest proof that it strikes against the air which the movable thing draws behind it; when two things collide this causes the reflex movement of each, and these reflex movements are converted into whirling movements which are carried by the air that fills up the vacuum left by the movable body, and it is impossible for the movement of the mover to be increased by the movement of the movable body in the same time, because the mover is always more powerful than the movable thing.[2]

At about the same time, and in another context, he nevertheless showed himself less than wholly committed to this view: 'Impetus is the impression of local movement transmuted from the mover to the movable thing and maintained by the air or by the water as they move in order to prevent the vacuum.'[3] Furthermore, he had clearly entertained the older idea a few years earlier, at about the time of the composition of *Sul Volo degli Uccelli*:

> Impetus is a power transmitted from the mover to the movable thing, and maintained by the wave of the air within the air which this mover produces; and this arises from the vacuum which would be produced contrary to the natural law if the air which is in front of it did not fill up the vacuum, so causing the air which is driven from its place by the aforesaid mover to flee away. And the air that goes before it would not fill up the place from which it is divided if it were not that another body of air filled up the place from whence this air was divided; and so of necessity it follows in succession. And this movement would continue to infinity if the air were capable of being condensed to infinity.[4]

[1] MacCurdy, p. 567, MS G, f. 73^r, 1510–15.

[2] MacCurdy, p. 569, MS G, f. 85^v, 1510–15.

[3] MacCurdy, p. 526, *Codice Atlantico*, f. 168^{v-b}, *ca.* 1515. (For the dates of the folios of the *Codice Atlantico*, see C. Pedretti, *Studi Vinciani*, Genève, 1957, pp. 264–92.)

[4] MacCurdy, p. 529, *Codice Atlantico*, f. 219^{v-a}, 1505–8.

These comments have to do with inanimate objects, while the case of 'self-movers' like birds was of course different. Leonardo certainly did not believe that birds were in any way propelled by a wind at the rear, even though some such wind was produced as a result of their self-generated *impetus*:

> [The air] runs after the vacuum which the bird leaves of itself as it pierces the air as much as the bird flies forward in the air which continually receives its contact. Consequently it is not the closing up of the air behind the bird that drives the bird before it but the impetus which moves the bird forward opens and drives the air, which becomes a sheath and draws the air behind it.[1]

He did, however, attach great importance to the presence of the 'slip-stream':

> If as the bird descends it moves its wings back as though they were oars the bird will make swift movement; and this comes about because the wings are striking in the air which is continually flowing in the wake of the bird to fill up the void from whence it has departed.[2]

These considerations led Leonardo to suppose that on the downstroke the bird squeezes together the 'fingers' of its wings, so as to compress the air and give the wing greater purchase:

> The big finger . . . of the hand . . . is that which when the hand is lowered comes to lower itself more than the hand, in such a way as to close and prevent the exit of the stream of air compressed by the lowering of the hand, in such a way that in this place the air becomes condensed and offers resistance to the oarage of the wing.[3]

He saw no reason to question the standard view that birds move their wings downwards and backwards in a rowing or swimming action: 'A bird makes the same use of wings and tail in the air as a swimmer does of his arms and legs in the water.'[4] His concept of the nature of this swimming action led him to draw several more false conclusions which serve to explain the theoretical basis of some of the complexities of his designs. Although Leonardo guessed that a bird is sustained by a region of relatively high pressure under the wing, he was mistaken in his view of how that pressure is developed:

> When the bird desires to rise by beating its wings it raises its shoulders and beats the tips of the wings towards itself, and comes to condense the air which is interposed

[1] MacCurdy, p. 487, MS E, f. 53ʳ, 1513–15.
[2] MacCurdy, p. 432, *Sul Volo*, f. 12 (11)ʳ.
[3] MacCurdy, p. 435, *Sul Volo*, f. 14 (13)ᵛ.
[4] MacCurdy, p. 431, *Sul Volo* (*fogli mancanti*), f. 11 (10)ᵛ.

between the points of the wings and the breast of the bird, and the pressure from this air raises up the bird . . .

Since the wings are swifter to press the air than the air is to escape from beneath the wings the air becomes condensed and resists the movement of the wings; and the motive power of these wings by subduing the resistance of the air raises itself in a contrary movement to the movement of the wings.[1]

The greatest obstacle to Leonardo's formulation of a satisfactory theory of flight was the inadequacy and uncertainty of his ideas about relative motion. He accepted the view, propounded as early as the fourteenth century by Nicole of Oresme (*ca.* 1325–82),[2] that a falling object will appear to follow a straight path even if the earth and the upper elements are all in uniform circular motion: 'The arrow shot from the centre of the earth to the highest part of the elements will ascend and descend by the same straight line although the elements may be in a movement of circumvolution round their centre.'[3] He failed, however, to extend these principles to the lateral movement of an object in a fluid medium. In a steady horizontal wind a bird is effectively flying through still air, as far as its aerial manoeuvres are concerned. Except at take-off and landing, its relative motion is not produced by the natural wind, but is a function of the bird's own propulsive efforts. Although Leonardo realised, of course, that a bird may be blown along by the wind, relative to the ground, he did not see that a freely floating object quickly reaches the same velocity as that of the medium. As a consequence of this failure of insight, his notebooks are filled with detailed comments on the function of the wind in making flight possible. He repeatedly speaks of the sustaining 'wedge-like' action of the air under the bird's wing, treating the bird as if it were subject to wind pressures identical to those which enable a tethered kite to fly. While it is apparent that his remarks sometimes refer to the effects of wind gradients and sudden gusts, he attributes what is fundamentally the same action to a steady wind, using this idea to explain the movements of birds which soar and circle without beating their wings. The soaring capacity of birds is properly ascribed to their ability to sense and respond to rising air currents and variations of wind speed at differing heights, but although Leonardo was well aware of the possibility of a bird's doing this, he treated it as a special case, failing to realise, in particular, how important a part the upward currents play in normal flight patterns:

[1] MacCurdy, pp. 425, 430, *Sul Volo*, ff. 6 (5)ᵛ, 11 (10)ʳ (*fogli mancanti*).
[2] A. C. Crombie, *Augustine to Galileo*, London, 1952, pp. 256–7.
[3] MacCurdy, p. 565, MS G, f. 54ᵛ, 1510–15.

The bird maintains itself in the air by imperceptible balancing when near to the mountains or lofty ocean crags; it does this by means of the curves of the winds which strike against these projections and, being forced to preserve their initial impetus, bend their straight course towards the sky with various turbulent movements, before which the birds come to a stop with their wings open, receiving underneath themselves the continual buffetings of the reflex course of the winds . . .[1]

The erroneous belief about motion relative to the air and to the earth was of course made by many others both before and after Leonardo, being responsible in particular for innumerable eighteenth- and nineteenth-century designs for sail-driven balloons and airships, all of them utterly useless.

Still pursuing his swimming approach to flight, Leonardo concluded that on the downstroke the feathers of a bird's wing lie together to form a solid surface, while on the upstroke they separate to allow the wing to pass through the air with less resistance:

I have seen the sparrow and the lark fly upward in a straight line when they were in a level position. And this happens because the wing raised with swift movement remains filled with holes, and only rises with the impetus it has acquired, and this is renewed in the lowering of the wings, for the wing then reunites and presses one feather in beneath another . . .[2]

To a limited extent Leonardo was right in his observation. In the flight of most birds some of the feathers do indeed separate in order to lessen the pressure on the wing during the upstroke, while during the downstroke the secondaries, in particular, tend to lie close together. The swimming analogy nevertheless made it impossible for him to understand another part of the truth, which is very nearly the opposite of what he supposed.

In 1919, Handley Page patented an aeronautical device consisting of a narrow, curved slat fixed parallel to and slightly in front of the leading edge of an aeroplane wing. The gap between the slat and the wing directed the flow of air over the wing surface, reducing turbulence and allowing the aeroplane to fly at a greater angle of attack before stalling. Such an arrangement is known as a slotted wing. The principle, which can be extended to form multi-slotted wings, is now widely adopted in various forms. The leading primary of a bird's wing is often so shaped that its trailing edge leaves a gap or slot between it and the rest of the wing. In

[1] MacCurdy, p. 471, MS E, f. 42ᵛ, 1513–15.
[2] MacCurdy, p. 447, *Codice Atlantico*, f. 160ʳ⁻ᵇ, *ca.* 1515.

some birds not only the leading primary but as many as eight feathers are slotted in this way. In such cases the air pressure forces the feathers apart, creating a multi-slotted wing which acts as a highly efficient anti-stalling device. Although some of Leonardo's sketches show that he had observed the separation of the primaries, he could not have guessed the true explanation.

A similar function is performed by the *alula*, or bastard wing, which is attached to the leading edge of the bird's 'hand' and looks like a small feathered equivalent of the human thumb (Fig. 1). As the wing approaches the stalling angle the *alula* lifts to form a slot.[1] Leonardo's notes contain scores of references to the *alula* whose action he did not, however, understand, and which he took to be a steering device.

Leonardo's ideas about bird-flight may be summarised as follows. The bird rises into the air by pushing down, especially with its wing-tips, on layers of air compressed by the beating and 'squeezing' action of the wings. The upstroke is prevented from creating a counterbalancing layer of compressed air on the upper surface both by the curvature of the wing and, in the case of some birds, by the separation of the feathers, which allows the air to pass through. In normal flight the bird gains forward *impetus* by making backward rowing movements of the wings which are pushed against the compressed air lying in its wake. During the downstroke the bird inclines its wings at a slight downward angle (negative angle of attack), which increases its velocity. During the upstroke the angle of attack becomes positive, enabling the bird to glide forward without losing height. By using the same alternation of angles while turning in circles, the bird may rise without beating its wings, provided a wind is blowing (Plate 54). Gliding flight in a steady wind is achieved by a similar manipulation of the angles of attack so as to make use of the wedge-like lifting force of the wind. For two reasons a bird will very seldom fly in the same direction as the wind: first, because its feathers will be ruffled the wrong way; second, because in the absence of the wedge action of the wind, the bird will need to beat its wings more strenuously in order to stay aloft.[2]

In addition to his comments on the mechanism of flight itself, Leonardo made many detailed analyses of the techniques used by birds to exercise directional control. Although these are by no means entirely accurate, they contain a number of insights into the complex functions of the tail feathers.

While it is perhaps a matter of regret that Leonardo did not grasp the true

[1] K. Simkiss, *Bird Flight*, London, 1963, pp. 36–9.
[2] MacCurdy, p. 464, MS E, f. 37ʳ, 1513–15.

principles of bird flight, his misconceptions led him to produce some interesting and highly ingenious, if also sometimes cumbersome, designs for transmitting power to a wing in such a way as to make it beat in the rowing and 'squeezing' fashion. Leonardo, aware that man's muscular strength was proportionately less than that of a bird, nevertheless concluded that if properly applied it might be sufficient to enable him to fly by means of such apparatus:

> You will perhaps say that the sinews and muscles of a bird are incomparably more powerful than those of a man, because all the girth of so many muscles and of the fleshy parts of the breast goes to aid and increase the movement of the wings, while the bone in the breast is all in one piece and consequently affords the bird very great power, the wings also being all covered with a network of thick sinews and other very strong ligaments of gristle, and the skin being very thick with various muscles. But the reply to this is that such great strength gives it a reserve of power beyond what is ordinarily used to support itself on its wings, since it is necessary for it whenever it may so desire either to double or treble its rate of speed in order to escape from its pursuer or to follow its prey . . . for it needs but little force in order to sustain itself, and to balance itself on its wings, and flap them above the oncoming stream of the wind and direct the course of its flight; and a slight movement of the wings is sufficient for this, and the movement will be slower in proportion as the bird is greater in size.[1]

In estimating the degree of muscular strength needed in order to sustain flight, Leonardo had of course been led into error by his belief that birds make use of steady horizontal wind currents. His supposition that the wind provided a large part of the necessary energy allowed him to conclude that the power of human muscles might be great enough to supply the remainder.

In order to achieve the most efficient application of the human muscles, Leonardo designed several machines for applying both leg and arm power to the wings, while in some cases he also made use of the head and neck for directional control. In many of the machines he simulated the general configuration of the bird by having the aeronaut lie prone, with his feet in stirrups which were connected by ropes and pulleys to the wings. While working his legs the aeronaut used his arms to apply various forms of supplementary power. Fig. 28 shows the general shape of such a machine, the details of whose structure are represented in Fig. 29. The legs, when straightened, make the downstroke, while the upstroke, requiring less effort, is achieved by the hands which hold the inverted T-shaped handle to

---

[1] MacCurdy, pp. 438–9, *Sul Volo*, f. 17 (16)ʳ.

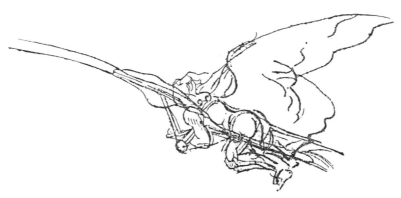

Fig. 28. General configuration of a prone ornithopter. Leonardo,
Codice Atlantico, f. 276^{r-b}, *ca.* 1487

the left of the diagram. The oblique bar immediately to the right of the handle
serves to twist the main spar as it is drawn down, so providing that backward
swimming stroke which Leonardo took to be essential. A later and more sophisticated design for producing the same general movement is shown in Plate 55, which
provides for separate flexing of each of the 'bat-fingers'. In order to simulate the
supposed opening and closing of the feathers of the wing on the up and down

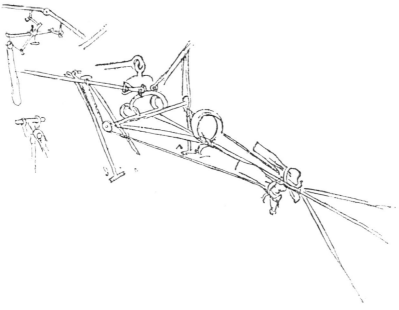

Fig. 29. Mechanism of the ornithopter sketched in Fig. 28

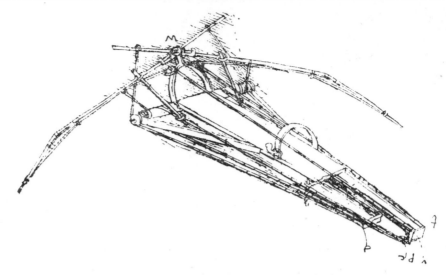

Fig. 30. Prone ornithopter. Leonardo, MS B, f. 74ᵛ, 1486–90

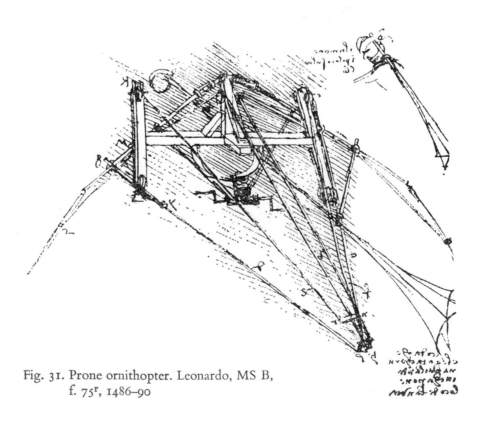

Fig. 31. Prone ornithopter. Leonardo, MS B,
f. 75ʳ, 1486–90

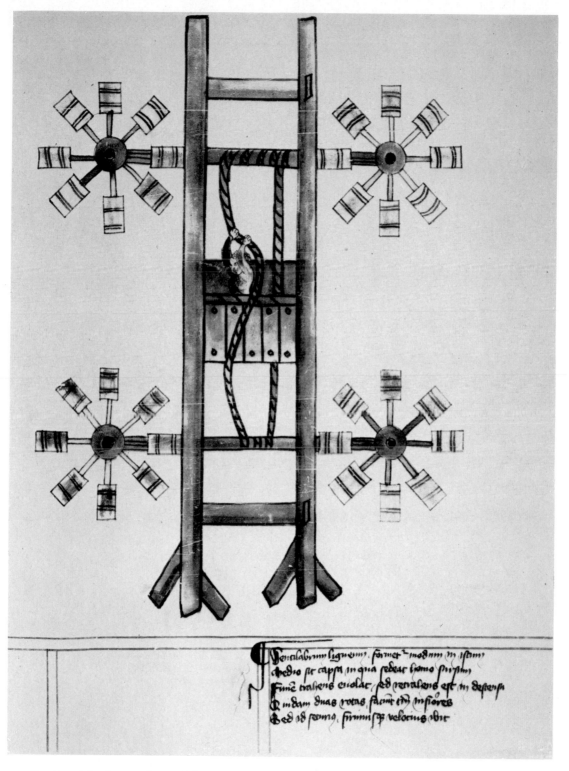

53. Rotary airbrakes used on a lifting and lowering mechanism. Göttingen, Niedersächsische
Staats- und Universitätsbibliothek, codex philos. 63, f. 134ʳ, 1405

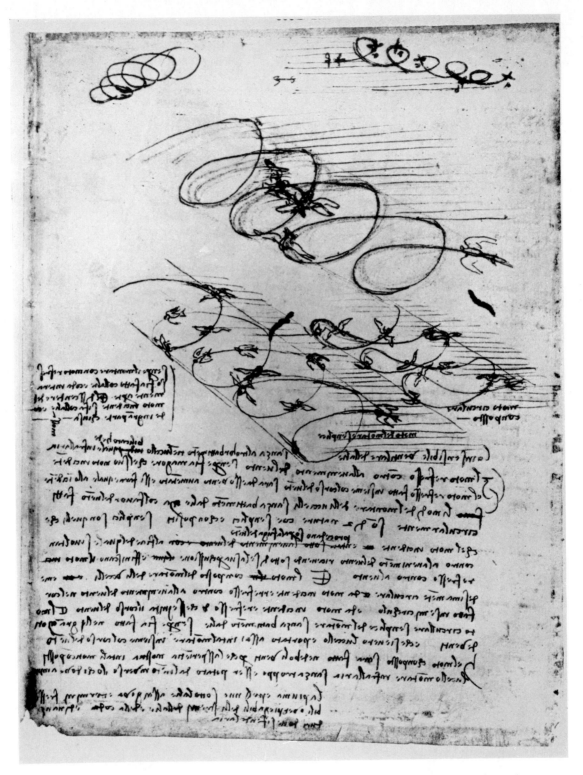

54. Leonardo's ideas about ways in which a bird may rise by circling in a horizontal wind.
Codice Atlantico, f. 308r-b, *ca.* 1505

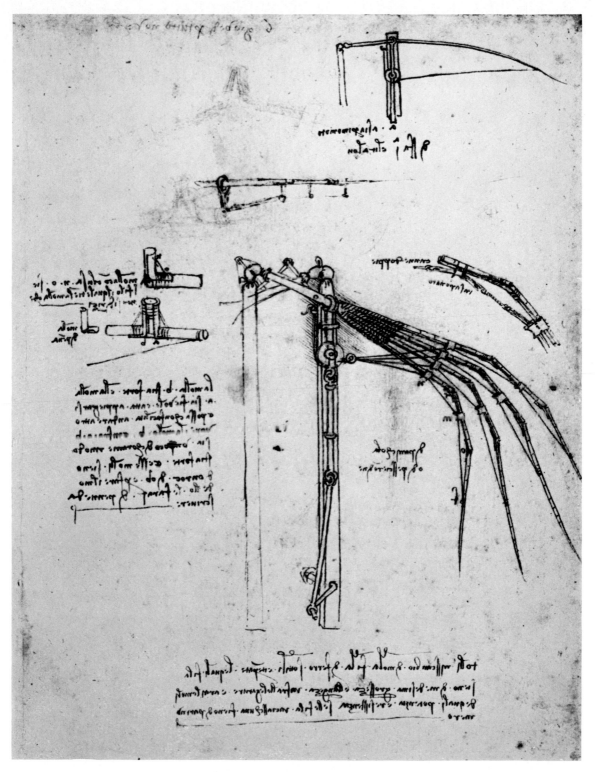

55. Flapping, twisting, and 'squeezing' mechanism for the wing of an ornithopter. Leonardo, *Codice Atlantico*, f. 308ʳ⁻ᵃ, 1495–97

56. Design for an ornithopter wing with flap valves operating under nets. Leonardo,
    Codice Atlantico, f. 309^{v-b}, 1487–90

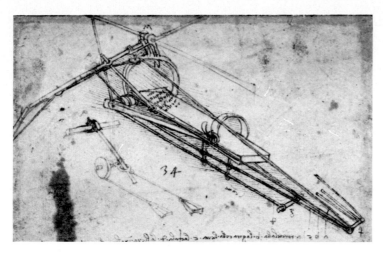

57. Prone ornithopter. Leonardo, *Codice Atlantico*, f. 302^{v-a},
    ca. 1487

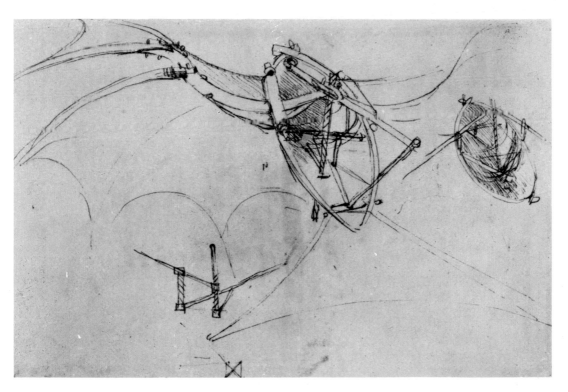

58. Ornithopter with boat-shaped hull. Leonardo, *Codice Atlantico*, f. 313^{v-a}, *ca.* 1487

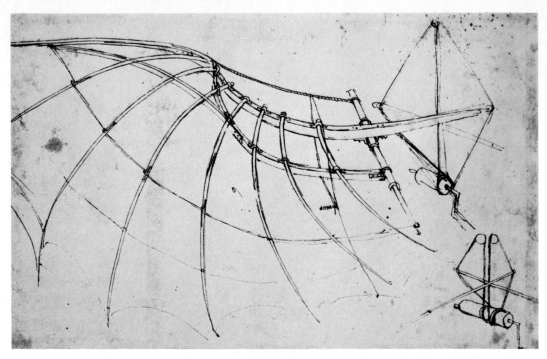

59. Winch-operated wings for an ornithopter. Leonardo, *Codice Atlantico*, f. 313^{r-a}, *ca.* 1487

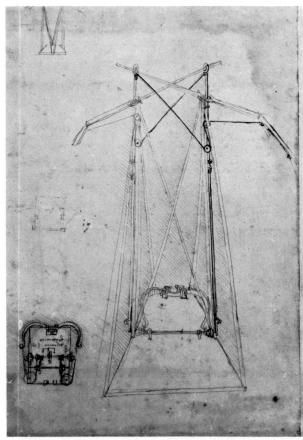

60. Ornithopter powered by a bow-string motor. Leonardo, *Codice Atlantico*, f. 314^{r-b}, 1495-97

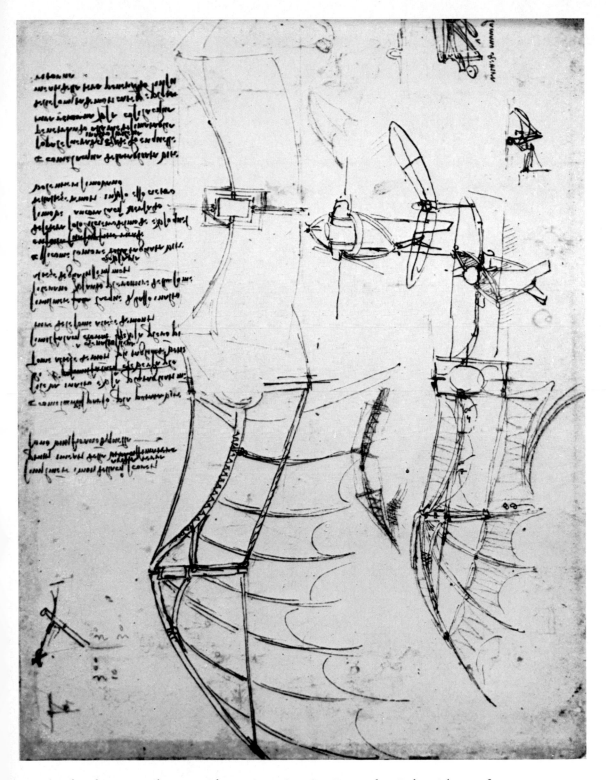

61. Sketches for an ornithopter with moving wing tips. Leonardo, *Codice Atlantico*, f. 309^{v·a},
1497–1500

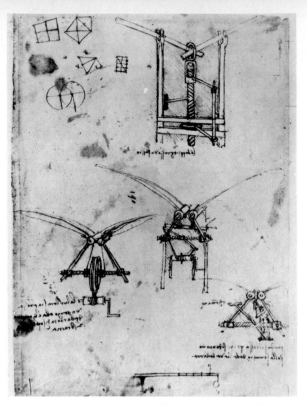

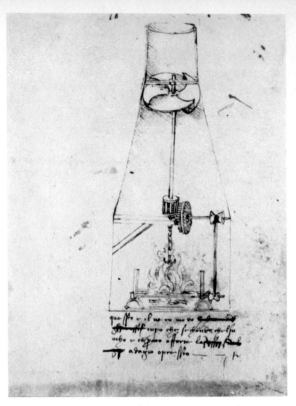

62. Mechanisms for flapping wings. Leonardo,
    Codice Atlantico, f. 278$^{\text{v-a}}$, *ca.* 1485

64. Roasting spit turned by air rising in the
    smoke-stack. Leonardo, *Codice Atlantico*, f.
    5$^{\text{v-a}}$, 1480–82

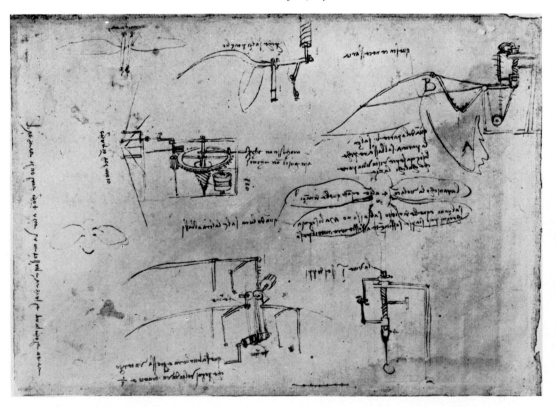

63. Mechanisms for flapping wings, with a sketch of a dragon fly. Leonardo, *Codice
    Atlantico*, f. 377$^{\text{v-b}}$, *ca.* 1485

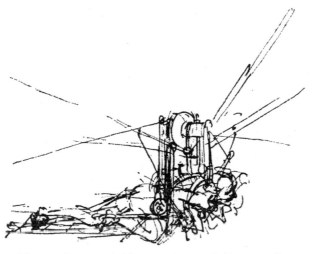

Fig. 32. Prone ornithopter. Leonardo, MS B, f. 79ʳ,
1486–90

strokes, Leonardo sketched some designs for artificial wings with flap-valves (Plate 56). He proposed the use of hinged panels which would be held in place, on the downstroke, by a network of cords stretched between the rigid fingers of the wings, while on the upstroke the flaps would fall, allowing the air to pass through the nets.

Although most of Leonardo's comments on natural flight concern birds, his artificial wings are usually bat-derived, so avoiding the necessity for such a complication as the valves introduced:

> Remember that your bird should have no other model than the bat, because its membranes serve as an armour or rather as a means of binding together the pieces of its armour, that is the framework of the wings.[1]

And, again: 'Dissect the bat, study it carefully, and on this model construct the machine.'[2] Such calm acceptance of the bat contrasts markedly with the traditional, mediaeval suspicion and fear of the creature. Renaissance anatomy and engineering had begun to weaken the earlier tendency to rely on natural affinities.

With wings of bat-shape, Leonardo designed flying machines which were, so to speak, half way between the ornithopter and the flying chariot. The boat-

[1] MacCurdy, p. 437, *Sul Volo*, f. 16 (15)ʳ.
[2] MacCurdy, p. 489, MS F, f. 41ᵛ, *ca.* 1508.

9

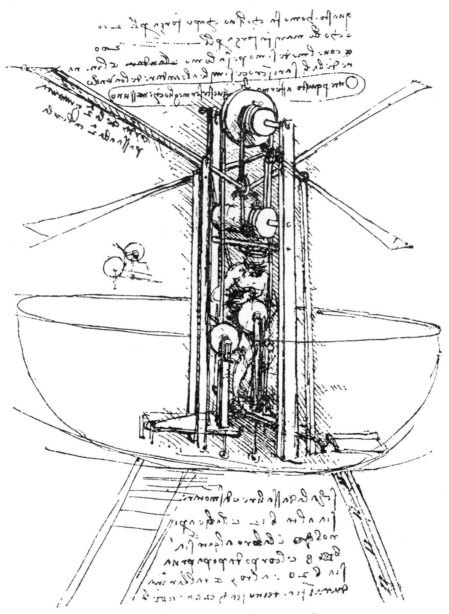

Fig. 33. Standing ornithopter. Leonardo, MS B, f. 80r, 1486–90

shaped hull of Plate 58 and the bowl of Fig. 33 are intended to enable the aeronaut to stand or sit in comparative comfort while working the wings.

Moving, no doubt unconsciously, towards the separation of the systems of

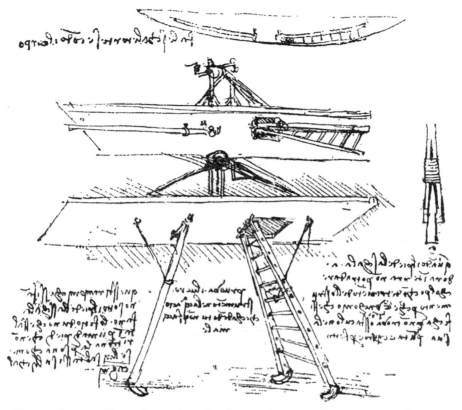

Fig. 34. Retractable undercarriage for the standing ornithopter. Leonardo, MS
B, f. 89^r, 1486–90

propulsion and lift which was to be necessary before manned flight could be
achieved, Leonardo sketched a 'semi-ornithopter', only the wing-tip of which was
designed to move. Having appreciated that the wing-tip does most of the work of
propulsion (but without, it seems, realising that the inner wing provides most of
the lift) he produced a design which economised on effort while adding to the
machine's rigidity (Plate 61). The aeronaut was to hang on a harness suspended
below the hole in the centre, a system which prefigures the famous hang-gliders
used by Lilienthal in the early 1890s. One might suppose that, having progressed
so far, Leonardo would immediately have moved on to the principle of the fully
rigid glider. We must, however, put hindsight aside and remember how obvious
it seemed, even to so great a genius as Leonardo, that the imitation of birds (or
bats) was the right path to follow. Although towards the end of his life he did
indeed jot down some notes about the movement through the air of a rigid plane

surface, based on his observation of the swinging movement of a falling sheet of paper, he did not pursue the application of these principles to human flight:

> This man will move to the right if he bends his right arm and extends his left arm; and he will then move from right to left by changing the position of the arms.[1] (Fig. 35.)

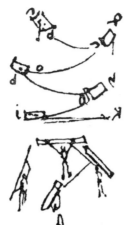

Fig. 35.
Glider control, based
on the movements of
a falling sheet of paper.
Leonardo, MS G,
f. 74[r], 1510–15

Most spectacular, and probably most famous, of all of Leonardo's aeronautical designs is that for the screw helicopter (Fig. 36):

> Let the outer extremity of the screw be of steel wire as thick as a cord, and from the circumference to the centre let it be eight braccia.

Fig. 36. Design for a helicopter, using a full helical
screw. Leonardo, MS B, f. 83[v], 1486–90

[1] MacCurdy, p. 495, MS G, f. 74[r], 1510–15.

Fig. 37. Balance mechanism for testing an ornithopter wing.
Leonardo, *Codice Atlantico*, f. 381ᵛ⁻ᵃ, *ca.* 1485

I find that if this instrument made with a screw be well made—that is to say, made of linen of which the pores are stopped up with starch—and be turned swiftly, the said screw will spiral into the air and it will rise high.

Take the example of a wide and thin ruler whirled very rapidly in the air, you will see that your arm will be guided by the line of the edge of the said flat surface.

The framework of the above-mentioned linen should be of long stout cane. You may make a small model of pasteboard, of which the axis is formed of fine steel wire, bent by force, and as it is released it will turn the screw.[1]

In comparison with the use of separate rotor blades, the full helix is inefficient, but the design might be made to work after a fashion, and the last sentence of the description has suggested to some that Leonardo may have built and flown a model.

Among the most interesting of Leonardo's ancillary aeronautical designs are those reproduced in Figs. 37–9. Of the wing-testing machine in Fig. 37 he writes:

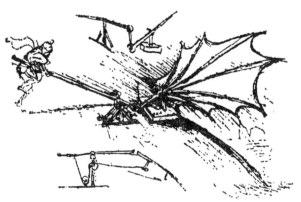

Fig. 38. Mechanism for testing an ornithopter
wing. Leonardo, MS B, f. 88ᵛ, 1486–90

[1] MacCurdy, pp. 517–8, MS B, f. 83ᵛ, 1468–90.

If you wish to ascertain what weight this wing will support, place yourself upon one side of a pair of balances and on the other place a corresponding weight so that the two scales are level in the air; then if you fasten yourself to the lever where the wing is and cut the rope which keeps it up you will see it suddenly fall; and if it required two units of time to fall of itself you will cause it to fall in one by taking hold of the lever with your hands; and you lend so much weight to the opposite arm of the balance that the two become equal in respect of that force; and whatever is the weight of the other balance so much will be supported by the wing as it flies; and so much the more as it presses the air more vigorously.[1]

Needless to say, his analysis is faulty, but here as elsewhere Leonardo is at pains to apply a genuinely quantitative approach to the problem, rather than rely on the hit-and-miss methods of so many of his predecessors.

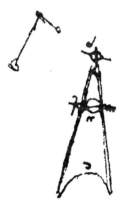

Fig. 39.
Directional control
unit, to be operated by
the head. Leonardo,
MS L, f. 59ʳ, 1499–
1503

Fig. 39 is a highly ingenious device for enabling an aeronaut to operate, with his head, a control surface shaped like that of a bird's tail. A head harness, represented by the circle in the middle of the diagram, is connected to the ribs by means of two rings which can slide back and forth along the spars, thus opening and closing the surface like a fan in emulation of the expanding and contracting movements of a bird's tail. (Leonardo does not consider the difficult problem of how to maintain the tension in the covering of the fan.) By tilting the head from side to side the aeronaut can also make the surface function as a rudder.

Although he was much more interested in ideas themselves than in putting ideas into practice, there is some reason to believe that Leonardo built models of some of his machines, and even that he tried full-scale versions of one or more of

[1] MacCurdy, p. 515, *Codice Atlantico*, f. 381ᵛ⁻ᵃ, *ca.* 1485.

his ornithopters. As I have mentioned in Chapter Six, there was a tradition, beginning no more than a generation after his death, that he had unsuccessfully attempted to fly. The manuscripts contain a number of brief and tantalising passages which indicate that he contemplated the actual construction of some of his designs. He gave careful thought to the appropriate materials, which were to have included cane, reed, linen, taffeta, fustian, paper, greased leather thongs, and springs made of wire or ox-horn. Since Leonardo pays great attention to the need for supple and powerful thongs to move the wings, the following passage has been interpreted by MacCurdy and others as a reference to a flying machine:

> Tomorrow morning on the second day of January 1496 I will make the thong and the attempt . . . To make the paste, strong vinegar, in which dissolve fish-glue, and with this glue make the paste, and attach your leather and it will be good.[1]

Although this interpretation is at best doubtful, a brief comment at the end of *Sul Volo degli Uccelli* is less ambiguous: 'From the mountain which takes its name from the great bird [Monte Ceceri, 1450 ft.], the famous bird will take its flight, which will fill the world with its great renown.'[2] While no other direct evidence of such an attempt has survived, MacCurdy has suggested that a report of the experiment, which would have taken place in 1505, could have been the source of the passage in Cardano.

Leonardo certainly hoped to 'fill the world' with the renown of his flying-machines, which he took very seriously. In a passage in the *Codice Atlantico* which may perhaps refer to one of them, he wrote: 'See tomorrow to all these matters and the copies, and then cancel the originals and leave them at Florence, so that if you lose those that you take with you the invention will not be lost . . .'[3] He made careful plans for the testing of his machines, which he wisely thought of trying over water in the first instance, even planning to take the precaution of providing himself with a life-belt: 'This machine should be tried over a lake, and you should carry a long wineskin as a girdle so that in case you fall you will not be drowned.'[4] Although he hoped for fame as a result of his invention, Leonardo was also, it seems, fearful of the derision, and perhaps worse, that might follow if he were known to have made an unsuccessful attempt. In one of the most interesting of all

[1] MacCurdy, p. 513, *Codice Atlantico*, f. 318[v-a].
[2] MacCurdy, p. 441, *Sul Volo*, f. 18[v].
[3] MacCurdy, p. 451, *Codice Atlantico*, f. 214[r-d], 1505–8.
[4] MacCurdy, p. 516, MS B, f. 74[v], 1486–90.

the notes which may refer to a flying machine he wrote the following memo to himself:

> Close up with boards the large room above, and make the model large and high, and you will have space upon the roof above, and it will be more suitable in all respects [?] than the Piazza d'Italia.
>
> And if you stand upon the roof at the side of the tower the men [at work] on the cupola cannot see you.[1]

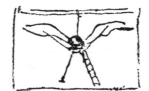

Fig. 40. Sketch of an ornithopter
suspended from the roof.
Leonardo, *Codice
Atlantico*, f. 361v–b,
ca. 1487.

These two notes are accompanied by a rough sketch of an ornithopter suspended from the roof by means of a rope (Fig. 40). That the 'model' was indeed to be large is indicated by the use of an undercarriage including a ladder. Leonardo appears to have conceived the cautious but not altogether practical plan of climbing into the suspended machine, retracting the undercarriage, and then working the wings to see whether he could produce sufficient lift to rise and slacken the tension on the rope. In order to make this experiment work he would, of course, have had to flap in such a way as to rise almost vertically. The cupola to which he refers in the second of the notes was evidently that of the cathedral in Milan.

While this and the other passages that I have quoted suggest that cautious attempts of some kind were indeed made, Leonardo never followed them up with any notes on the results of his experiments. This may well have been due to a reluctance to commit to paper any record of failure. One can in any case say with some confidence that Leonardo never launched himself from the top of a building in the manner ascribed to his contemporary Danti. As Mr Gibbs-Smith says:

[1] MacCurdy, p. 514, *Codice Atlantico*, f. 361v–b, *ca.* 1487.

It is just possible, but highly unlikely, that Leonardo built one of his prone orni-thopters, and lay in it fruitlessly flapping its wings: its weight alone would have kept it firmly earthbound. But he certainly never had himself launched into the air; the machine's weight, together with the rapid movement of the centre of pressure rearwards the moment he made the first down-and-back-beat of the wings, would have immediately led to a disastrous crash, with death or serious injury for the pilot.[1]

As most of the manuscripts lay unread until the nineteenth century, Leonardo's aeronautical work remained unknown, and hence had no influence on the subsequent development of the subject. Comments about him were widespread during his lifetime and later, but apart from the story of failure which seems to have begun with Cardano, the only sixteenth-century suggestion that Leonardo actually under-took aeronautical experiments is found in Vasari's *Life*. In a brief and ambiguous passage he tells how, when Leonardo was on his way to Rome for the coronation of Pope Leo X in March 1512/3, he made 'a paste of wax, and, while he was walking, shaped very thin animals, full of wind, blowing into which he made them fly through the air, but they fell to the ground when the wind ceased.'[2] This account, which seems totally garbled, cannot be interpreted with any certainty. It may be that the last words should be taken to refer to the flight of a kite,[3] but Vasari's statement that Leonardo 'blew into' the wax animals seems rather to imply that he had in mind something akin to Archytas' dove. As the unconvincing tone of the passage suggests the activities of a lay miracle worker casually revealing wonders while he walks towards the great ceremony, the story is probably best dismissed as apocryphal. In such circumstances even Leonardo is unlikely to have been able to build mechanical birds powered either by compressed air or by rockets. It is nevertheless possible that there is some tenuous factual basis for the account. At some time, perhaps, Leonardo, who was of course deeply interested in firearms and war-machines, may have experimented with a rocket powered flying model (some-thing not elsewhere attested). Again, the dependence of the animals on 'wind' may be a reference not only to the motive and sustaining power derived from the atmosphere and from rockets, but also, in a confused fashion, to the supposed *antiperistasis* process. One can do no more than speculate.

[1] Gibbs-Smith, *Leonardo da Vinci's Aeronautics*, p. 35.
[2] G. Vasari, *Le Vite de piu eccellenti architetti*, . . ., Firenze, 1550, p. 573.
[3] Mr Gibbs-Smith's tentative interpretation. *Leonardo da Vinci's Aeronautics*, p. 36.

Almost all of Leonardo's designs for flying machines are both wrong in principle and hopelessly impractical as examples of mechanical engineering. He understood virtually nothing of the mechanisms of bird flight, and only once, in the case of the proto-helicopter which he pursued no further, did it occur to him to depart from the example provided by living creatures. While we may regret his failures of insight and the crippling dominance of the idea that nature should be imitated in detail, Leonardo remains by far the most remarkable aeronautical experimenter before 1600. The partial successes ascribed to others may, paradoxically, have resulted from their having been the attempts of lesser men. Eilmer, Danti, and Guidotti, while aspiring to flap their wings, may have constructed them in such a way that they were able to support short and relatively stable glides; Leonardo's astonishing ingenuity led him, on the other hand, to design, and perhaps build, remarkably lifelike wings which were so complex as to render such partially satisfactory function virtually impossible. *Vincius ... tentauit & frustra: hic pictor fuit egregius.*

CONCLUSION

It was more than a hundred years before aeronautical technology advanced beyond the achievements of Leonardo. With the 'New Science', the creation of the Royal Society, and the acceleration of technological progress in the seventeenth century, interest in the possibilities of flight began to take on a different character. Approaches to the problem became more generally rational, and the subject lost its air of mystery. The New Science changed old ideas about the universe and about man's place in it. Although man still had his right and proper station in the scheme of things, he now had rather more physical and conceptual mobility. As a consequence one sees the gradual falling away of the old belief that attempts at flight were presumptuous. The prejudice was, of course, long in dying (indeed, it lingers on today) but it began to have very much less effect on intellectual technicians after 1600 than it had had in previous centuries. The tone of Flayder's oration, delivered in 1617, is indicative of the change. In answer to the traditional objections made by the 'antagonist' whose introductory remarks preceded his address, Flayder denied the charge that there is any presumption in man's attempts to fly. By his art man should create those things (including wings) which nature and God have denied him, and in doing so he will make proper use of his God-given wit and intelligence.[1] The change is also revealed in new attitudes to the work of the early experimenters. For almost the first time there arose a serious concern with what was reported to have been achieved in the past. Many seventeenth-century books on technology contain a passage summarising the various kinds of aeronautical trials which had been made since the time of Daedalus, and the summaries show

[1] F. H. Flayder, *De arte volandi*, [Tübingen,] 1627, pp. 54–5.

that the way to flight had been prepared in a practical as well as in a conceptual sense. By 1600 virtually all of the major forms of flight had been either tried or proposed in detail. Gliders, flappers, kites, the parachute, the hot-air balloon, the helicopter, the rocket, had all grown familiar to those interested in exploring the subject. Before sustained flight became a reality there remained only the creation of a proper combination of constituent parts and the availability of a prime mover. There is little doubt that if an adequate form of prime mover had been to hand in, say, 1603, men would have conquered the air long before 17 December 1903.

Appendix A

A Summary Chronology to 1600

B.C. *ca.*	400	The wooden dove of Archytas.
A.D. *ca.*	60	Attempts at flight in the Roman arena.
	?60	Heron's windmill-operated pipes.
ca.	200	*Draco* standard adopted by the Romans.
ca.	250	Flight of King Shapur's architect.
ca.	630	Kites known in Islam.
ca.	850	*Draco* standard in the *Psalterium aureum*.
ca.	875	'Abbas b. Firnās.
ca.	900	Mechanical birds in Islam.
	1002–10	al-Djawharī.
	1000–10	Eilmer of Malmesbury.
	1162	Turk in Constantinople.
ca.	1185	Horizontally shafted windmills in Europe.
	1232–3	Buoncompagno.
	1241	(9 April) Battle of Wahlstatt. *Draco* standards.
ca.	1250	Roger Bacon's thoughts on flying machines.
ca.	1325	First illustration of a *moulinet* (possibly a toy helicopter).
	1326/7	First illustration of a European kite (Milemete).
ca.	1350	Pennon kite in Nizhni-Novgorod.
	1405	Fair copy of *Bellifortis*.
ca.	1420	Rocket bird in Fontana's *Metrologum*.
ca.	1430	Kite and rocket bird in Vienna Codex 3064.
	1432/3	First European illustration of a vertically shafted windmill (Taccola).

ca. 1440	Illustration of a rocket bird in Fontana's *Bellicorum instrumentorum liber*.
1452	Birth of Leonardo.
1473/4	(February–March) Regiomontanus' eagle.
ca. 1480	Proto-parachutes in B.M. Add. MS 34113.
ca. 1485–99	Period of Leonardo's most important aeronautical work.
1498/9	Danti.
1505	Leonardo's *Sul Volo degli Uccelli*.
1507	(October) Damian.
1512/3	(March) Leonardo flies kites?
1519	Death of Leonardo.
1530	(10 June) Kite flown for Charles V in Munich.
1557–8	Torriano flies model birds for Charles V at St Yuste.
1558	della Porta's description of a kite.
1578	Bourne speculates on mechanical birds.
ca. 1580	Italian makes an attempt to fly from the Tour de Nesles?
ca. 1600	Guidotti.

Appendix B

Laying some Aeronautical Ghosts

In order to keep the main text free from a polemical tone, I have placed here notes on four matters of controversy.

The ventilabrum in the Kyeser hexameters

The editor of the facsimile edition of *Bellifortis*, Dr Götz Quarg, who is convinced that the *draco* was indeed intended to be three-dimensional, supports his interpretation by offering a translation of the word *ventilabrum* which differs from mine. He renders *medio ventilabro mota* by *in der Mitte mit einem Gebläse* ('in the middle with a bellows').[1] Dr Quarg believes that Kyeser intended the mouth of the dragon to hold some form of bellows which would be operated by the dragon's movement through the air as it was pulled by the horseman, blowing up the cloth kite like a balloon and so providing (imaginary) lift. In a voluminous correspondence with me (31 July 1967–4 October 1967), Dr Quarg answered objections to the unlikelihood of such an arrangement by re-emphasising, with some cogency, that many of the devices depicted in such manuscripts must be considered as entirely fanciful. His interpretation, which fails to explain the use of the word *mota*, nevertheless seems to me to be unduly complex. Furthermore, my reading 'reel' has the advantage of referring to something depicted in the miniature.

The word *ventilabrum*, which originally meant winnowing-fork, or flail, was used in later Latin to refer to fans in general, but especially to fans of the long-handled

[1] G. Quarg, ed., *Conrad Kyeser aus Eichstätt: Bellifortis*, 2 vols., Düsseldorf, 1967, 'Umschrift und Übersetzung', pp. 78–9. Some egregious errors in the transcription, here and elsewhere, undermine one's confidence in these handsomely printed volumes.

kind and of the kind used as ceremonial fly-flaps.[1] Although it was never, as far as I know, used to mean windmill, it was applied in the fifteenth century, and later, to rotating, fan-like airbrakes (see above, p. 118). While this usage might reasonably be thought to support the reading 'bellows', I believe that in the absence of any other Latin name for the cranked reel held by the horseman, Kyeser called it *ventilabrum*, both because he saw in it some similarity to the primitive hinged flail, and also because of its rapidly rotating action. This kind of reel, although cumbersome and inefficient, can be made to function adequately if one whirls it much as one may whirl a child's wooden rattle. Further, and in my view decisive, support for my reading is provided by the unambiguous translation of *ventilabrum* as *haspel* (= reel) in Colmar MS 491, f. 72^r.

Birds in Cyprus

Duhem places great importance on what he believes to be reports of flying models of great intricacy made in Cyprus in the sixteenth century and earlier.[2] After citing some passages about the so-called *oiselets de Chypre*, which were sometimes spoken of as highly prized and which Duhem finds surrounded with an atmosphere of mystery and awe, he goes on to discuss in detail a short poem in Juan de Valcaçar's *Relacion de las Exeqvias*:[3]

> Véritablement extraordinaire est l'intérêt d'une petite pièce de vers latins, composée par un jésuite qui, célébrant après d'autres les vertus de la reine défunte, et prenant pour thème emblématique la colombe d'Archytas, assure dans ce livre que le secret n'en est point perdu, et qu'une école d'artisans, à Chypre, fait encore dans son temps des oiseaux supérieurs à celui du Tarentin. Non seulement, dit-il, ces oiseaux sont capables de voler, mais ils chantent, picorent, fuient, trompent le chasseur, rompent le filet et semblent même gémir quand le plomb les a frappés. Soit que le jésuite ait vu de ses yeux les automates chypriotes, soit qu'il en parle par ouï-dire, il ne met point en doute qu'ils surpassent ceux des anciens. Il les donne enfin pour des engins qui existent encore, et il est le dernier à le dire.

The poem, which I give below, will not bear any such interpretation. In the first

---

[1] See, for example, du Cange's *Glossarium*.

[2] J. Duhem, *Histoire des idées aéronautiques avant Montgolfier*, Paris, 1943, pp. 130–2.

[3] J. de Valcaçar, *Relacion de las Exeqvias qve se celebraron en Napoles, en la Mverte de la Serenissima Reyna Margarita Señora nuestra*, 2 pts., En Napoles, 1612, pt. 2, p. 16.

place, the *Cypria . . . auis* which sings from its dead throat is surely not a Cypriot bird but a copper one. Second, the whole poem, which Duhem seems thoroughly to have misconstrued, is merely an imaginary extended metaphor of a conventional kind, addressed to the dead queen Margarita, and is without any implication of historical accuracy with respect to automata.

Architæ columba artificioso suspensa
volatu

Natiuum mentita genus mouet ardua pennas,
Cypriaque exanimi gutture cantat auis.
Sæpe dolos lusit venantum, & retia rupit,
Sæpe tulit duro spicula fixa sinu.
Architæ miraris opus? ne temne, doloris
Non est mæror iners ingeniosus amor.
Nam sine te ficto vitæ iam viuimus usu,
Siqua mouet gemitus vis, dolor arte mouet.

As for the *oiselets de Chypre*, the suggestion that they had anything to do with mechanical birds is entirely unfounded. They were in fact small, decorated sachets for holding perfumes of various kinds. The perfume was extracted by squeezing the sachets, which were made to represent birds and may sometimes have been covered with feathers. They were occasionally kept in boxes appropriately built in the shape of a cage.[1]

The Nürnberg Cantor

Especially since the publication of Hennig's influential article of 1918, historians of aeronautics have commonly attributed to the Nürnberg cantor 'the unlikely name Senecio'.[2] The attribution is more than unlikely: it is almost certainly wrong.

---

[1] L. de Laborde, *Notice des émaux exposés dans les galeries du Musée du Louvre*, vol. 2, Paris, 1853, pp. 424–5. The *oiselets de Chypre* date from at least as early as 1380.

[2] R. Hennig, 'Beiträge zur Frühgeschichte der Aeronautik,' *Beiträge zur Geschichte der Technik und Industrie*, vol. 8, 1918, p. 115.

Although *Senecio* was indeed a Roman family name, there is no need to assume that the sixteenth-century Nürnberger was so improbably called. *Senecio* is also a common noun, a simple variant of *senex*: 'A [little] old man, who was a cantor . . .' His name remains unknown.

Helicopters and Whirligigs

The substantial hand-grip and the thick cord associated with several of the *moulinets*, including the one by Taccola, suggest that the vanes were made to spin very fast, which would be necessary if lift were being provided for the blades of a helicopter. Return-toys of the 'whirligig' type are usually made to spin less rapidly. I nevertheless found that, even to produce the whirligig effect, a reproduction of a *moulinet*, using wooden bearings, required a fairly strong pull for which a hand-grip on the cord proved convenient. The vanes of a whirligig are usually painted in bands of colour, to make pretty patterns. Even if the sail-like frames of the *moulinets* were not so painted, a whirligig of this kind would have been capable of providing as much simple amusement as might be derived from many of the toys of the period.

The details of the structure of the *moulinets*, on which any interpretation of their function must ultimately depend, are unclear and ambiguous. The simplest form of construction would consist of a single shaft passing through the hollow nut, the vanes either spinning in direct contact with the top of the nut or being held above it by means of an intermediate bearing. To operate such a *moulinet* one would need to hold the nut while pulling the string, a method shown in several of the illustrations. While this is the probable form of construction of some of them, other forms may have been made. If the position of the hand in Plate 52 is not an illustrator's error, the lower part of the shaft must have been independent of the upper. This also seems to be true of the tapered lower shaft in Plate 51, which looks like a hand-grip. The use, in the cruciform *moulinets*, of a divided shaft whose short upper part is held at its base by a socket, would have lightened the load of a helicopter whose vanes and shaft were intended to rise together. Such a method of construction would be pointless in a whirligig. Although it is more complex, the helicopter interpretation appears to explain the available evidence more satisfactorily.

Appendix C
The Original Documents

I reproduce here, in their original form, what I believe to be the most important texts on aerodynamic subjects written or published in Europe before 1600, together with one or two of slightly later date. Leonardo's notes, which are widely available, have been omitted. Most of the passages, a number of which are printed here for the first time, are translated in full in the main body of the book, while the remaining few have been either paraphrased or translated in part. The sequence of passages in the main text and in the Appendix is the same. Page numbers following the headings indicate the relevant pages of the main text.

S. AUGUSTINE ON REGIONS OF THE ATMOSPHERE (See pages 23–4)
De Genesi, liber imperfectus, XIV. 44.

> Nubes autem aqua est, quod omnes sentiunt quibus contingit in montibus inter nubila, vel etiam in campis inter nebulas ambulare. In hoc quippe aere volare aves dicuntur. Nam in illo sublimiore atque puriore, qui vere aer ab omnibus appellatus est, nequeunt: non enim earum pondus tenuitate sua sustinet. In illo autem neque nubes concrescere asseruntur, neque aliquid procellosum existere: quippe ubi ventus adeo nullus est, ut in vertice Olympi montis, qui spatia hujus humidi aeris excedere dicitur . . .

MONGOL DRAGON STANDARD (See page 35)
Długosz, J., *Historiae polonicae libri xii*, Leipzig, 1711–12, col. 679. (Written in the fifteenth century.)

Erant in *Tartarorum* exercitu inter alia signa vexillum perimmane, in quo tale signum X depictum videbatur. In summitate verò hostilis vexilli, imago capitis tetri & nigerrimi cum mento barbato habebatur. Signifer itaque illius vexilli, *Tartaris* ad vnius stadii spatium pedem referentibus, in fugamque procliuibus, caput quod hastili supereminebat fortius quo poterat quatire cœpit, de quo illicò vapor, fumus, & nebula tam fœtidissimè exhalauit, in totumque *Polonorum* exercitum se superfudit, vt præ horrendo & intolerabili fœtore pugnantes *Poloni* penè exanimes & extincti, & ad pugnandum imbelles & inualidi redderentur.

THE KYESER DRACO (See pages 36, 39, 41)

Bellifortis, Göttingen, codex philos. 63, f. 105[r].

> *Draco volans iste formetur capite perga*
> *Medium sit lineum cauda tamen sericea sit*
> *Colores diuersi fine capitis sit tripla zona*
> *Ligno coadiuncta medio ventilabro mota*
> *Capud versus ventum ponatur quo tunc assumpto*
> *Duo leuent capud tertius ventilabrum portet*
> *Equo sequatur eum corda mota mouetur volatus*
> *Sursum deorsum dextrorsum & sinistrorsum*
> *Capud sit depictum rubeo colore que fictum*
> *Medio lunaris coloris fine diuersi*

Bellifortis, Colmar, MS 491, f. 72[r].

> *Diss ist ain fliegender track der sol also gemacht sin*
> *das hopt von bermet mittel und schwantz von*
> *siden von mangerlay farwen ussgenomen das*
> *hopt ain trifaltige schnur sol man binden an das*
> *register mit aim gelaich Item dise schnur sol haften*
> *an ainem haspel die sol also lang sin als hoch*
> *man den tracken gan wil laufen und wen man*
> *inn uff wel laufen so ker im das hopt gegen dem*
> *wind wenn der darin kumpt so heb inn by*
> *der schnur uff der ainen hapdt uff der hand hat*
> *so gat er uff in die luft so du im hengest.*

Bellifortis, Vienna, codex 3062, f. 128ʳ.

> Ain tracken mach von dünem duech
> als du waist speys den kopf mit
> firnysse und zund es an so geit
> ez grossen flamen.

ARCHYTAS (See page 49)

Aulus Gellius, *Noctium atticarum libri xx*, X.12.8–10.

> Multa autem videntur ab hominibus istis male sollertibus huiuscemodi com-
> menta in Democriti nomen data, nobilitatis auctoritatisque eius perfugio
> utentibus. Sed id quod Archytam Pythagoricum commentum esse atque
> fecisse traditur, neque minus admirabile neque tamen vanum aeque videri
> debet. Nam et plerique nobilium Graecorum et Favorinus philosophus,
> memoriarum veterum exequentissimus, affirmatissime scripserunt simulacrum
> columbae e ligno ab Archyta ratione quadam disciplinaque mechanica
> factum volasse; ita erat scilicet libramentis suspensum et aura spiritus inclusa
> atque occulta concitum. Libet hercle super re tam abhorrenti a fide ipsius
> Favorini verba ponere: Ἀρχύτας Ταραντῖνος, τὰ ἄλλα καὶ μηχανικὸς ὤν, ἐποίησεν
> περιστερὰν ξυλίνην πετομένην· ὁπότε καθίσειεν, οὐκέτι ἀνίστατο. μέχρι γὰρ τούτου ✱✱✱

MAGICAL FIRE BIRDS (See page 51)

De mirabilibvs mvndi, [Venice, 1472?] f. 26ᵛ.
Attributed to Albertus Magnus.

> Licinium: quod cum accenditur in domo uidebis res uolantes uirides, ut
> passeres, & aues, accipe pannum exequiarum recentem, & pone in eo cerebrum
> auis, & panas [*sic*] caude eius, & inuoluendo fac ex eis licinium, & pone ipsum
> in lampade noua uiridi, accende ipsam in domo cum oleo oliue: & quæ res
> erunt in domo fient uirides ualde, & uidebitur quasi uolent aues uirides, &
> nigræ.

FONTANA'S ROCKET BIRD (See pages 19, 53–7, 94–5, 110–11)

Metrologum de pisce cane et volucre, ff. 95ᵛ–104ᵛ.
[Numbers in brackets show the beginnings of folios.]

> [95ᵛ] Capitulum septimum de motu per aerem et alijs ad hoc accomodatis. Est

tercius nobis motus considerandus quo res ad altum feratur per aerem et hic similiter uarijs modis fieri contingit. Nam quedam manibus pelluntur sursum ad ethera ueluti lapides uel iacula cum prohiciuntur quadam balista uel arcu tenduntur in altum sicut sagitte uel a machina uel a bombarda uel ab alijs generibus instrumentorum prohiciendi.

Sed ego uidi et expertus sum fistulam pulueribus ignibilibus plenam ascendentem ad aerem. Hec enim cum incenditur uirtute ignis qui post egreditur sursum uelociter ducitur donec combusti sunt pulueres. Quare semel ymaginatus fui formas corui et formas dyaboli ex carta depicta et ligno subtili facere cum alis apertis super ferrum uel es tremulum constitutis in quorum uentribus tales canne pulueribus conculcate situabam et capita que igniri debebant ad subcaudam terminabantur ut de ibidem ab ano uideretur ignis egredi atque ualeret eas formas rectas pellere sursum tenentes capita. Cumque mouerentur tremebant ale et uidebantur ac si fuissent ueri dyaboli sub forma propria uel in spetiem corui mutati uoluantes per aerem et relinquentes post se fumum et fetorem.

Similiter magnus draco et admirationis non parue subtiliter fabricatus ex lignis et tela et carta per aerem uolare facies si modo predicto in longitudine uentris interiori grossa longaque canna puluerum firmaueris cuius ignis per anum egrediatur. Sed ut ignis potencia maior esset et ex ore ipsius ignis egredi uideretur aliam cannam similem de collo procedentem ad posteriora uerso facias quomodo ignis ex ea per os exiens et qui per anum egreditur ad partem eandem uersi unite magis pellerent ipsum draconem.

Sed opus est in hijs animalia longam caudam continere posterius tensam que sufficiat formas [96^r] sursum erectas tenere si quidem hec cauda non poneretur ignis superiora petens formas euerteret nec illas duceret per aerem ut deberet. Cauda preterea non eciam construatur nimis grauis ne uirtuti resistat ignis ad motum sursum ideo in hoc sicut et in alijs artificijs proportio neccessaria uidetur quare cum artifex hec uel similia facere uoluerit consideret primo potenciam ignis ut quantum pondus elleuare possit in aerem et non agat rem mobilem ab illo uel equali grauiorem quod cum frequenter expertus fuerim iudicaui cereum uel candelam fore possibile quod se ipsum ignitum per notabile tempus in aere substineret facta materie et ignis proportione equalitatis fere. Cum enim primo uidissem ignem potentem candelam sursum ferre feci postea candelam grauiorem notabiliter cum equali uirtute puluerorum et consequenter ignis et inueni quod in terra residebat nec ab igne elleuabatur propter sui grauitatem. Postmodum de medio concipiens formare nimis [MS: minus] grauiorem candella prima et leuiorem secunda ad equalitatem deueni proportionis ignis ipsius ad resistenciam grauitatis materie. Talis enim in omni loco aeris posita stat. Non cnim cadit neque sursum uadit eo quod duorum grauitatis scilicet ipsius tocius et leuitatis ipsius ignis inuicem contra operantia resistit.

Sed aduertendum ne sit cereum uel candela uel aliquod tale compositum quod ab igne sursum duci uel suspendi debet ex graui materia constructum et forma indebita quoniam nimis de igne requereretur et multum consequenter de pulueribus uel re combustibili ex quibus uel opus esset magnum uel parue durationis. Preterea debet ignis esse ex generibus illorum qui cum difficultate extinguntur. Si facile separaretur ignis ab ipso combustibili caderet subito extinctum ad terram grauitate sua. Comete [96ᵛ] quidem qui sub celo apparent in aere substinentur quia cum materia sit ignibilis et fortase uiscosa ignis in ipsa remanet inseperabiliter donec uratur materia et ipsa leuitate sua sedet in aere quare proportionata materia leuitati et ignitioni sursum in loco perdurat.

Quidam uero de numero eorum qui se tenent architectos et male phylosophantur dixit fore possibile quod homo per aerem ascenderet beneficio cuiusdam artificij. Et ymaginabatur pyramidem ex grossa tella et circulis de ligno componi multe quantitatis cuius conus sursum esset, et in dyametro circuli super basem transuersale lignum construi et fortiter ligari super quod homo sederet uel equitaret tenens in manibus suis lumenarias ardentes ex pice et seppo uel alia materia ignibili forti perdurante multiplicanteque fumum multum et grossum.

Putauit enim quod propter ignem illum aer intra piramidem inclusus continuo fieret leuior et rarior et consequenter regionem petens altiorem et cum naturaliter egredi non posset subleuaret pyramidem et hominem sedentem in ea ad quod similiter multum conferre putabat uaporem a luminaribus procreatum in pyramide interclusum sursumque coactum ascendere. Dixit tamen rem non habere locum cum pyramis parua fuisset uel nimis grauis uel habens per cohoperturam suam exspirationem aliquam uel quoniam paruus ignis fuisset uel paucitas includeretur uaporum predictorum.

Sed ego non parus admiratus fui de opinione huius uiri et magis quam de illo qui sub aqua uolebat descendere cum uegete. Sunt enim hic multa contraria nec non et pericula maxima. Primo nescitur qualiter in tanta raritate caliditateque aeris atque fumo grosso quibus uult artificium hoc non egere sed superhabundare respiratio possit in homine construari.

[97^r] Item timendum ne ab oportuno tanto calore comburatur pyramis et sequatur hominis ustio uel casus cum potuerit aer et fumus expirare particula tele combusta.

Tercio si cuncta que dixit essent adhuc uera queritur quomodo descendet homo sine ruina et periculo quia donec ardebunt facces ascenderet pyramis. Cumque fuerint consumpte defficiente motore sursum et quolibet suspendente uertitur pyramis ab aere et cadit inferius repentine sicut et res quedam que a turbine sursum feruntur cum uentus deficit qui leuabat illas ruunt grauitate sua.

Pretermitto reliquas contrarietates. Uir quidem iste non respexit ad finem quoniam de ascensio ne tantum cogitauit sed insufficienter rationes et argumenta sua. De descensu uero certo non hiunt considerationem ueluti multi que presumunt incipere quod finire nesciunt uel nequeunt.

Alexander uero ut fertur cum uoluisset aeri preesse melius fuit opinatus sedens super grifones fortes et uolantes tenens in ueru carnes assatas in altum. Grifones quidem odorem cibi sencientes supra capud suum ut comederent nitebantur ascendere. Cumque peruenisset alexander altissime et descendere uoluisset uertit carnes deorsum infra griffonum ora. Illi uero similiter cibum appetentes ut illum caperent inferius uolare cogebantur et ad terram duxerunt alexandrum incolumen sine periculo. Hoc certe siue uerum siue fabulosum dictum sit rationis tamen habet ingenij fundamentum sed de nimia uiri indicet animositate. Dedalus eciam ut poete narrant ex paruis plumis et cera condidit alas sibi quas sua industria quassare dixerunt et petere aeris regionem et ycareum mare uolando pertransisse.

Ego quidem non dubito iungi posse alas homini artificialiter actas quibus se leuabit in aere et per illum se [97^v] ualebit transferre et turres ascendere et aquas pertransire de quo iamdudum scribere cepi et fantasiam explanare. Sed alijs distractus occupationibus non perfeci. Sunt et plures ascensus alij per cordas et scalas et quedam ingernata. Sed illa pretermitto dicturus alias cum tempus dabitur magis ydoneum.

[After the fish and the dog.] [100^r] Capitulum decimum de uolucre que altitudines metiri ualebit. Ad mensurandas altitudines aquilam uel pauonem uel yrundinem uel alterius spetiei ex generibus uolatilium componas animal quod ad altum ualeat ascendere. Hoc ex materia leuissima in qua tamen aeris et ignis dominetur uirtus ut illud per aerem sursum trahere possit non nimia celeritate qualiter ante fore possibile declaratum est. Sed cum eius motus pigrior fuerit erit mensura certior et sufficiet tibi si de carta uel tella uel subtilissimo leuissimoque ligno uel metallo componatur auis intus uacua in cuius uentre canna pulueris incensibilis sit preparata terminata ad posteriora eiusdem sub cauda. Ibidem ignis incendi debet et sit longe caude ut fiat motus rectior. Mouetur quidem sagitta recte magis per aerem longior quam breuior. Nam si breuis est uolutando quandoque reflectitur et inordinate mouetur propterea fulmen existens breue sintomatier discurrit per ethera et per loca que comburit et dissipat. Si quidem in longitudinem multum fuisset pertensa ipsius forma moueretur sicut sagitta. Erit ergo cauda ut themon gubernationis motus eius sicut est themon nauis. Ap, tetur tamen ignis taliter quod caudam non comburat uel fiat cauda ex materia incombustibili ab ipso igne quasi ex subtilissimo ere uel [100ᵛ] fero. Quibus preparatis habeas horologium ex numero predictorum uel similium cum quo metiaris primo uelocitatem auis ad aliquam altitudinem notam hoc modo. Stans in pede turris cognite longitudinis gratia exempli centum brachiorum tenensque caudam auis perpendiculariter pendentem ponas ignem in pulueres et permitte subito illam ascendere et simul incipiat horologium et cum uideris auem ad summum altitudinis uentam esse tunc signa horologium tuum quia tempus uel differencia ipsius horologij est correspondens illi motui cum illa uelocitate ad altitudinem centum brachiorum. Postea illam eandem auem si recipere ualebis si cadet in terram et fuerit incombusta quia ex metallo facta aut aliam illi similem omnino in figura et grauitate et potencia ignis incenda[n]s in base alterius altitudinis incognite et apta tuum horologium et nota signum in ipso quando peruenerit auis ad altitudinis terminum. Et similiter considera differenciam in horologio tuo quam compares ad differenciam eiusdem uel similis habitam in prima experiencia et in qua proportione se habuerit in eadem se habebit altitudo incognita ad altitudinem illam centum brachiorum quare si proportio differencie secunde ad primam fuerit dupla erit altitudo secunda ducentorum brachiorum.

Sed si non possit auis ascendere per perpendicularem lineam ad terminum altitudinis quod contingere potest uel quia est altitudo obliqua sicut mons uel quia non est accessus ad basem altitudinis propter aliqua impedimenta uel quia mensurator uult distanter stare ab ipsa altitudine tunc est habenda diligencia in

situacione auis cum debet incendi propter quod ymaginatus sum rem geomet-
rice rationis. Sub ala ipsius iuxta radicem ale pendeat filum subtile cum parus
plumbino quod sit grauitatis minoris dragma uel tante quod sufficiat tenere
filum extensum et sit longitudo fili parum infra uentrem auis.

Cum igitur uoluero altitudinem [101ʳ] metiri tenebo auem manu et ponam
oculum iuxta finem caude respiciamque per dorsum auis altitudinem et si
uidero terminum eius bene quidem. Sin autem elleuabo uel deprimam auis
caput donec per directum dorsi eiusdem quasi per caudam et caput illum uidero
et non mota eadem de tali situ notabo sub uentre locum quem filum tensum
designat et ponam ibidem notam cum cera uel aliter. Et signabo locum ubi
sint pedes mei, quod sit F. Post hoc ueniam ad alium locum ubi sit altitudo
nota michi et tenens in manu ut prius auem cum filo cadente super notam
presignatam in uentre eiusdem acedam huc et illuc donec respiciens per dorsum
eius uidero terminum altitudinis note cadente filo in loco predicto et tunc
parato ut supra horologio incendam pulueres et permittam auem moueri
usque ad altitudinis terminum que recte per lineam uisualem mouebitur si bene
fuerit composita. Quando uero illuc peruanerit [sic] notabo differenciam in
horologio que gratia exempli sit .a. et sit altitudo hec nota 50 pedum. Postea
accipiam illam auem cum ad terram ceciderit uel aliam omnino similem et
accedens ad locum primum F signatum stansque tenebo illam simili modo
respiciens terminum altitudinis prime incognite et incenso puluere simul
incipiat horologium et auis discurrere. Quando uero peruenerit ad altitudinem
notabo differenciam in ipso horologio que sit b.

Quibus expeditis credere debeo quod sicut se habebit b ad a sic se habebit
altitudo prima incognita ad altitudinem secundam que est 50 pedum quare si b
fuerit triplum ad a erit altitudo prima 150 pedum.

Nam si bene consideretur operatio causantur ibidem trianguli equianguli et
consequenter laterum proporcionalium quoniam ex radio uisuali uel linea ab
aue discripta ab oculo usque ad terminum altitudinis tamquam ex latere
longiori et ex linea recta ab ipso oculo ymaginabiliter intellecta uersus
altitudinem protracta et linea a termino altitudinis perpendiculariter descen-
dente orthogonaliter secantibus se iuxta basem uel inferiorem partem altitudinis
ocultam uel manifestam tamquam ex duobus alijs lateribus triangulus formatur
orthogonius [101ᵛ] utrobique consimilis quem geometra intelligit et sic habebis
aliorum altitudinem per similes modos mensurationis.

Uerumtamen sicut de aqua dicebatur quod essent consimiles sic est aduertendum de aere ne fiant hij motus in locis quorum unus aerem grossum uel caliginosum uel perspicuum magis quam alter habere uideatur. Euitentur eciam uenti et pluuie et reliqua que experiencie contradicere possunt in ceteris instrumenti conditionibus semper obstruando paritatem.

[102ʳ] . . . Et hec que dixi de pisce cane et uolucre explicare decreui non ut precisam certitudinem mensure in ipsis esse cognoscam et uelim sed ut ingenio nouo curam darem et ad subtiliora inuenienda principium et fundamentum atque mensurationum artis genus nouum haberetur numquam ab alijs taliter explicatum.

[103ᵛ] . . . Nunc uero siue moueantur equaliter siue non per aquam terram uel acrem animalia predicta poteris cum hoc ingenio non minus certe quam in mensuratorio uiatorio scire submersionem piscis progressum quadrupedis et uolatum auis ubi non erit eciam opus horologij.

Fac igitur corditenum in axe ualde faciliter uolubilem que manu teneri possit et circa corditenum duc filum uel cordulam [104ʳ] longam tractabilem note quantitatis ut exempli gratia centum passuum et possis in ea si uolucris passus distinguere et numerari facilius illos ualeas. . . . Similiter si formaueris auem ducendam ab lgne uel aliter pulsam ab ymo usque ad terminum altitudinis taliter cordam caude ipsius apponas fortiter ligatam et quando ducetur auis per aerem extendetur filum uel cordula extra corditenum. Cum uero peruenerit auis ad terminum altitudinis tene corditenum non plus extendatur et nota signum in corda quam postea retrahe et habebis longitudinem uolatus auis. Et si super perpendicularem lineam sursum ascendat erit eadem altitudinis mensura. Si uero per obliquam iterum fac de altitudine nota minori ut ante narrauimus quoniam ex ratione triangulorum similium uenies in noticiam altitudinis incognite. . . . Sed in huius experiencia oportunitas est ut non dimittatur corditenum nimis celeriter uolui ne plusquam requiratur labatur cordula quod faciliter contingeret cum impetus in corditeno impressus esset. Teneatur ergo manus leuiter super ipsum corditenum uel circa cordulam que ab ipso disoluitur et permittatur illum paulatine reuolui. Sic extendetur corda sufficienter [104ᵛ] et percipi melius poterit quando fuerit animal in termino sui motus. Sed si non uelles uel non posses animal motum ad te conuertere cum illud fuerit in termino mensurationis quod uidere posses in aere uel in plano et comprehenditur in aqua cum non plus de corda trahitur eo quod plumbum fundum tangit nota signum corde iuxta corditenum et uide quantum de corda remansit circa ipsum et illam quantitatem deme de tota quantitate cordule et quod remanet est uera quantitas corde que inter corditenum et animal fuit extensa et sic habebis consequenter mensuram uerissimam loci quam optabas.

VIENNESE ROCKET BIRD (See page 59)

Vienna, Nationalbibliothek, codex 3064, ff. 21ʳ⁻ᵛ.

Item wildu ein fliegund fewer machen oder ain vogel so mach ain form als ein vogel geschaffen ist von ierdeim oder von holcz uberzeuch das mit bapir und sneids und leyms mit aim täschler leym das es gancz und wol auff der forem anligen werd doch das es an aim ortt offen weleib das die forem daraus müg und tue den vogel puluer in also das es im vor pey dem haup lig [21ᵛ] und ist der vogel als ain amsel gröss oder der selbigen mass so sey des puluers alls ain ponnuss. Und wen das puluer dar ein kumpt so leyms wol zue mit dem täschler leym oder ain taiglein das es gancz werd. Und par ein löchlein mit einem spriczigen hölczlein dar in hinnen pey und durch den auss und stoss dar in einen federkiel der gefult sey mit püchsen puluer und ains vingers langk sey und der ain tail hin ein und das andertail heraus räkg und secz den vogel auff die erden oder wo du wellest und zündt das puluer hinder in dem feder kiell an und gang da von und ist güt daz das puluer so in dem vogel ist vor pey dem haupt oder in dem haupt sey. So du es an zündest und wen du es angezündest so macht ains wurffs oder zwairr verr da von gan wo du wilt ee es sein strass vertt.

KIRCHER'S ROCKET BIRD (See pages 59–60)

Mundus subterraneus, Amstelodami, 1665, p. 480.

Quamvis aquila eodem modo in aëre exprimi possit, quo Draco, sunt tamen nonnulli pyrotechni, qui rochetttis [sic] quoque instructam in aëre exhibeant, quemadmodum ego in Germania me vidisse memini. Aquilam efformant ex rochettis constructam ea proportione pulveris, ut una rochetta ignem altius non projiciat alterâ, sed juxta pennarum in alis proportionem; deinde totum aquilæ corpus pulvere, aqua vitæ & camphora imbuunt, quæ materia vi rochettæ principalis in altum sublata aërem, & accensa perfectam specie aquilam exhibet, quam deinde rochettarum explosio, imò fumus ipse in aëre exprimet. Hoc pacto quamcunque rem exhibere poteris; materia enim pulveris cum cæteris admixta in superficie statuæ aut cuicunque tandem figuræ inspersa suaviter ardet, & unà flammulis suis perfectam figuram exhibet.

Est hæc inventio plena admirationis & mirè opportuna ad hostes hoc spectaculo deterrendos, præsertim si literis nomen aliquod in aëre exprimentibus instituatur: negotium industriosum artificem desiderat, ut desideratum successum sortiatur; debet enim machina perfecte æquilibrari, deinde perpendiculari situ projici in aërem vi rochettæ principalis sufficientis roboris ad machinam in notabilem altitudinem elevandam.

THE VIENNA PENNON KITE (See pages 65–7)

Vienna, Nationalbibliothek, codex 3064, ff. 4ᵛ–7ʳ.
[Numbers in brackets show the beginnings of folios.]

Nota wie du ainen tracken artificialiter machen und regieren solt das er in dem lufft swebt und fert als er lebendig sey [5ʳ] Nim ein rot oder grüen oder einer anderen farbein seydein tuech oder von farben gestukcht würmischen ob du wilt, Aber von rotem ist es aller scheinbarist wen es dikch in dem lufft erscheint und wesunder gegen der sunnen als ob es etwas fewrem sey. Auch möchtest du von vergultem ding dar zu nemen oder machen das zumal scheinpar und fewrischen wer. Doch das es als von gar liechtem ding sey. Und lass dir den trakchen von dem tuech schneiden und formiern nach ordenung und gestalt der hernach gemachten gegenwürtigen figur. Und also das er ein haupp hab von einer hautt lindtz pergames und die doch starchk genueg sey als im das angesicht wegreifft. Und also bedarff er zu einer sämleichen gröss des hauptz was ein brayte hautt pergames begreiffen mag, das im das corpus hinder dem haupt auff aindleff ellen lang sey mit dem swancz, und mit aller leng. Und das das corpus an der haut dem haupt als braytt sey als das haupt, und das es enmitten zu den seytten etwas büchischen oder flügilischen erseczt sey das es ein würmisch gestalt hab wesunder wer im guet wen er als gancz gerecht wer das man in den auff dem ruken enmitten von dem hauppt hin auff zwair oder dreyr ellen lang auff schnit und im denn ain stukch seydeins tuech enmitten auff anderhalb span brayt mynner oder mer und an beden örten zue gespiczt nach forme des corpus dar in säcztte und vernäte. Wen dan der lufft dar an schlüeg

so sakctt es sich nach weis ains segels und trib in der lufft vil dester ringer auff
und gewun ein gestalt ains erhaben leibs oder rukken das er vil dester besser und
ausrichtiger wer als du auch in der nachgeschriben figur vindest. Ist aber das
du daz nicht dar in machest noch denn ist er ze mal guet. Wen nu das corpus
also gemacht ist so lass dir an die hautt pergamess den kchopff malen ein
scheinpars wurmisch angesicht, das vast weiss und scheinpar welib von ringen
liechten varben. Und nä dan den kopff an das corpus und mach dan an yedes
ortt der hautt zwai rinkli oder drein die drivalt oder vierrvalt von vadem
seindt und das die hautt an beden seytten pey dem rinklin mit klainen pergamen
plëczlin [5ᵛ] welait sey das die rinkli dester minder durch die haut schneiden.
Und hab dan klaine schinle die von gueten newen zahem tenneynen stekchen
gespalten und geschniten sind in der braytt als ain vinger und in der dikch als
ain halber rokkenhalben die schinle span krewcz weis über ein ander uber das
angesicht und hefft es in die ringkli also das sy enmitten auff zwen twerch finger
von dem angesicht herauswerts gepogen seindt doch also das sy auch enmitten
umb das krewcz mit ainem rinklin etwas fur den wind gehefft seindt als du
an der figur gezaichentt findest. Ob auch der wind etwas zestarchk wer das du
entzäschist daz sich der kchoph etwast zevast biegen wurd, und das siech die
schinen zerzärten so macht du das geleich ein schinen auswendig dem trakchen
uber den kopph machen auch ain ringklin und uber twerchs alls dyser ains
oder zerichts uber den schedel von mitten koph herauff als er an dem rukken
stöst untcz an die stiernen. Ist auch der wind zu gueter mass starck so macht du
das selb schinlein dester dikcher machen. Oder ob er gar zemal starck wer so
möchtest du im einen stekchen pey ains vingers gross uber den schedel legen
von dem rukken gegen den stiernen herauff als vorgeschriben ist. Darnach
macht du dreir ringkli entzwischen den augen von der stiernen her ab uber
die nasen als da aygenleich figuriert ist. Und stöss den vaden dar an du den
trakken füren wilt durch das ain oder durch die zwai und pint in an das dritt
das ist das nidrist als du auch gezaichent vindest. Ist aber der wind ze gueter
mass starckh so stoss den vaden durch das öbrist und windt in an das mittlist.
Ist der wind noch sterkcher so wind in allain an das öbrist. Ist er aber zu mal
starckh so wind im den dikchen stekchen uber den koph als vorgeschriben ist und
bind den vaden ze öbrist an der stiernen an den stekchen und lass in sein strass
varen. [*I.e.*, let it fly straight out like a pennon instead of rising.] Item wen
du in nu wilt lassen fliegen so gang da du lufft habest und halt in gerad auff also

das im der wind in das angesicht und in das corpus schlach und wen der lufft icht
krefftig sey so heb in vast auff und heng im mit dem vaden so gett er auff und
heng im alleweg zu hübschleich und wen der lufft etwas swach well sein, so
[6ᵛ] gang gegen den lufft das er da gegen werd streben also treibst du in mit
dem lufft auff als hoch du wild. Wenn er nun ains turens oder zwair hoch in die
höche kumen ist das in der lufft nu wol ergriffen hat und welhes landes aushin
du in denn füren wilt das macht du mit dem regimen zuebringen als verr das land
eben ist das du gewandeln macht. Wildu in gegen den lufft füeren so zeuch in
hubschleich und heng im alleweg zu damit so wiert er yelenger ye höcher.
Wildu in dem luft nach lassen streichen so muest im nach gan und hübschleich
hengen und den muess er hinder sich gan. Darumb stät es wol das man im gar
muessiklich henge als ob er still stuend so chumpt er in swebunder weis als verr
du wilt das man nicht sprech er gang hindersich. Und wenn er dan uber ain stat
oder gepirg gegangen ist so macht du in dan wider umb oder entwerchs hin
ziehen als verr du wilt. Aber du solt merchken ob der lufft zc krankch wer.
Wenn der trakch dan den kopff henkcht oder neben sich wendt so müst du snel
lauffen gegen den lufft das in der lufft erblass und das er sich auff richt. Wan aber
er den kopff auf richtet so macht in nach der vernufft regieren wo du wilt als
vorgeschriben ist. Wan du in auch wider nider ziechen wilt so far einer weiten
stat umb das wen er vast nider kchum ob es dann zevast windstill wurd das er
nicht zu der erden chüm e das du zu dir bringest oder er möcht in ainen pawm
oder stauden wehangen. Wolten auch die lewt dich uberlauffen und sehen was
es wer an dem niderziechen so gib dcinem gesellen den faden in die hant als ob
er in niderzug und nym den vaden under dic ainen ellenpogen und in die ander
handt ob er in der ellenpogen bräch das du in doch in der hant behebest und lauff
anhin uncz das er zu der erden kchüm und ze stett zeuch im die schindel auss
und walg im dem kchoph zu samen und slach das corpus darumb und verbirg
in. Ouch ist es güt wen du in mit dem vaden regierest das du zestätt ainen
gesellen habest der eben und geradt under dem trakchen gang alls verr er
gewandeln mag umb das ob der vaden bräch das er sech wo sich der trakch
niderlass das er nicht verloren werd. Wen wo der trakch swebt da sinchkt er
geleich under sich nider das er nicht umb ains rayspiess oder zwair [7ʳ] lenge
hinder nach fur vellet das in der selb knecht nicht verlieren kann. Auch ist der
knecht dar zü guet das villeuts wenen mag er regier den trakchen das man auff
den der in regiert dester mynner acht hat willdu auch das der trachk sich an

stetten nider lass als ob er zu der erden oder zu den lewten schiess das macht du auch mit dem regimen nach vernufft zuebringen. Nota des geleich nach vernufft möchtest du zuwegen bringen das der trakchen vier oder sechs kleiner und grösser mit einander flugen als ob die iungen mit dem alten flugen und das ainer ob dem ander flug und doch mit ainem vaden oder ainer snuer regiert wurden. Nota nach vorgeschribener weis macht auch du den trakchen zu mal gröss machen das man gross wunder dar ab nympt. Explicit.

REGIOMONTANUS (See page 69)

Ramus, P., *Scholarum mathematicarum libri unus et triginta*, Basileae, 1569, lib. II, p. 65.

At inter artificum noribergensium Regiomontani mathematis eruditorum delitias est, muscam ferream ex artificis manu velut egressam convivas circumvolitare, tandemque veluti defessam in domini manum reverti: Aquilam ex urbe adventanti imperatori longissimé obviam sublimi aëre procedere, atque adventantem ad urbis portam comitari. Desinamus itaque Archytæ columbam mirari, cum muscam, cum aquilam geometricis alis alatam Noriberga exhibeat.

KITE IN MUNICH, 1530 (See pages 70-1)

Ain kurtze anzaygung . . . [Munich,] 1530, [A4ʳ].

Als die ding wie angezaigt begangen, haben sich jr baide Maie. nach der Statt vnd einzug gewendt, vnd mittelwegs ist ain fliegender Tracke in den lüfften vast wercklich zugericht gewest, der hat inn der höhe also lange geschwebet, biss der zug fürüber kommen.

LEONARDO'S WAX ANIMALS (See pages 72, 137)

Vasari, G., *Le Vite*, Firenze, 1550, p. 573.

Andò a Roma col Duca Giuliano de Medici nella creazione di Papa Leone, che attendeua molto a cose Filosofiche, & massimamente alla alchimia, doue formando vna pasta di vna cera, mentre che' caminaua faceua animali sottilissimi pieni di vento, ne i quali soffiando, gli faceua volare per l'aria: ma cessando il vento, cadeuano in terra.

DELLA PORTA'S KITE (See pages 73-4)

Magiae naturalis . . . libri iiii, Neapoli, 1558, pp. 69-70.

Draco volans,

Vel Cometæ sydus dicitur, cuius talis sit constructio: E subtilioribus arundinum paxillis quadrangulum constituatur, vt longitudo latitudini hemioliæ sit proportionis, diametri duo & ex oppositis partibus, vel angulis immittantur, quarum intersecatione funiculus illigetur, & eiusdem quantitatis, cum duobus aliis iungatur, e capitibus machinæ prouenientibus: sic papyro, vel subtili lino obtegatur, ne quod graue in ea sit: inde è turris, montis, vel altioris loci fastigio, æqualibus, & vniformibus ventis credenda, non validis ne disrumpatur machina, nec leuibus: si vndique silebit aura, nam eam non sublimat, ventorum'que segnities irritum faciat laborem, ipsa recto non incedat tramite, sed obliquè, quod efficit funis tractus è capite vno, ex altero longa cauda, quam è restibus effinges æquidistantibus, & papyris passim religatis, sic leui tractu immissa, artificis manibus committenda, qui nec segniter, nec oscitanter, sed validè impellat: & sic volitans carbasus aera petit, vbi paululum fuerit eleuatum (hic enim ex domorum anfractu disruptus est ventus) vt vix manibus compesci, vel retineri queat. Laternam aliqui supra locant, vt cometa videatur. Sclopum alii charta, & pyrio puluere inuolutum, & cum in aere quiescit, immittitur per restim accensus funiculus, anulo, vel lubrico aliquo, statim'que velum petens, ignem ori admouet, maximo'que tonitru, in plures machina dissilit partes, & ad terram procumbit. Aelurum aliqui, vel catulum ligant, ac per aera immissas auscultant voces. Hinc auspicari poterit ingeniosus principia, quonam pacto, & homo volare possit, ingentibus alis cubito, & pectori deligatis, eas autem à pueritia paulatim iactare assuescat, loco semper sublimiori. Quod si quispiam id mirum putauerit, aspiciat ea, quæ Archytam Pythagoricum commentum esse, atque fecisse traditur: plærique enim nobilium græcorum, & Fauorinus Philosophus memoriarum veterum exequentissimus, affirmatissimè scripserunt, simulachrum columbæ è ligno ab Archyta ratione quadam disciplina'que mechanica factum volasse, ita erat scilicet libramentis suspensum, & aura spiritus inclusa, atque occulta concitum.

MECHANICAL BIRDS (See pages 50–2, 81–2)

Cardano, G., *De rerum varietate libri xvii*, Basileae, 1557, p. 440.

> quæri enim solet an columbam ligneam, qualem Architam Tarentinum ex Gellio alibi narrauimus fabricasse, facere liceat? scilicet quæ sponte uolet, ubi tamen quieuerit, immota maneat? Nam imagines statuasque ambulantes super mensam, rotarum abditarum ui, aliquoties uidimus. Volantem etiam auem, sed funi insitam: per se, nondum. Ergo que se sponte eleuet, uix fieri potest: quoniam firma oportet esse uincula, quæ moueant: atque ideo grauiora, quàm ut agi proprijs possint uiribus. mota uerò ab initio & impulsa & maximè uento flante secundo, ob alarum magnitudinem & uim rotarum quæ illas agat, nihil prohibet. Conueniat igitur leuitas corporis, alarum magnitudo, & robur rotarum, atque uenti auxilium: quod & anseres & grauiores aues non negligunt, ut columba euolet certo ordine, incerto autem ignis ui, quemadmodum & lampades. Sic enim & sponte se eleuabit & alas mouebit, sed statim desinet, quoniam ignis non manet: & materiam citra pondus, suppeditare non licet.

Scaliger, J. C., *Exotericarum exercitationum liber*, Lutetiae, 1557, f. 444^v.

> Quid enim non sordeat nobis, præ uolandi arte? At quamobrem artem de motu perpetuo non commemorasti? Sola nanque deerat, ad tam insignem cumulum, insania hæc. Volantis tamen columbæ machinulam, cuius autorem Architam tradunt, uel facillimè profiteri audeo. Nauiculam sponte mobilem, ac sui remigij autorem faciam, nullo negotio. Eadem ratio cum uolante auicula. Materia ex iunci medulla parabilis, uesiculis amicta, aut pelliculis, quibus auri bracteatores, atque foliatores (sic enim libet nunc) utuntur, neruulis obuoluta: ubi semicirculus rotam unam impulerit, motum præstabit aliarum, quibus alæ agitabuntur.

Lauretus Laurus, quoted by G. Schott, *Magia universalis*, Herbipoli, 1657–9, vol. 3, pp. 271–2.

> Ovorum gallinaceorum cortices, matutino rore repleti, & bene occlusi, si Solis radijs exponantur, arcanis modis attolluntur in sublime, & extasim aliquamdiu patiuntur. Quid si majorum olorum ova, vel folles tenui pelle consuti, replerentur nitro purissimo sulphure, hydrargyro, alijsquam hujus modi, quæ vi caloris

rarefiunt, & exteriùs vestirentur in speciem aliquam columbarum; volatum fortè aliquem simularent. Si ligneam & ponderosam velimus machinam impellere ad volandum, adhibeamus ignem. Si timetur incendium, columba vestiatur asbestino, stannei inserantur tubi, ut innocenter ignis foveatur in sinu. Ad impediendum stridorem, & exspiramentum favillarum, pyrius pulvis auripigmento deliniatur, & butyro imminuatur halinitrum, guttur formetur, ut pro stridere referat gemitum columbarum, ut in tauro olim infaustè nimiùm docuit Perillus. Ita addere aliquid possumus, quod in Architæ opere videbatur defuisse, quòd scilicet columba non exurgeret, cùm resedisset: conjungi enim facilè possent tubi, ut alter post alterum accenderetur, & intervalla interponerentur pro arbitratu, ut viva omnino columba videretur.

ROMAN BIRD MEN (See page 89)

Sabellicus, *Exemplorum*, Argentoraci, 1509, f. 98[r].

Romæ sub Cæsaribus inter spectacula populo exhibita productus est, qui per aduersum parietem felis modo reptando scanderet, & qui fabrefactis sibi alis altiuscule a terra volans per aerem auis modo veheretur.

EILMER (See page 92)

William of Malmesbury, *De gestis regum*, lib. II, para. 225.

Is erat litteris, quantum ad id temporis, bene imbutus, ævo maturus, immanem audaciam prima juventute conatus: nam pennas manibus et pedibus haud scio qua innexuerat arte, ut Dædali more volaret, fabulam pro vero amplexus, collectaque e summo turris aura, spatio stadii et plus volavit; sed venti et turbinis violentia, simul et temerarii facti conscientia, tremulus cecidit, perpetuo post hæc debilis, et crura effractus. Ipse ferebat causam ruinæ quod caudam in posteriori parte oblitus fuerit.

BUONCOMPAGNO (See page 94)

Salimbene de Adam, *Cronica*, Bari, 1966, vol. I, pp. 109–10.

. . . iste magister Boncompagnus, videns quod frater Iohannes intromittebat se de miraculis faciendis, voluit et ipse se intromittere et predixit Bononiensibus quod, videntibus eis, volare volebat. Quid plura? Divulgatum est per Bononiam. Venit dies statuta, congregata est tota civitas, *a viro usque ad mulierem, a puero usque ad senem*, ad radicem montis qui appellatur Sancta Maria in Monte. Fecerat sibi duas alas et stabat in cacumine montis aspiciens eos. Cumque se diu mutuo aspexissent, protulit istud verbum: 'Ite cum benedictione divina, et sufficiat vobis vidisse faciem Boncompagni.' Et recesserunt cognoscentes se derisos.

DANTI (See pages 95–6)

Alessi, C., *Elogia civivm pervsinorvm . . . centvria secvnda*, Romae, 1652, pp. 204–7.

Admirari iam libet Ioannem Baptistam Dantium Perusinæ Vrbis Dædalum, qui cum Mathematicis studijs plurimum insudasset, præexcellentis ingenij acumine, preter multa de suo in ea facultate inuenta, Alarum remigium debita corpori suo proportione aptauerat, illoque ad benè volandum concinnato, eius periculum non semel in Transimeno lacu fecerat: cumque voluntati suæ optimè responderet. De hoc etiam publicè experiri Perusiæ constituit; atque cum in hanc Vrbem magnus summorum Virorum Cœtus ad solemnes Ioannis Pauli Balionis Sororis Nuptias conuenisset, quæ Bartholomæo Aluiano strenuissimo Duci nuptui tradebatur, & frequens Populus ad hasti ludium in magnam Plateam conuenisset, eccè sibi repentè ex altiori nostræ Ciuitatis parte ingenti sibilo per aera volantem Dantium pinnis varijs inuolutum, magnoque alarum remigio supra Plateam transeuntem, tanto omnium stupore, atque non nullorum etiam timore, vt Monstrum aliquod magnum, ac portentosum videre crederent: At ille sui sublimitatem ingenij, dum humili solo relicto, membris etiam in aerem sublimem elatis assequi contendit, fortuna tanto ausu indignata, ferrum, quo sinistra Ala regebatur inuida perfregit, & Dantius alterius Alæ auxilio corporis molem sustinere non valens, supra Sanctæ Mariæ tecta prouolutus cecidit, & magnoque sui, omniumque dolore crus offendit: Hunc postea valetudine confirmatum, Ioan. Paulus Balionus, vt Mathematicum insignem cum honore, ac stipendio magno Venetias secum adduxit, vbi digito ab omnibus, vt quondam Demostthenes [sic], indicabatur, proque Viro admirabili suspiciebatur ab omnibus, qui ingenij acumine homines quoque volare posse docuisset; at non dum quadragenarius dira febri correptus meritorum suorum pennis tutius, quam mentitis viuens alis ad Cælestia, vt sperare licet volauit an. MDXVII. *De eo habetur in antiquis manuscriptis.*

JOHN DAMIAN (See page 97)

The following is from the later, Latin version of Lesley's book (Romae, 1578, p. 346).

Is, affixis vtrique lateri alis (quas ex plumis diuersarum auium conficiendas sibi curauerat) ex altis mœnibus arcis Striuelingensis sese in aera, tanquam in viam, dedit. Sed ecce tibi impostorem in terram subito casu præcipitatum, qui astabant, incerti vtrum hominis amentiam insectarentur, an potius illius doloris commiseratione tangerentur, concurrunt: Abbatem iam tùm alatum percunctantur, qui ualeret.

NÜRNBERG CANTOR (See page 99)

Burggravius, J. E., *Achilles*, Amsterodami, [1612], p. 52.

Senecio quidam *Noribergæ* præcentor erat, qui alarum geminarum præsidio vel remigio elatus in aëre, instar alitis, vagabatur: & prapetis instar rursus devolabat, etsi casu denique ex imprudentia commisso (quo rotulæ, nescio quæ, alis affixæ, volatumque concitantes, vel implicatæ, vel non rite applicatæ & præpeditæ;) præcipitatus brachia & crura diffringeret. Cui simile quid *Lutetiæ* Gallorum dicitur contigisse patrum memoriâ.

THE ITALIAN ON THE TOUR DE NESLES (See pages 99–101)

Lou banquet d'Augié Gailliard, Paris, 1584, f. 17^{r-v}.

> . . . *Coumun Icarus fec, quant coumo vno pasero*
> *Voulguec passa la mar an sas allos de cero:*
> *Et quant voulec trop naut, lou soulel li fondec*
> *Las allos qu'el abio, peis dins la mar toumbec:*
> *Que me fa soubeni d'vno autro grand fadeso,*
> *Qu'vn gran sot Italien abio aital entrepreso,*
> *(De fadeso iamai degus nou ne gueris)*
> *Dos allos se fec fa de telo dins Paris,*
> *Epeissos el mountec de sus la tour Denelo,*
> *Disen quel voullario coumo vno tourtourelo*
> *Que cinq cens milo gens o may fec amounta.*

Quant passa la ribieiro el sanabo vanta,
Et prenguec la voulado an sas allos de telo,
Et toumbec coumo vn porc pres de la tour Denelo,
Que se penssec trinqua, so m'a lon dih lou col.

WINGED TIGHTROPE WALKERS (See page 100)

Boaistuau, P., *Bref discovrs de l'excellence et dignité de l'homme*, Paris, 1558. f. 20ʳ.

Que reste donc plus à l'homme que l'air, qu'il ne penetre par tous les elemens, & qui ne se rende familier d'iceux? encores se trouue il vn Leonard Vincius lequel a cherche l'art de voler & a presque sorty heureusement son effaict, sans mettre en compté ces histrions que nous auons veu de nostre temps voler sur la corde en l'air auec telle dexterité & peril, que les yeux mesmes des princes & grands seigneurs qui les regardoient ne les pouuans souffrir, en estoient espouuentez.

GUIDOTTI (See page 101)

Baldinucci, F., *Notizie de' professori . . .*, vol. 4, Firenze, 1700, pp. 249–50.

[Among many other stories about Guidotti's achievements was the assertion of] Matteo Boselli Pittore, Uomo degnissimo d' ogni fede, e stato per lungo tempo nella di lui Scuola, che Paolo si messe una volta in testa questo concetto, che e' potesse trovarsi il modo di volare, e con grand' artifizio, e fatica compose d' osso di Balena alcune ali, coprendole di penne, dando loro la piegatura mediante alcune molle, che egli si congegnava addosso sotto le braccia, acciocche anche fussero d' ajuto a lui, per alzar l'ali medesime, nell' atto del volo, e che dopo essersi molte, e molte volte provato, finalmente s' espose al cimento, spiccandosi da luogo eminente, e che coll' ajuto delle medesime si portò avanti per la quarta parte d' un miglio in circa, non volando, secondo me, ma cadendo più adagio di quello, che senza l' ali egli averebbe fatto, perche io tengo ferma opinione, e ne ho ragioni, e mie e d' altri molto sode, che tal' Arte per verun modo possa trovarsi per altr' uso, che per discostarsi alquanto da un tal posto, cadendo sempre al basso, ma con maggiore intervallo di tempo, che altri precipitandosi non farebbe. Così dunque fece il Guidotti, il quale stanco finalmente dal faticoso muovere delle braccia, cadde sopra d' un Tetto, il quale si roppe, ed esso per l' apertura si trovò nella Stanza di sotto, spiccando dal suo volo la rottura d' una Coscia, che lo condusse a mal partito.

Lo stesso Boselli pure affermava, d' aver veduto con gli occhi propri i frammenti di quell' arredo, e l' ali stesse, di che si servì il Maestro.

S. AGOBARD'S FLYING SHIPS (See page 105)

Saint Agobard, *Contra insulsam vulgi opinionem de grandine et tonitruis*, II.

Plerosque autem vidimus et audivimus tanta dementia obrutos, tanta stultitia alienatos, ut credant et dicant quamdam esse regionem, quæ dicatur Magonia, ex qua naves veniant in nubibus, in quibus fruges, quæ grandinibus decidunt, et tempestatibus pereunt, vehantur in eamdem regionem, ipsis videlicet nautis aereis dantibus pretia Tempestariis, et accipientibus frumenta vel cæteras fruges. Ex his item tam profunda stultitia excæcatis, ut hæc posse fieri credant, vidimus plures in quodam conventu hominum exhibere vinctos quatuor homines, tres viros, et unam feminam, quasi qui de ipsis navibus ceciderint: quos scilicet per aliquot dies in vinculis detentos, tandem collecto conventu hominum exhibuerunt, ut dixi, in nostra præsentia, tanquam lapidandos.

THE FLYING SHIP IN ENGLAND (See page 105)

Geoffroi de Vigeois, *Chronica*, Paris, 1657, vol. 2, pp. 299–300.

Nauis sursum, in aëre, velut nauta (natans) in æquore visa est in Anglia, iactâ anchorâ vrbis in medio à ciuibus Londoniarum impeditur. Mittitur à nautis quidam, qui solueret anchoram, sed retentus à pluribus, qui mersus aquis exspirauit. Clamantes nautæ aëra denuò sulcant, fune anchoræ secto.

NAVIGATING THE AIR (See pages 105–6)

Albert of Saxony, *Questiones . . . in octo libros Physicorum Aristotelis*, Parisiis, 1516, IV.vi.2.3.

ignis multo subtilior et rarior et leuior est aere: patet hoc: nam sicut se videtur habere ad aerem: sic aer se habet ad aquam: modo aer est multo rarior et multo subtilior & leuior quam sit aqua: ergo sic est de igne respectu aeris. ergo. Ex hoc sequitur vt posset diffusius ostendi ex scientia de ponderibus: quod aer supra vbi est contiguus igni est nauigabilis sicut aqua vbi est contigua aeri: vnde si nauis esset supra aerem interim quod non repleretur aere sed igne non submergeretur in aere: sed quamcito esset repleta aere submergeretur in aere: sicut in aqua interim quod nauis esset repleta aere & non aqua nataret et non mergeretur: sed quando est repleta aqua tunc submergitur.

ROGER BACON (See page 106)

De mirabili potestate artis et naturae, Paris, 1542, f. 42^{r-v} (written *ca.* 1250).

possunt fieri instrumenta volandi, vt homo sedens in medio instrumenti reuoluens aliquod ingenium, per quod alæ artificialiter compositæ aërem verberent, ad modum auis volantis.

... certum est quòd sit instrumentum volandi, quod non vidi, nec hominem qui vidisset cognoui, sed sapientem qui hoc artificium excogitauit explicite cognosco.

THE WINDMILL LIFT (See page 118)

Bellifortis, Göttingen, codex philos. 63, f. 134^r.

> *Ventilabrum ligneum formetur modum in istum*
> *Medio sit capsa in qua sedeat homo sursum*
> *Funem trahens euolat sed retrahens est in descensu*
> *Quidam duas rotas faciunt tamen inferiores*
> *Sed id securius firmiusque velocius ibit.*

Appendix D

Dunbar's two poems on Damian are the most substantial literary works in English to have been inspired in part by early aeronautical experiments. They are here quoted from W. Mackay Mackenzie's edition, London, 1970, pp. 67-71.

THE FENYEIT FREIR OF TUNGLAND

As yung Awrora, with cristall haile,
In orient schew hir visage paile,
A swevyng swyth did me assaile,
  Off sonis of Sathanis seid;
Me thocht a Turk of Tartary
Come throw the boundis of Barbary,
And lay forloppin in Lumbardy
  Full lang in waithman weid.
Fra baptasing for to eschew,
Thair a religious man he slew,
And cled him in his abeit new,
  For he cowth wryte and reid.
Quhen kend was his dissimulance,
And all his cursit govirnance,
For feir he fled and come in France,
  With littill of Lumbard leid.
To be a leiche he fenyt him thair,
Quhilk mony a man micht rew evirmair,
For he left nowthir seik nor sair
  Unslane, or he hyne yeid.

Vane organis he full clenely carvit,
Quhen of his straik so mony starvit,
Dreid he had gottin that he desarvit,
    He fled away gud speid.

In Scotland than the narrest way
He come, his cunnyng till assay;
To sum man thair it was no play
    The preving of his sciens.
In pottingry he wrocht grit pyne,
He murdreist mony in medecyne;
The jow was of a grit engyne,
    And generit was of gyans
In leichecraft he was homecyd;
He wald haif, for a nicht to byd,
A haiknay and the hurt manis hyd,
    So meikle he was of myance.
His irnis was rude as ony rawchtir,
Quhair he leit blude it was no lawchtir,
Full mony instrument for slawchtir
    Was in his gardevyance.

He cowth gif cure for laxatyve,
To gar a wicht hors want his lyve,
Quha evir assay wald, man or wyve,
    Thair hippis yeid hiddy giddy.
His practikis nevir war put to preif
But suddane deid, or grit mischeif;
He had purgatioun to mak a theif
    To dee withowt a widdy.
Unto no mes pressit this prelat,
For sound of sacring bell nor skellat;
As blaksmyth bruikit was his pallatt
    For battering at the study.

Thocht he come hame a new maid channoun,
He had dispensit with matynnis cannoun,
On him come nowther stole nor fannoun
   For smowking of the smydy.

Me thocht seir fassonis he assailyeit,
To mak the quintessance, and failyeit;
And quhen he saw that nocht availyeit,
   A fedrem on he tuke,
And schupe in Turky for to fle;
And quhen that he did mont on he,
All fowill ferleit quhat he sowld be,
   That evir did on him luke.
Sum held he had bene Dedalus,
Sum the Menatair marvelus,
Sum Martis blaksmyth Vulcanus,
   And sum Saturnus kuke.
And evir the cuschettis at him tuggit,
The rukis him rent, the ravynis him druggit,
The hudit crawis his hair furth ruggit,
   The hevin he micht not bruke.

The myttane, and Sanct Martynis fowle,
Wend he had bene the hornit howle,
Thay set aupone him with a yowle,
   And gaif him dynt for dynt.
The golk, the gormaw, and the gled,
Beft him with buffettis quhill he bled;
The sparhalk to the spring him sped,
   Als fers as fyre of flynt.
The tarsall gaif him tug for tug,
A stanchell hang in ilka lug,
The pyot furth his pennis did rug,
   The stork straik ay but stynt.

The bissart, bissy but rebuik,
Scho was so cleverus of hir cluik,
His bawis he micht not langer bruik,
   Scho held thame at ane hint.

Thik was the clud of kayis and crawis,
Of marleyonis, mittanis, and of mawis,
That bikkrit at his berd with blawis
   In battell him abowt.
Thay nybbillit him with noyis and cry,
The rerd of thame rais to the sky,
And evir he cryit on Fortoun, Fy!
   His lyfe was in to dowt.
The ja him skrippit with a skryke,
And skornit him as it was lyk;
The egill strong at him did stryke,
   And rawcht him mony a rowt.
For feir uncunnandly he cawkit,
Quhill all his pennis war drownd and drawkit,
He maid a hundreth nolt all hawkit
   Beneth him with a spowt.

He schewre his feddreme that was schene,
And slippit owt of it full clene,
And in a myre, up to the ene,
   Amang the glar did glyd.
The fowlis all at the fedrem dang,
As at a monster thame amang,
Quhill all the pennis of it owsprang
   In till the air full wyde.

And he lay at the plunge evirmair,
So lang as any ravin did rair;
The crawis him socht with cryis of cair
   In every schaw besyde.

Had he reveild bene to the ruikis,
Thay had him revin all with thair cluikis:
Thre dayis in dub amang the dukis
   He did with dirt him hyde.
The air was dirkit with the fowlis,
That come with yawmeris and with yowlis,
With skryking, skrymming, and with scowlis,
   To tak him in the tyde.
I walknit with the noyis and schowte,
So hiddowis beir was me abowte;
Sensyne I curs that cankerit rowte,
   Quhair evir I go or ryde.

THE BIRTH OF ANTICHRIST

Lucina schynnyng in silence of the nicht,
The hevin being all full of sternis bricht,
To bed I went, bot thair I tuke no rest,
With havy thocht I wes so soir opprest,
That sair I langit eftir dayis licht.

Off Fortoun I complenit hevely,
That scho to me stude so contrariowsly;
And at the last, quhen I had turnyt oft,
For weirines on me ane slummer soft
Come with ane dremyng and a fantesy.

Me thocht Deme Fortoun with ane fremmit cheir
Stude me beforne and said on this maneir,
Thow suffer me to wirk gif thow do weill,
And preis the nocht to stryfe aganis my quheill,
Quhilk every warldly thing dois turne and steir.

Full mony ane man I turne unto the hicht,
And makis als mony full law to doun licht;
Up on my staigis or that thow ascend,
Trest weill thy truble neir is at ane end,
Seing thir taikinis, quhairfoir thow mark thame rycht.

Thy trublit gaist sall neir moir be degest,
Nor thow in to no benifice beis possest,
Quhill that ane abbot him cleith in ernis pennis,
And fle up in the air amangis the crennis,
And as ane falcone fair fro eist to west.

He sall ascend as ane horrebble grephoun,
Him meit sall in the air ane scho dragoun;
Thir terrible monsteris sall togidder thrist,
And in the cludis gett the Antechrist,
Quhill all the air infeck of thair pusoun.

Under Saturnus fyrie regioun
Symone Magus sall meit him, and Mahoun,
And Merlyne at the mone sall him be bydand,
And Jonet the weido on ane bussome rydand,
Off wichis with ane windir garesoun.

And syne thay sall discend with reik and fyre,
And preiche in erth the Antechrystis impyre,
Be than it salbe neir this warldis end.
With that this lady sone fra me did wend;
Sleipand and walkand wes frustrat my desyre.

Quhen I awoik, my dreme it was so nyce,
Fra every wicht I hid it as a vyce;
Quhill I hard tell be mony suthfast wy,
Fle wald ane abbot up in to the sky,
And all his fethreme maid wes at devyce.

Within my hairt confort I tuke full sone;
'Adew,' quod I, 'My drery dayis ar done;
Full weill I wist to me wald nevir cum thrift,
Quhill that twa monis wer sene up in the lift,
Or quhill ane abbot flew aboif the mone.'

Bibliography

The nature of the material is such that no form of classification, even into primary and secondary sources, is entirely satisfactory. I have therefore divided the bibliography into three main parts only: A, manuscripts, i, Kyeser, ii, other; B, printed material written before 1600; C, printed material written after 1600. I have not thought it necessary to cite the original Leonardo manuscripts, the well-known facsimiles and transcriptions of which are listed in Section B. Where it has seemed useful to do so, I have included brief explanatory comments in parentheses after items.

A: MANUSCRIPTS

i: Kyeser

Chantilly
    Musée Condé. MS XX.C.14, f. 135^r. (Early fifteenth century.)

Colmar
    Bibliothèque de la ville de Colmar. MS 491, f. 72^r. (Late fifteenth century. Text only; illustration lost owing to mutilation.)

Cologne
    Historisches Archiv. Codex W fo. 232X, f. 79^r. (Fifteenth century.)

Donaueschingen
    Fürstliche Fürstenbergische Hofbibliothek. Codex 860, f. 117^r. (Mid fifteenth century. Windmill operated bells.)

Erlangen
    Universitätsbibliothek. MS 1390, f. 169^v. (Ludwig v. Eyb zum Hartenstein, Kriegsbuch. 1500. Kyeser *draco*.)

Göttingen

Niedersächsische Staats- und Universitätsbibliothek. Codex philos. 63, ff. 104^v, 105^r. (1405.) Codex philos. 64, ff. 92^r, 134^r. (Early fifteenth century. *Draco*; rotary air-brakes.)

Facsimile of Codex philos. 63, edited with introduction, transcription, translation, and commentary, by G. Quarg: *Conrad Kyeser aus Eichstätt: Bellifortis.* 2 vols. Düsseldorf, 1967.

Innsbruck

Museum Ferdinandeum. Codex 16.0.7, f. 103^r. (Early fifteenth century.)

Karlsruhe

Badische Landesbibliothek. Codex Durlach II, f. 119^r. (*Ca.* 1410?)

Strasbourg

Bibliothèque nationale. MS 2259, f. 27^r. (Fifteenth century.)

Vienna

Österreichische Nationalbibliothek. Codex 3062, ff. 127^v, 128^r. (Fifteenth century.) Codex 3068, f. 88^r. (Fifteenth century.) Codex 5278, ff. 144^v, 145^r, 173^r. (1428. *Draco*; horizontally shafted windmill.)

Weimar

Thüringische Landesbibliothek. Codex fol. 328, f. 218^v. (*Ca.* 1430.)

ii: *Other Manuscripts*

Arras

Bibliothèque municipale. MS 657 (139), f. 89^r. ('Chansonnier d'Arras'. Probably Arras. Late thirteenth century. Man with bat wings.) MS 1043, f. 7^r. (Compilation d'anciennes histoires. Arras. Late thirteenth century. Grotesques with bat wings.)

Musée Diocésain. MS 47, f. 31^r. (Psalter and Hours, Saint-Omer calendar. North French. Early fourteenth century. Man with bat wings.)

Baltimore

Walters Art Gallery. MS 82, f. 207^r. (Psalter and Hours. Flemish. Early fourteenth century. Ape with toy windmill.)

Berlin

Staatsbibliothek der Stiftung Preussischer Kulturbesitz. Hs. germ. fol. 94, f. 198^r. (Johann von Nassau. Rüst- und Feuerwerksbuch. *Ca.* 1540. Rocket-dragon.)

Bologna

Biblioteca Universitaria. MS 2705, ff. 95^v–104^v. (Giovanni da Fontana. *Metrologum de pisce cane et volucre. Ca.* 1420?)

Copenhagen

Det Kongelige Bibliotek. MS 3384.8°, f. 27^r. (Psalter. Flemish. First quarter of the fourteenth century. String-pull helicopter?)

Florence

Biblioteca Nazionale Centrale. MS Palat. 766, f. 37^r. (Taccola. Notebook. 1432/3. Vertically shafted windmill.)

Frankfurt am Main

Stadt- und Universitätsbibliothek. MS II, 40, f. 104^r. (Rüst- und Feuerwerksbuch. German. *Ca.* 1490. Rocket-dragon.)

London, British Museum

Birch 4459, f. 11^r, item 3. (Notesheets. Seventeenth century. Worcester's mechanical bird.)

Royal 2.B.VII, f. 163^v. ('Queen Mary's Psalter'. English. First quarter of the fourteenth century. Men with flying insects attached to threads.)

Sloane 2156, ff. 83^v, 112^v–113^r. (Fifteenth century. Roger Bacon.)

Additional 34113, ff. 189^v, 200^r. (Italian. Late fifteenth century. Siennese parachutes.)

Stowe 17, f. 89^v. (Hours. ?Maastricht. *Ca.* 1300. Windmill.)

London, Wellcome Historical Medical Library

MS 272, ff. 123^v–124^v. (Fireworks book. South German. 1584. Bird carrying a fire bomb.)

MS 763, f. 5^v. (Johann Staricius. *The Newly Reformed Warriours-treasure.* English. *Ca.* 1650. Translation of *Ernewerter und Künstlicher HeldenSchatz*, n.p., 1616, Biii^r–^{v}. Nürnberg Cantor.)

Munich

Bayerische Staatsbibliothek. Codex icon. 242, ff. 37^r, 63^v. (Giovanni da Fontana. *Bellicorum instrumentorum liber. Ca.* 1440. Title of comparatively recent date. Rocket bird; automaton.) Codex lat. 197, ff. 74^v, 87^r. (Taccola. Notebook. *Ca.* 1438. Toy helicopter; vertically shafted windmill.)

New York

Pierpont Morgan Library. MS 102, f. 2^r. ('Windmill Psalter'. East Anglian. Late thirteenth century. Horizontally shafted windmill.)

Oxford

Bodley MS 264, f. 80^v. (*The Romance of Alexander*. Flemish. *Ca.* 1340. Alexander's flight.)

Bodley MS 266, ff. 32^v–35^r. (Michael Scot. *Liber introductorius*. Fifteenth century. Seven regions of the air.)

Christ Church MS 92, ff. 77^v–78^r. (Walter de Milemete. *De nobilitatibus sapientiis et prudentiis regum*. 1326/7. Pennon kite. Facsimile edition by M. R. James, London, 1913, pp. 154–5.)

Paris

Bibliothèque nationale. MS 1104, f. 22^v. (Villard de Honnecourt. Album. *Ca.* 1235. Eagle automaton. Facsimile edition by H. R. Hahnloser, Wien, 1935, pp. 137–8 and Plate 44.)

St Gallen

Stiftsbibliothek. Codex 22, p. 140. (*Psalterium aureum*. Ninth century. *Draco* standard. See also J. R. Rahn, *Das Psalterium aureum von Sanct Gallen*, St Gallen, 1878, p. 33 and Plate X.)

Turin

Biblioteca Reale. MS Mil. 238, ff. 43^v, 45^r. (Francesco di Giorgio. *Trattura di Architettura*. Sixteenth century. Vertically shafted windmills.)

Valenciennes

Bibliothèque municipale. MS 838, f. 55^r. (Calendrier-obituaire. French. Late thirteenth century. Windmill.)

Vienna

Österreichische Nationalbibliothek. Codex 3064, ff. 4^v–7^r; 21^{r-v}. (Büchsenbuch. South German. *Ca.* 1430. Pennon kite; rocket bird.)

B: PRINTED MATERIAL WRITTEN BEFORE 1600

Agobard, Saint. *Contra insulsam vulgi opinionem de grandine et tonitruis*, II. (J. P. Migne, *Patrologiæ cursus completus*, Series Lat., vol. 104, Parisiis, 1851, col. 148.)

Ain kurtze anzaygung und beschreybung Römischer Kayserlicher Maiestat einreyten, Erstlich von Innspruck gen Schwatz, volgendt zu München, und zuletst gen Augspurg auf den Reychstag, und was sich mittler zeyt daselbst täglich verlauffen unnd zugetragen hatt. [Munich,] 1530, [A4^r].

Albert of Saxony. *Questiones subtilissime Alberti de Saxonia in libros de celo & mundo.* Venetijs, 1492.

——. *Questiones eximij Doctoris magistri Alberti de Saxonia in octo libros Physicorum Aristotelis*, IV.vi.2.3. First printed Padua, 1493: Hain, 578. Edition used: *Quæstiones & decisiones physicales insignium virorum*, Parisiis, 1516, f. 47ʳ.

Albert Magnus. *De celo & mundo.* Venetijs, 1495.

——. [?] *De mirabilibvs mvndi.* [Venice, 1472?] f. 26ᵛ. (Magical fire birds.)

——. [?] *De motibvs animalivm*, II.iii: 'De motu volantium & natantium'. Edition used: *Opera quæ hactenus haberi potuerunt.* 21 vols. Lugduni, 1651. Vol. 5, p. 129.

Aldrovandus, U. *Ornithologiae hoc est de avibus historiae libri xii*, vol. 1. Bononiae, 1599, p. 695.

Ambrose, Saint. *Hexaemeron*, V.xiv.45; V.xxiv. 87. (J. P. Migne, *Patrologiæ cursus completus*, Series Lat., vol. 14, Parisiis, 1845, cols. 225–6, 240.)

Ammianus Marcellinus. *Rerum gestarum libri qui supersunt*, XVI.10.7. (*Ammianus Marcellinus.* Ed. and trans. by J. C. Rolfe. Vol. 1, London and Cambridge, Mass., 1963, pp. 244, 245. Loeb Classical Library.)

Aristotle. *The Physics.* 2 vols. Ed. and trans. by P. W. Wicksteed and F. M. Cornford. Rev. edn. London and Cambridge, Mass., 1957, 1960. (Loeb Classical Library.)

——. *On the Heavens.* Ed. and trans. by W. K. C. Guthrie. London and Cambridge, Mass., 1960. (Loeb Classical Library.)

——. *Meteorologica.* Ed. and trans. by H. D. P. Lee. London and Cambridge, Mass., 1962. (Loeb Classical Library.)

——. *Movement of Animals. Progression of Animals.* Ed. and trans. by E. S. Forster. London and Cambridge, Mass., 1961. (Loeb Classical Library.)

Arrian. *Tactics*, 35.2 ff. (*Flavii Arriani Qvae Exstant Omnia.* 2 vols. Ed. A. G. Roos. Lipsiae, 1967–8. Vol. 2, p. 167.)

Augustine, Saint. *De Genesi, liber imperfectus*, XIV.44. (J. P. Migne, *Patrologiæ cursus completus*, Series Lat., vol. 34, Parisiis, 1845, cols. 237–8.)

——. *De Genesi contra Manichæos*, I.15. (J. P. Migne, *Patrologiæ cursus completus*, Series Lat., vol. 34, Parisiis, 1845, col. 184.)

——. *Soliloquiorum libri duo*, II.xi.20. (J. P. Migne, *Patrologiæ cursus completus*, Series Lat., vol. 32, Parisiis, 1845, col. 894. Daedalus.)

——. *De Trinitate libri quindecim*, III.ix.18. (J. P. Migne, *Patrologiæ cursus completus*, Series Lat., vol. 42, Parisiis, 1845, col. 879. Possibility and legitimacy of flight.)

Aulus Gellius. *Noctium atticarum libri xx*, X.12.8–10. (*The Attic Nights of Aulus Gellius*. Ed. and trans. by J. C. Rolfe. Vol. 2, London and New York, 1927, pp. 244, 245. Loeb Classical Library.)

Bacon, R. *De mirabili potestate artis et naturae*. Lutetiae Parisiorum, 1542, f. 42^{r-v}. (Translation published as *Frier Bacon, his Discovery of the Miracles of Art, Nature, and Magick. Faithfully translated out of Dr. Dees own copy, by T. M. and never before in English*, London, 1659, pp. 17–19.)

Bartholomaeus Anglicus. *De proprietatibus rerum*. [Cologne, 1472?], f. c^{v}.

Basil, Saint. *Homilia VIII in Hexaemeron*, 2. (J. P. Migne, *Patrologiæ cursus completus*, Series Gr., vol. 29, Parisiis, 1857, col. 169.)

Belon, P. *L'Histoire de la nature des oyseaux auec leurs descriptions, & naïfs portraits retirez du naturel*. Paris, 1555.

Besson, J. *Théâtre des instrumens mathématiques et méchaniques*. Lyon, 1578, plate 50. (Written before 1569.)

Boaistuau, P. *Bref discovrs de l'excellence et dignité de l'homme*. Paris, 1558, f. 20^{r}. (Appended to *Le Theatre dv monde*, Paris, 1558.)

Bourne, W. *Inuentions or Deuises. Very necessary for all Generalles and Captaines, or Leaders of men, as wel by Sea as by Land*. London, [1578,] pp. 98–9.

Cardano, G. *De subtilitate libri xxi*. Norimbergae, 1550, pp. 314, 318.

——. *De rerum varietate libri xvii*. Basileae, 1557, p. 440.

Cassiodorus, Flavius Magnus Aurelius. *Epistola* xlv. (J. P. Migne, *Patrologiæ cursus completus*, Series Lat., vol. 69, Parisiis, 1848, col. 540.)

Cellini, B. *Vita*, I.xxiii. (Trans. by R. H. H. Cust as *The Life of Benvenuto Cellini*. 2 vols. London, 1910. Vol. 2, pp. 20–2.)

Curione, C. A. *Sarracenicae historiae libri III*. Basileae, 1567, p. 127.

Dio Chrysostom. *Discourses*, 21.9. (*Dio Chrysostom*. Ed. and trans. by J. W. Cohoon. Vol. 2, London and Cambridge, Mass., 1961, pp. 280, 281. Loeb Classical Library.)

Długosz, J. *Historiae polonicae libri xii*. Lipsiae, 1711–12, col. 679.

Dunbar, W. 'The Fenyeit Freir of Tungland,' and 'The Birth of Antichrist'. *The Poems of William Dunbar*. Ed. W. Mackay Mackenzie. London, 1970, pp. 67–70, 70–1.

Fabyan. [*The Chronicle*.] 1516, f. viii^{r}. (Bladud.)

Favorinus. *Favorin von Arelate, der erste Teil der Fragmente*. Ed. E. Mensching. Berlin, 1963, p. 154.

Favorinus. *Opere*. Ed. A. Barigazzi. Firenze, 1966, pp. 241–2. (Archytas.)

Fenton, E. *Certaine secrete wonders of Nature, containing a description of sundry strange things, seming monstrous* . . . London, 1569, ff. 114ʳ–116ᵛ. (The *apis indica*.)

Frederick II of Hohenstaufen. *De arte venandi cum auibus*. Augustae Vindelicorum, 1596. (Trans. by C. A. Wood and F. M. Fyfe and published as *The Art of Falconry, being the De arte venandi cum avibus of Frederick II of Hohenstaufen*, Stanford University, California and London, 1943.)

Fulke, W. *A Goodly Gallery with a Most Pleasaunt Prospect, into the Garden of Naturall Contemplation, to Beholde the Naturall Causes of All Kind of Meteors*. London, 1571, ff. 10ʳ–11ʳ. (The meteorological *draco volans*.)

Geoffrey of Monmouth. *Britannie utriusque regum et principum origo et gesta insignia*. [Paris,] 1508, f. xiiiʳ. (Bladud.)

Geoffroi de Vigeois (or, du Breuil). *Chronica Gaufredi cœnobitæ*, XL. 1584. (P. Labbe, *Nouæ bibliothecæ manuscript. librorum*, 2 vols., Paris, 1657, vol. 2, pp. 299–300.)

[Godwin, F.] *The Man in the Moone: Or, a Discourse of a Voyage thither*. By Domingo Gonsales. London, 1638. (Written *ca*. 1600.)

Heron of Alexandria. *Heronis Alexandrini opera qvae svpersvnt omnia*. 5 vols. Ed. W. Schmidt. Lipsiae, 1899–1914. Vol. 1, 'Pnevmatica et avtomata,' pp. xxxix–xl, 202–7.

Ibn al-Faḳīh. *Compendium libri Kitâb al-Boldân*. Ed. M. J. de Goeje. Lugduni-Batavorum, 1885. (*Bibliotheca Geographorum Arabicorum*, part 5. Flying architect. Original Arabic text.)

Isidor. *Isidori Hispalensis Episcopi etymologarvm sive originvm libri xx*, XII. vii, viii. Ed. W. M. Lindsay. Oxonii, 1911. ('De avibvs,' 'De minvtis volatilibvs.')

Kalender of Sheepeherds. London, [1560?] Miᵛ. (Meteorological *draco volans*.)

Latini, B. *El tesoro*, I.99, 100. Triviso, 1474. (Elements of air and fire.)

Lees, B. A. (ed.) *Records of the Templars in England in the Twelfth Century: the Inquest of 1185*. London, 1935, p. 131. (First mention of a European windmill.)

Leonardo da Vinci. *Il Codice Atlantico di Leonardo da Vinci* . . . *Trascrizione diplomatica e critica di Giovanni Piumati*. 8 vols. Milano, 1894–1904.

——. *Codice sul Volo degli Uccelli*. Parigi, 1893. (Transcription and translation, ed. by G. Piumati and C. Ravaisson-Mollien.)

——. *I Fogli Mancanti al Codice di Leonardo da Vinci su'l Volo degli Uccelli nella Biblioteca di Torino*. Torino, 1926. (Facsimile and transcription, ed. by E. Carusi.)

——. *I Libri del Volo* . . . *nella Ricostruzione critica di Arturo Uccelli*. Milano, 1952.

Leonardo da Vinci. *Manuscrit B (2173 et 2184) de l'Institut de France. Traduction française de Francis Authier . . . Transcriptions du Dr Ing. Nando de Toni . . . Introduction d'André Corbeau.* 2 vols. Grenoble, 1960. (With facsimile.)

——. *Les manuscrits de Léonard de Vinci . . . Facsimilés . . .* 6 vols. Paris, 1881–91. (The manuscripts of the Institut, and B. N. Ash. 2038, 2037. With transcriptions and French translations, ed. by C. Ravaisson-Mollien.)

——. R. Giacomelli (ed.) *Gli Scritti di Leonardo da Vinci sul Volo.* Roma, 1936.

——. E. MacCurdy (ed. and trans.) *The Notebooks of Leonardo da Vinci Arranged, rendered into English and Introduced.* 2 vols. London, 1938.

Lesley, J. *The Historie of Scotland.* Edinburgh, 1830, p. 76. (Original version, written 1568–70. John Damian.)

——. *De origine moribus, et rebus gestis scotorum libri decem.* Romae, 1578, p. 346. (Latin version.)

——. *The Historie of Scotland.* Trans. Fr. James Dalrymple (1596). Ed. Fr. E. G. Cody and W. Murison. 2 vols. Edinburgh and London, 1888, 1895. Vol. 2, pp. 124–6. (Translation of the Latin version.)

Lestoire de Merlin. Ed. H. O. Sommer. Washington, 1908, pp. 225, etc.

Livingstone, M. (ed.) *The Register of the Privy Seal of Scotland. Vol. I. A.D. 1488–1529.* Edinburgh, 1908, pp. 259–60. (Damian.)

Lucian. *How to Write History*, 29. (*Lucian.* Ed. and trans. by K. Kilburn. Vol. 6, London and Cambridge, Mass., 1959, pp. 42, 43. Loeb Classical Library.)

Lupton, T. *A Thousand Notable things, of sundry sortes. Wherof some are wonderfull, some straunge, some pleasant, diuers necessary, a great sort profitable and many very precious.* London, 1579, pp. 269, 281, 282.

Manasses, C. Συνοφις Ἱστορικη, lines 4798 ff. (J. P. Migne, *Patrologiæ cursus completus*, Series Gr., vol. 127, Parisiis, 1864, col. 400.)

Martial. *On the Spectacles*, VIII. (*Martial: Epigrams.* Ed. and trans. by W. C. A. Ker. Vol. 1, London and New York, 1925, pp. 8, 9. Loeb Classical Library.)

Nicetas Choniates. *Nicetae Acominati Choniatae LXXXVI annorum historia . . .* Basileae, 1557, p. 60.

Paul, Sir J. B. (ed.) *Accounts of the Lord High Treasurer of Scotland. Vol. IV. A.D. 1507–13.* Edinburgh, 1902, pp. 83, 89, etc. (Damian.)

Pliny. *Natural History*, X, XI. (Birds, insects. *Natural History*, vol. 3, ed. and trans. by H. Rackham, London and Cambridge, Mass., 1947, pp. 292–611. Loeb Classical Library.)

Polo, Marco. *The Description of the World.* Ed. A. C. Moule and P. Pelliot. 2 vols. London, 1938. Vol. 1, pp. 356–7.

Porta, G. B. della. *Magiae naturalis…libri iiii.* Neapoli, 1558, pp. 69–70. (Translation by T. Young and S. Speed, *Natural Magick … in twenty books*, London, 1658, p. 409.)

Ramelli, A. *Le diverse et artificiose machine; composte in lingua Italiana et Francese.* Parigi, 1588, f. 315^v.

Ramus, P. *Scholarum mathematicarum libri unus et triginta*, II. Basileae, 1569, p. 65. (Regiomontanus.)

Reisch, G. *Margarita philosophica nova*, VII.I.41. Ex Argentoraco veteri, 1515. (Woodcut, regions of the air. Not in first edition, 1496: Hain, 13852.)

Remigius, N. *Dæmonolatreiæ libri tres*, I.25. Lugduni, 1595, pp. 158–62. (Magical flight.)

Reusner, J. *Emblemata … partim ethica, et physica: partim verò historica, & hieroglyphica … *Francoforti, 1581, p. 140. (Daedalus and Icarus.)

Sabellicus (Marcus Antonius Coccius). *Exemplorum libri decem*, X.9. Argentoraci, 1509, f. 98^r.

Salimbene de Adam. *Cronica.* 2 vols. Ed. G. Scalia. Bari, 1966. Vol. 1, pp. 109–10. (Buoncompagno.)

Scaliger, J. C. *Exotericarum exercitationum liber quintus decimus de Subtilitate, ad Hieronymum Cardanum.* Lutetiae, 1557, f. 444^v.

Schedel, H. *Registrum hujus operis libri cronicarum …* Nuremberge, 1493, f. cclv^r. (The 'Nuremberg Chronicle'; passage on Regiomontanus.)

Schmidlap, J. *Künstliche vnd rechtschaffene Fewerwerck zum Schimpff, vormals im Truck nie auszgangen.* Nürnberg, 1564, A5^v–A6^r. (Written about 1560.)

Stenton, Sir Frank (ed.) *The Bayeux Tapestry.* London, 1957, Plate 71. (*Draco.*)

Strabo. *Geography*, X.2.9. (*The Geography of Strabo*. Ed. and trans. by H. L. Jones. Vol. 5, London and New York, 1928, pp. 32–5. Loeb Classical Library.)

Sturm, J. *Lingvae latinæ resoluendæ ratio.* Argentorati, 1581, p. 40. (Written *ca.* 1573.)

Suetonius Tranquillus, Gaius. *De vita Caesarum*, VI.XII.2. (*Suetonius.* Ed. and trans. by J. C. Rolfe. Vol. 2, London and New York, 1914, pp. 104, 105. Loeb Classical Library.)

Vasari, G. *Le Vite de piu eccellenti architetti, pittori, et scultori italiani …* Firenze, 1550, p. 573.

Vegetius, Flavius Renatus. *Epitoma institvtorvm rei militaris*, II.13 (14). Romae, 1487. (Unnumbered pages.)

Veranzio, F. *Machinae novae Fausti Verantii Siceni*. Venezia, [1615–16]. (Composed *ca.* 1595.)

Wecker, H. J. *De secretis libri xvii*. Basileae, 1582, pp. 690–2, 936–8. (Quotations from della Porta.)

Whitney, G. *A Choice of Emblemes, and other devises, for the moste parte gathered out of sundrie writers, Englished and Moralized. And divers newly devised*. Leyden, 1586, p. 28. (Icarus.)

William of Malmesbury. *De gestis regum anglorum libri quinque*, II.225. (2 vols. Ed. W. Stubbs. London, 1887, 1889. Vol. 1, pp. 276–7.)

C: PRINTED MATERIAL WRITTEN AFTER 1600

Agricola, G. A. *Neu- und nie erhörter doch in der Natur und Vernunfft wohlgegründeter Versuch der Universalvermehrung aller Bäume, Stauden, und Blumen-Bewächse* . . . 2 vols. Regenspurg & Leipzig, 1716–17. Vol. 1, pp. 121–2.

Alessi, C. *Elogia civivm pervsinorvm qui patriam, rerum, pace, ac bello, gestarum gloria illustrarunt, centvria secvnda*. Romae, 1652, pp. 204–7. (Danti.)

Aymar, G. C. *Bird Flight*. London, 1936.

Babington, J. *Pyrotechnia; or, a Discourse of Artificiall Fire-works* . . . London, 1635, pp. 40, 44–6. (Funicular rocket-dragons; earliest use of the word 'kite' in application to the artificial object.)

Baier, J. W. and Bühel, J. A. *De aquila et musca ferrea, quæ mechanico artificio apud Noribergenses quondam volitasse feruntur*. Altorfiae, 1707.

Baldinucci, F. *Notizie de' professori del disegno* . . . 6 vols. Firenze, 1681–1728. Vol. 4, 1700, pp. 248–50. (Guidotti.)

Bassermann-Jordan, E. von. *Alte Uhren und ihre Meister*. Leipzig, 1926, pp. 64–6. (Kite in Munich, 1530.)

Bate, J. *The Mysteryes of Nature, and Art; conteined in foure seuerall Tretises, the first of Water workes, the second of Fyer workes, the third of Drawing, Colouring, Painting, and Engrauing, the fourth of divers Experiments* . . . London, 1634, pp. 80–2. (Kites.)

Baudoin, J. *Recveil d'emblemes divers. Avec des discovrs moravx, philosophiqves, et politiqves* . . . 2 vols. Paris, 1638–39. Vol. 1, 1638, pp. 114, 362. (Daedalus and Icarus.)

Becher, J. J. *Närrische Weiszheit und weise Narrheit: oder ein hundert so politische alss physicalische, mechanische und mercantilische Concepten und Propositionen.* Franckfurt, 1682, pp. 164–68.

Beck, Th. *Beiträge zur Geschichte des Maschinenbaues.* 2nd edn. Berlin, 1900.

Beltrami, L. *Leonardo da Vinci e l'aviazione.* Milano, [1912].

Berthelot, M. 'Histoire des machines de guerre et des arts mécaniques au moyen âge.' *Annales de chimie et de physique,* 7th series, vol. 19, 1900, pp. 289–420. (Study and reproduction of *Bellifortis.*)

Birkenmajer, A. 'Zur Lebensgeschichte und wissenschaftlichen Tätigkeit von Giovanni Fontana (1395?–1455?).' *Isis,* vol. 17, 1932, pp. 34–53.

Boeheim, W. *Handbuch der Waffenkunde.* Leipzig, 1890, pp. 501–6. (*Draco* standard.)

Boffito, G. *Il Volo in Italia.* Firenze, 1921.

Borelli, G. A. *De motu animalium.* 2 vols. Romae, 1680, 1681. Vol. 1, 1680, pp. 322–26.

Bourdeilles, P., abbé et seigneur de Branthôme. *Oeuvres complètes.* 13 vols. Paris, 1858–95. Vol. 5, p. 80. (Simulation of flight.)

Bourgeois, D. *Recherches sur l'art de voler.* Paris, 1784.

Burggravius, J. E. *Achilles πάνοπλος redivivus.* Amsterodami, [1612], p. 52. (Archytas; Nürnberg cantor.)

The Cambridge Medieval History, IV.1. Cambridge, 1966, p. 236. (Date and context of the flight of the Turk.)

Campanella, T. *De sensu rerum et magia, libri quatuor,* IV.vi. Francofurti, 1620, p. 282. (Archytas; Regiomontanus.)

Cats, J. *Silenus Alcibiadis, sive Proteus.* Middelburg, 1618. Pt. 2, plate between pp. 106, 107; text pp. 108–9. (First printed European illustration of a kite.)

Chapuis, A. and Gélis, E. *Le monde des automates, étude historique et technique.* 2 vols. Paris, 1928.

Chapuis, A., and Droz, E. *Les automates.* Neuchatel, 1949.

Crispolti, C. *Perugia augusta.* Perugia, 1648, pp. 360–1. (Danti.)

Crombie, A. C. *Augustine to Galileo: The History of Science A.D. 400–1650.* London, 1952, pp. 212ff. (For a convenient summary of the *impetus* theory and reactions against Aristotelianism in general.)

Delisle, L. 'On the Origin of Windmills in Normandy and England.' *The Journal of the British Archaeological Association*, vol. 6, Jan. 1851, pp. 403–6.

Denk, F. 'Zwei mittelalterliche Dokumente zur Fluggeschichte und ihre Deutung.' *Sitzungsberichte der Physikalischmedizinischen Sozietät in Erlangen*, vol. 71, 1939, pp. 353–68. (Erlangen, 1940.)

Dircks, H. *The Life, Times, and Scientific Labours of the Second Marquis of Worcester.* London, 1865, pp. 440–3, 556.

Doppelmayr, J. G. *Historische Nachricht von den Nürnbergischen Mathematicis und Künstlern.* Nürnberg, 1730, p. 23.

Drachmann, A. G. 'Heron's Windmill.' *Centaurus*, vol. 7, no. 2, 1961, pp. 145–51.

Duhem, J. 'Les aérostats du moyen-âge d'après les miniatures de cinq manuscrits allemands.' *Thalès*, vol. 2, 1935, pp. 106–14.

——. *Histoire des idées aéronautiques avant Montgolfier.* Paris, 1943.

——. *Musée aéronautique avant Montgolfier.* Paris, 1943.

——. *Histoire des origines du vol à réaction.* Paris, 1959.

——. *Histoire de l'arme aérienne avant le moteur.* Paris, 1964.

Egger, A. *De Archytæ tarentini, pythagorici, vita, operibus et philosophia disquisitio.* Parisiis, 1833.

The Encyclopedia of Islam, new edition. Ed. H. A. R. Gibb, *et al.* Leiden and London, 1960, etc. ('al-Djawharī,' by L. Kopf.)

Fabri, H. *Physica, id est scientia rerum corporearum.* 4 vols. Lugduni, 1669–71. Vol. I, 1669, p. 154.

Feldhaus, F. M. *Luftfahrten einst und jetzt.* Berlin, 1908.

——. *Ruhmesblätter der Technik.* Leipzig, 1910, pp. 280–368.

——. *Die Technik der Vorzeit, der geschichtlichen Zeit und der Naturvölker.* Leipzig und Berlin, 1914.

——. *Die Technik der Antike und des Mittelalters.* Potsdam, 1931.

——. *Die Maschine im Leben der Völker.* Basel und Stuttgart, 1954.

Flayder, F. H. *De arte volandi, cujus ope quivis homo . . . semet ipsum promovere potest.* [Tübingen], 1627.

Fuente la Peña, Antonio de. *El Ente Dilucidado*, IV.6.1780–1836. Madrid, 1675.

Fumagalli, G. and Fabretti, A. (eds.) *Giornale degli eruditi e curiosi*, III, 1885, pp. 162–3, 205–6, 265–6. (Danti.)

Gachard, L. P. *Retraite et mort de Charles-Quint au monastère de Juste.* 3 vols. Bruxelles, 1854, 1855.

Garibbo, L. *Cenni storici sull'Aeronautica.* Firenze, 1838.

Gassendi, P. *Nicolai Copernici, Georgii Peurbachii, & Joannis Regiomontani Astronomorum celebrium Vita.* Parisiis, 1654, p. 91.

Gibbs-Smith, C. H. *Leonardo da Vinci's Aeronautics.* London, 1967.

——. *Aviation: An Historical Survey from its Origins to the end of World War II.* London, 1970.

Gille, B. *Les ingénieurs de la Renaissance.* Paris, 1964. (English translation published as *The Renaissance Engineers,* London, 1966.)

González Palencia, A. *Moros y Cristianos en España Medieval.* Madrid, 1945, pp. 30–1. (al-Djawharī; 'Abbas b. Firnās.)

Grosse, R. *Römische Militärgeschichte von Gallienus bis zum Beginn der byzantinischen Themenverfassung.* Berlin, 1920, pp. 231–3.

Guyot, E.-G. *Nouvelles récréations physiques et mathématiques . . .* 3rd edn. 3 vols. Paris, 1786. Vol. 2, pp. 327–8, and plate 44 (opposite p. 320, 'Dragon volant').

Haddon, A. C. *The Study of Man,* London, 1898, pp. 232–54. (Kites.)

Hart, C. 'Early English Kites and an Ante-dating of O.E.D.' *Notes and Queries,* n.s., vol. 14, no. 3, March 1967, p. 92.

——. *Kites: an Historical Survey,* London, 1967.

——. 'Mediaeval Kites and Windsocks.' *Aeronautical Journal,* vol. 73, Dec. 1969, pp. 1019–26.

Heninger, S. K., Jr. *A Handbook of Renaissance Meteorology.* Durham, N.C., 1960.

Hennig, R. 'Beiträge zur Frühgeschichte der Aeronautik.' *Beiträge zur Geschichte der Technik und Industrie,* vol. 8, 1918, pp. 100–16.

——. 'Zur Vorgeschichte der Luftfahrt.' *Beiträge zur Geschichte der Technik und Industrie,* vol. 18, 1928, pp. 87–94.

Heydemann, H. 'Drachenspiel.' *Archäologische Zeitung,* vol. 25, Dec. 1867 (*Denkmäler und Forschungen,* no. 228), cols. 125–6.

Hooke, R. *The Diary of Robert Hooke.* Ed. H. W. Robinson and W. Adams. London, 1935, p. 146.

Huelsen, C. 'Der "Liber instrumentorum" des Giovanni Fontana.' In *Festgabe Hugo Blümner überreicht zum 9. August 1914 von Freunden und Schülern.* Zürich, 1914, pp. 507–15.

Jose de Siguenza. *Tercera parte de la Historia de la Orden de San Gerónimo,* I.36–40. Madrid, 1605, pp. 190–212. (Charles V in retirement.)

Kircher, A. *Magnes, sive de Arte Magnetica.* Romae, 1641, pp. 358–60.

Kircher, A. *Ars magna lucis et umbrae*. Romae, 1646. Pt. 2, pp. 826–7.

——. *Musurgia universalis sive ars magna consoni et dissoni*. 2 vols. Romae, 1650. Vol. 2, p. 354.

——. *Mundus subterraneus*. Amstelodami, 1665. Pt. 2, pp. 479–80.

——. *Athanasii Kircheri e Soc. Jesu. phonurgia nova*. Campidonae, 1673, pp. 147–8. (Reprint of the *Musurgia* passage, with a new cut.)

Klinckowstroem, C. von. 'Tito Livio Burattini, ein Flugtechniker des 17. Jahrhunderts.' *Prometheus*, no. 1100, 26 Nov. 1910, pp. 117–20.

Knolles, R. *The Generall Historie of the Turkes*. London, 1603, p. 37. (Flying Turk.)

Laborde, L. de. *Notice des émaux exposés dans les galeries du Musée du Louvre*. 2 vols. Paris, 1852, 1853. Vol. 2, pp. 424–5.

Laufer, B. *The Prehistory of Aviation*. Chicago, 1928.

Leônij, L. *Vita di Bartolommeo di Alviano*. Todi, 1858, pp. 48–9. (Danti.)

Lévi-Provençal, E. *La Civilisation arabe en Espagne*. Paris, 1848, pp. 76–7. ('Abbas b. Firnās.)

Levis, H. C. *The British King Who Tried to Fly*. London, 1919. (Bladud.)

Leybourn, W. *Pleasure with Profit: Consisting of Recreations of Divers Kinds* ... London, 1694. Pt. 3, pp. 19, 24–5.

Lobkovitz, J. Caramuel. *Mathesis biceps*. Campaniae, 1670, pp. 740–62.

Loomis, R. S. 'Alexander the Great's Celestial Journey.' *The Burlington Magazine*, vol. 32, April, 1918, pp. 136–40; May, 1918, pp. 177–85.

Mackay, Ae. J. G. *William Dunbar 1460–1520: a Study in the Poetry and History of Scotland*. Edinburgh, 1889, pp. xlvi–xlvii, cxvii–cxix, ccxiv–ccxvi. (Damian.)

Maiolus, S. *Dies caniculares, hoc est colloquia tria et viginti physica, nova et penitus admiranda ac summa iucunditate concinnata*. 2 vols. Moguntiae, 1607, 1608. Vol. 1, 1607, pp. 9 (*draco* meteor), 762 (Archytas).

al-Maḳḳarī. *The History of the Mohammedan Dynasties in Spain*. Trans. by P. de Gayangos. 2 vols. London, 1840, 1843. Vol. 1, 1840, p. 148. (Written in the early seventeenth century.)

The Marriage of Prince Frederick, and the Kings Daughter ..., London, 1613. (Somers' *Tracts*, 2nd edn., ed. Walter Scott, London, 1809, etc., vol. 3, pp. 35–43.)

Mersenne, M. *Questions inouyes, ou récréation des scavans*. [Paris,] 1634, pp. 1–5. ('A sçavoir si l'art de voller est possible ...')

Meyer, C. *Sechs und Zwanzig nichtige Kinderspiel*. Zürich, [*ca.* 1650,] plate 12. (Kite-flying.)

Milizia, F. *Le Vite de' più Celebri Architetti d'ogni Nazione et d'ogni Tempo Precedute da un Saggio sopra l'Architettura.* Roma, 1768, pp. 326–7. (Guidotti.)

Mormino, G. *Storia dell'Aeronautica dai Miti Antichissimi ai nostri Giorni.* 2nd edn. Milano, 1940.

Muratov, P. P. *Les icones russes.* Paris, 1927, p. 137. (Pennon kite at Nizhni-Novgorod.)

Needham, J. *Science and Civilisation in China*, IV.2. Cambridge, 1965, pp. 163–4, 555–99.

Nicolson, M. H. *Voyages to the Moon.* New York, 1948.

Norton, R. *The Gunner, shewing the whole practise of Artillerie.* London, 1628, plate opposite p. 96. (Trajectories.)

Novarinus, A. *Schediasmata sacro-prophana*, V.113. Lugduni, 1635, p. 152. (Regiomontanus; from Ramus.)

Oldoini, A. *Athenaeum Augustum.* Perusiae, 1678, pp. 168–9. (Danti.)

Partington, J. R. *A History of Greek Fire and Gunpowder.* Cambridge, 1960, pp. 99, 162, 174, 242, 290.

Pasch, G. *Schediasma de curiosis hujus seculi inventis.* Kiloni, 1695, pp. 224–49.

Pascoli, L. *Vite de' Pittori, Scultori, ed Architetti Perugini.* Roma, 1732, pp. 59–60. (Danti.)

Peacham, H. *Minerva Britanna or a Garden of Heroical Deuises, furnished, and adorned with Emblemes and Impresa's of sundry natures, Newly devised, moralized, and published.* London, 1612, p. 168. (Toy windmill.)

Pearson, J. D. *Index Islamicus, 1906–1955.* Cambridge, [1958].

Pedretti, C. *Studi Vinciani. Documenti, analisi et inediti leonardeschi.* Genève, 1957.

Pegel, M. *Thesavrvs rervm, selectarvm, magnarvm, dignarvm, vtilivm, svavivm . . .* 1604, p. 123.

Pellini, P. *Dell'Historia di Perugia.* 3 pts. Venetia, 1664.

Plischke, H. 'Alter und Herkunft des Europäischen Flächendrachens.' *Nachrichten von der Gesellschaft der Wissenschaften zu Göttingen*, Phil.-Hist. Kl., N. F., Fachgr. 2, vol. 2, no. 1, 1936, pp. 1–18.

Quarg, G. 'Der BELLIFORTIS von Conrad Kyeser aus Eichstätt, 1405.' *Technikgeschichte*, vol. 32, no. 4, 1965, pp. 293–324.

Qvarnström, G. *Dikten och den nya Vetenskapen: det Astronautiska Motivet.* Lund, 1961. (Good summary of the aeronautical theme in literature to the seventeenth century.)

Randall, L. M. C. *Images in the Margins of Gothic Manuscripts.* Berkeley and Los Angeles, 1966. (The index lists a number of subjects of aeronautical interest.)

Rausch, H. A. 'Die Spiele der Jugend aus Fischarts Gargantua.' *Jahrbuch für Geschichte, Sprache und Literatur Elsass-Lothringens*, vol. 24, 1908, pp. 53 ff.

Renel, C. *Cultes militaires de Rome: les enseignes.* Paris, 1903, pp. 206–11.

Reti, L. 'Helicopters and Whirligigs.' *Raccolta Vinciana*, fasc. XX, 1964, pp. 331–38.

Rolt, L. T. C. *The Aeronauts: a History of Ballooning 1783–1903.* London, 1966.

Romanus, A. *Pyrotechnia, hoc est, de ignibus festivis jocosis, artificialibus et seriis variisque eorum structuris libri duo ex scriptoribus Latinis, Italis et Germanis collecti.* [Frankfurt,] 1611, pp. 22–3. (Funicular rocket-dragons.)

Romocki, S. J. von. *Geschichte der Explosivstoffe.* 2 vols. Berlin, 1895, 1896. Vol. 1, pp. 160–62.

Sauval, H. *Histoire et recherches des antiquités de la ville de Paris.* 3 vols. Paris, 1724. Vol. 2, p. 544. (Italian on the Tour de Nesles.)

Schott, G. *Magia universalis naturae et artis.* 4 vols. Herbipoli, 1657–59. Vol. 3, pp. 268–72.

Schweisguth, P. 'Note sur les jeux de cerf volants en Thailande.' *Journal of the Siam Society*, vol. 34, pt. 1, April, 1943, pp. 1–32.

Schwenter, D. *Deliciæ physico-mathematicæ. Oder Mathematische und Philosophische Erquickstunden.* 1st part. Nürnberg, 1636, pp. 472–5.

Segneri, P. *Il Cristiano instruito nella sua Legge Ragionamenti Morali dati in Luce.* 3 vols. Firenze, 1686. Vol. 3, III.2.8, pp. 21–2. (Archytas.)

Sepibus, G. de. *Romanii Collegii Societatis Jesu Musæum Celeberrimum.* Amstelodami, 1678, pp. 19–20.

Simkiss, K. *Bird Flight.* London, 1963.

Storer, J. H. *The Flight of Birds.* Michigan, 1948.

Strada, F. *De bello belgico decas prima.* Romae, 1632, p. 8. (Trans. by Sir Robt. Stapylton as *De bello belgico: the History of the Low-Countrey Warres*, London, 1650, p. 7.)

Thorndike, L. *A History of Magic and Experimental Science.* 8 vols., London, 1923, etc.

——. 'Marianus Jacobus Taccola.' *Archives Internationales d'Histoire des Sciences*, vol. 8, 1955, pp. 7–26.

Valcaçar, J. de. *Relacion de las Exeqvias qve se celebraron en Napoles, en la Mverte de la Serenissima Reyna Margarita Señora nuestra.* 2 pts. En Napoles, 1612. Pt. 2, p. 16.

Venturini, G. *Da Icaro a Montgolfier*. 2 vols. Roma, 1928.

V[erstegan], R. *A Restitution of Decayed Intelligence: In Antiquities. Concerning the most noble and renowned English nation*. Antwerp, 1605, pp. 52–3. (Regiomontanus.)

Vincioli, G. 'Lettera del Signor Abate Conte Giacinto Vincioli Concernente Tre Curiosi Fatti'. In D. Girolamo Baruffaldi, *Miscellanea di Varie Operette*, Venezia, 1740, pp. 454–60. (Danti.)

Wailes, R. 'A Note on Windmills'. In *A History of Technology*, ed. Ch. Singer, et. al., vol. 2, Oxford, 1956, pp. 623–28.

Waley, A. [Review article.] *Folklore*, vol. 47, no. 4, Dec. 1936, pp. 402–3. (Kites.)

Waller, R. 'The Life of Dr. Robert Hooke.' In *The Posthumous Works of Robert Hooke*, London, 1705, p. iv.

White, Lynn, Jr. 'Eilmer of Malmesbury, an Eleventh Century Aviator.' *Technology and Culture*, vol. 2, 1961, pp. 97–111.

——. 'The Invention of the Parachute.' *Technology and Culture*, vol. 9, no. 3, July 1968, pp. 462–7.

——. 'Medieval Uses of Air.' *Scientific American*, vol. 223, no. 2, August 1970, pp. 92–100. (See also correspondence in vol. 223, no. 4, October 1970, p. 6.)

Wilhelm, B., S.J. 'Schweikart und Mohr, zwei schwäbische Flieger aus alter Zeit.' *Illustrierte Aeronautische Mitteilungen*, vol. 13, 1909, pp. 441–5.

——. *Die Anfänge der Luftfahrt Lana-Gusmão. Zur Erinnerung an den 200. Gedenktag des ersten Ballonaufstieges (8. Aug. 1709–8. Aug. 1909)*. Hamm i. W., 1909. (Especially the early pages.)

Wilkins, J. *Mathematicall Magick; or, the wonders that may be performed by mechanicall geometry*. London, 1648, pp. 191–223.

Worcester, Edward Somerset, earl of. *A Century of the Names and Scantlings of such Inventions as at present I can call to mind to have tried and perfected* . . . London, 1663, p. 31 (invention 46). (Artificial bird.)

Zéki Pacha, A. 'L'Aviation chez les Arabes.' *Bulletin de l'Institut Egyptien*, 5th series, vol. 5, 1911, pp. 92–101. (al-Djawharī; 'Abbas b. Firnās. Reprinted, with minor changes, in his *L'Aviation chez les Musulmans*, Le Caire, 1912.)

Zingerle, I. V. *Das deutsche Kinderspiel im Mittelalter*. 2nd edn. Innsbruck, 1873.

Zinner, E. *Leben und Wirken des Joh. Müller von Königsberg genannt Regiomontanus*. Rev. edn. Osnabrück, 1968. (Especially pp. 214–5, for the eagle and fly.)

Index